Frank Selee

Frank Selee

*Hall of Fame Manager
of the Boston Beaneaters
and Chicago Cubs*

RICHARD BRESSLER

McFarland & Company, Inc., Publishers
Jefferson, North Carolina

All photographs are from the National Baseball Hall of Fame and Museum, Cooperstown, New York.

Also of Interest and by Author: *The Cubs and the A's of 1910: One Dynasty Ends, Another Begins* (McFarland, 2016); *The Thirteenth Century: A World History* (McFarland, 2018)

Frontispiece: Frank Selee, ca. 1890s

Library of Congress Cataloguing-in-Publication Data

Names: Bressler, Richard, author.
Title: Frank Selee : Hall of Fame manager of the Boston Beaneaters and Chicago Cubs / Richard Bressler.
Description: Jefferson, North Carolina : McFarland & Company, Inc., Publishers, 2021 | Includes bibliographical references and index.
Identifiers: LCCN 2020051542 | ISBN 9781476682044 (paperback : acid free paper) ∞
ISBN 9781476641041 (ebook)
Subjects: LCSH: Selee, Frank, 1859-1909. | Baseball managers—United States. | Chicago Cubs (Baseball team)—History. | Boston Braves (Baseball team)—History. | National Baseball Hall of Fame and Museum.
Classification: LCC GV864.S43 B74 2021 | DDC 796.357092 [B]—dc23
LC record available at https://lccn.loc.gov/2020051542

British Library cataloguing data are available
**ISBN (print) 978-1-4766-8204-4
ISBN (ebook) 978-1-4766-4104-1**

© 2021 Richard Bressler. All rights reserved

No part of this book may be reproduced or transmitted in any form or by any means, electronic or mechanical, including photocopying or recording, or by any information storage and retrieval system, without permission in writing from the publisher.

Front cover: Cabinet card photograph of Boston Beaneaters manager Frank Selee (Elmer Chickering)

Printed in the United States of America

*McFarland & Company, Inc., Publishers
Box 611, Jefferson, North Carolina 28640
www.mcfarlandpub.com*

Acknowledgments

I would like to thank everyone who helped me in the research and writing of this book. Jerry Goodbody loaned me his *Baseball Encyclopedia*, which covered 20th century information. Dick Goodbody helped me with the preparation of the photographs. George and Sally Stubbs put up with me and put me up on a visit to Melrose and Boston. The vast majority of the research for this book was looking at newspapers from 1884 to 1908. Most of this was done at the University of Illinois Library, particularly the newspaper collection in the History, Philosophy and Newspaper Library. Other newspaper research was done at the Wisconsin State Historical Library in Madison, University of Nebraska (Omaha) Library, Boston Public Library, and Pueblo Public Library. Thanks to all staff members at these institutions who helped me out. I made a couple of trips to the National Baseball Hall of Fame in Cooperstown, and received much help at the Giamatti Research Center. Particular thanks to Cassidy Kent and John Horne at that center. The remainder of the research took place at the Champaign Public Library and the Urbana Free Library. It is good to know one's tax dollars are used for institutions like this. Thanks to Mike Kulas for his help on getting the manuscript prepared on the computer, as my tech level is minuscule. Thanks to everyone at McFarland and Company, for the third time.

Table of Contents

Acknowledgments v

Introduction 1

1. Early Days and Start in Baseball 3
2. The Minors 20
3. Boston: The First Seven Years 35
4. Boston: The Last Five Years 92
5. Chicago 138
6. Endgame 175

Chapter Notes 189
Bibliography 192
Index 193

Introduction

One of the constants of sports is the mystery of what makes one person a fine leader. This book is a biography of one of the finest leaders in baseball history, a man who does not fit many of our common notions of how someone becomes a successful baseball manager. Going back to the beginnings of organized baseball, the manager was someone who had played the game, usually at the highest level. The first person who managed a professional baseball team, Harry Wright of the 1869 Cincinnati Reds, never played organized baseball but had been playing at the highest available level for several years before he invented the job of manager. Managers in the early years of the National Association and National League were usually active players, such as Albert Spalding and Cap Anson. If a player at the highest level wanted to stay in the game after his playing career was over, his choices were to become a manager or an owner. As is the case today, most chose to become managers (the first coach was not hired until the early 1900s).

Frank Selee did not fit this mold. As will be shown in this biography, his playing career was so marginal that it is not reported in most places where his career is discussed. He was working at a watch company when he decided to get into baseball. Nothing in his personal or professional background indicated he could become a successful leader of a baseball team. He had to overcome the preference of baseball executives to hire former or current players to manage their teams. He forged his own path to become a Hall of Fame manager.

Selee's career started in 1884 and ended in 1908. Until the first general manager was named by the Cleveland Indians in 1927, the functions of a general manager were fulfilled by either the manager, the owner, some other executive, or some combination thereof. The first executives who were involved in player selection but were not owners were Ed Barrow and Branch Rickey, in the early 1920s. Before then, the manager commonly scouted and selected the players he wanted, subject to the budgetary requirements of the owner (both Barrow and Rickey had been managers before 1920). Sometimes the manager negotiated the contracts, sometimes the owner. The managers inducted into the Hall of Fame for careers that started before 1920 had the player procurement duties of a general manager in their job description. This includes well-known managers such as John McGraw, Harry Wright, Ned Hanlon, and Connie Mack. Selee managed against these men and had a better winning percentage than any of them in the Major Leagues.

There are as many styles of managers as there are managers. However, there are a few broad categories that encompass these styles. These include Players' Manager; My Way or the Highway; Tough Guy; Fiery Leader; and the current Analytics-Driven Manager. Most managers are a descendant of the founding member of a school of management style. Since Harry Wright was the first manager of a professional team, all managers could be said to descend from him. But he continued to manage into the 1890s and encountered many other styles. Ned Hanlon spawned the largest school, what I would call the Fiery Leader. His Baltimore and Brooklyn teams of the 1890s had success playing a combative style, and this style was spread by John McGraw and his many disciples. Even Connie Mack, who was not a combative manager, played for Hanlon. Mack developed a different style. Mack had several players who became managers, some of whom had a similar style.

Frank Selee, a great manager in the majors from 1890 to 1905, had no disciples. As will be shown, he could be considered one of the founders of the Players' Manager style. But none of his players became successful managers at the Major League level using his style. His style does not seem to have been transferrable.

Join me in an exploration of the baseball world from 1884 through 1908. This was a different world from today's world in many ways. But there are other ways that are familiar to us today. Frank Selee became a successful Major League manager in that time, and I will try to explain how and why.

1

Early Days and Start in Baseball

Life Before Professional Baseball

Frank Selee was born into a different world from our current world. The fastest way to distribute and receive news on a mass basis was the newspaper. The fastest way to travel locally was by horse, and the fastest way to travel longer distances was by ship or rail. Even though the U.S. is still a religious nation, it was more so in the 1850s. Selee was born into a family heavily involved in religion.

Frank Gibson Selee was the first son born to Nathan and Annie Selee on October 26, 1859. In 1859, Nathan was a Methodist minister in Amherst, New Hampshire. Nathan had been a schoolteacher there and somehow secured the necessary education to become a minister. Soon afterward, he became the minister of a church in Truro, Massachusetts. That lasted a couple of years. In 1864, Nathan and Annie and family moved to Melrose, Massachusetts. Today, Melrose in a close-in suburb of Boston. In 1864, it was eight miles outside the city, a small town connected to Boston by the railroad. Nathan became the minister of the First Methodist Episcopal Church in Melrose. Along with this job came a house at 115 Emerson Street.[1]

Deep roots were established in Melrose by the Selee family. It is not clear how long Nathan remained the minister at First Methodist Episcopal. By the time Frank was a teenager, Nathan and Annie were running complementary businesses. Annie was a homeopathic doctor, practicing in Melrose. Nathan was a supplier of medicines for Annie's practice, and for other homeopathic physicians in the area. This led to modest prosperity, and there seems to have been no economic hardships suffered by this family.

A check of available records in Melrose does not show any educational records for Frank Selee. One can assume that he received primary education in the schools of Melrose. There is no record of his attending any school after that, mostly because there are no records at all about him as a child. My guess from his behavior in later life is that he had some secondary education locally in Melrose. It is unlikely that he went any further. He was known throughout his career as a smart, well-mannered man, which leads me to believe he had gone beyond primary school. However, this is an educated guess.

What is not a guess is Frank's love for baseball and its early manifestation. How he initially got involved with the sport is not known. The best parallel story is from a contemporary of his, Connie Mack.[2] Mack was born in 1862 in another small town in Massachusetts. Mack recalled much later that he started playing a game called four o' cat as soon as he could run around in the open field near his home. This game resembled cricket. A flat bat was used, and batters could be put out by catching a fly ball (no gloves) or by hitting a runner with a thrown ball. Cricket and Massachusetts town ball were morphing into baseball after the Civil War. Town teams sprang up all over the country, and this area was no exception. Through his playing around the town, Frank Selee made his way to playing for a town team.

Several sources state that Frank played for the Alpha team of Melrose. Check of the *Melrose Record* for the period from 1875 to 1882 did not reveal any stories about the Alpha team. There was coverage of base ball (two words through the career of Frank Selee). As a matter of fact, the first available day of the microfilm for the *Melrose Record* showed a box score. The game was between the Lightfoot and Trimountain teams. The shortstop for Trimountain was Selee. The article led me to believe that this was Frank Selee, because the players are referred to as young locals. Selee was 16 years old. The box score shows Selee as scoring three runs, making four putouts, and making 11 errors in a 33–32 win for Trimountain.[3]

Articles about Selee state that he played many more games than this in Melrose, but I could not find records for them. What we can discuss is the state of baseball at this period. In 1871, the first overtly professional baseball league was formed, the National Association of Base Ball Players. From the start, there was a team in Boston. That team was managed by Harry Wright, who had managed the pioneer professional team, the Cincinnati Reds of 1869–1870. The game of baseball was quite different from the modern version. No one wore gloves. The pitcher pitched, not threw, the ball. That means the pitcher had to initiate each pitch with his throwing arm somewhere below perpendicular to the ground. Some games still utilized the one bounce rule, which meant a batted ball caught on one bounce would be an out. Catchers stood well behind the plate, which was made of wood or concrete. The batter would call for a pitch to be high or low, and batters were expected to swing at any pitch that was in their preferred area. As we can see from Selee's line in the box score from the above game, fielding was the most important and most difficult part of the game. A line of four putouts versus 11 errors was not good, but not uncommon. In most games, errors outnumbered hits. That led to high scoring.

Selee played for amateur teams where he lived. There are no records of where he worked before 1884. I would expect that he lived in Melrose for some time and worked there. The one workplace shown in all the sources was the Waltham Watch Factory. Quoting Frank Selee directly, "I was working in the Waltham Watch Factory in 1884."[4] Check of Wikipedia shows a company that manufactured watches and clocks in Waltham from 1850 through 1957. The company went through many names. In 1884 it was called The American Watch Company. The name changed in 1885 to The American Waltham Watch Company, then in 1907 to The Waltham Watch Company. The wording of Selee's statement leads me to believe he worked as a manual laborer at this company.

Selee states, "With the approach of spring, I got baseball fever and induced some friends of mine to organize a stock company with a capital, I believe, of $1,000, most of which was put into grounds, fence and grandstand."[5] This action marks the start of Frank Selee's baseball career.

Waltham

Waltham is about 11 miles west of Boston. There was a train line from Boston west through Waltham in the 1880s. It is not known if Selee lived at home in Melrose while he worked at the Waltham Watch Factory or played with the Waltham ball club. It would have been possible to commute via rail by going through Boston. However, I expect he lived in a boarding house along with many other young, single men working in Waltham, a manufacturing center. It was home to the Boston Manufacturing Company, the first integrated textile mill in the United States, and the Waltham watch was becoming well known.

The team founded by Selee in 1884 played at a low level of organized baseball. There were no official designations of non-major leagues. In 20th-century baseball, leagues were designated as Class AAA, AA, A, B, C, D, Rookie, and so forth. In the late 19th century, these leagues were just being organized. Most of the teams grew out of town teams. As can be seen by Selee's statement, not a lot of money was required to start a team. A team would try to join an existing league or would form a new league. The Waltham team joined the Massachusetts State League. We might consider this team semi-pro, as the players had a monthly salary which could be supplemented by other work. The first mention of the Waltham team in the 1884 *Waltham Daily Tribune* was on April 10. A player was signed from the Boston Union League team, who also received other employment in

Waltham. The manager (Selee) was authorized by the directors to secure grounds and schedule games.[6] The lineup was given to the newspaper on April 12. It showed 12 players with no mention of the manager. Selee himself gives an example of the amounts of money involved, saying, "As an illustration of the salaries paid in those days I want to say that Connie Mack … agreed to sign with me for $60 a month and board; I would have agreed to the $60 but I could not see him on the board proposition."[7] Mack ended up signing with Meridian in the Connecticut State League, starting a professional career in baseball that lasted until 1950.[8]

Waltham started play on April 12 with an exhibition game at Lowell. Grading the ball field commenced on April 14. An article on April 17 states, "Manager Selee has given up his position in Ede's grocery store and will devote the greater part of his time attending to the wants of the ball club."[9] He was contacting teams to schedule games, as income was necessary. The next exhibition game was with Harvard in Cambridge, which was on the train line to Boston. On April 21, Harvard beat Waltham, 11–0, in a five-inning game. Waltham had no hits, and the newspaper article stated, "The only special feature of the game was the utter inability of the Walthams to field the ball."[10] The next game scheduled for the Walthams was with the Boston Union League team on April 26. An April 21 article stated that the Waltham grounds were "all graded and half sodded."[11] An ad on April 25 for the April 26 game stated that it would feature the Boston team (Champions of the World) and the Walthams. Admission would be 25 cents and the game would start at 4 p.m. Boston scored 14 in the first three innings and won, 14–0. The weather was good, but the crowd was small at 4 p.m. However, the nearby factory let out at 5 p.m., and the crowd increased notably. Per the report, Waltham fielded okay, but could not hit.

Even though the Waltham team was a start-up in a low minor league, they were able to secure an exhibition game with the National League Boston club. We will see this happen many times in this story. Baseball was taking baby steps toward becoming an organized league sport, and there was lots of interaction between Major League teams and teams in other leagues. In the lower leagues, many games were played outside the league as well. The next announcement in the Waltham paper was that Waltham would start the league season on May 1 at home against Springfield. Waltham played an exhibition game against the Unions on April 30, winning 11–0. Springfield told Selee they would not show on May 1, so he arranged a doubleheader in Waltham on May 1 against two local amateur teams.

Opening day in the Massachusetts State League took place on May 4 against Springfield. Waltham started their games at home at 4 p.m., to try to get factory workers to attend. This game was a 4–4 tie in 10 innings. Two of

1. Early Days and Start in Baseball

the next three games Waltham played featured a future Hall of Fame manager (Selee) and a future Hall of Fame pitcher. Selee signed Arthur "Candy" Cummings to pitch. Cummings made the Hall of Fame as the pitcher who developed the curve ball. He was from Massachusetts and was known for this skill in the state. In 1879 Connie Mack and the pitcher from his town team contacted Cummings to learn how to pitch the curve ball. The lesson cost $10, a large investment for a couple of teenagers in 1879.[12] It is not known how much Selee paid Cummings. Cummings pitched the next two league games. The first was a 20–19 win at Lawrence in a game that lasted 2½ hours. A week later, Cummings lost to the Boston Reserves (not the Major League team) 13–12. The catcher for Waltham was commended for his good fielding, even though he used no mask or glove. Catcher's gloves were starting to come in around this time, with fielding gloves soon to follow. In this same game, a Waltham player was called out after declining to take first base after six called balls during his at bat. At the beginning of each game, a coin was tossed to determine which team had the right to select when to bat. Either team could bat first. As will be noted many times, the rules for baseball were developing and changing.[13]

The final game of May was played on Decoration Day (now Memorial Day), May 28. Waltham had an unusual home doubleheader that day. The first game started at 9:30 a.m., an exhibition game won by Waltham, which took place in very cold weather per the reporter. The second game was supposed to start at 3 p.m. against Lawrence. The game was delayed a short time because Lawrence had neglected to bring their bats. Waltham won, 6–3. Waltham had only two hits. Waltham committed 11 errors, and Lawrence committed 22. By June 4, Waltham had played seven league games with a record of 5–2, and five exhibition games.[14] The other teams in the league were Lynn, Salem, Boston Reserves, Holyoke, Lawrence, Springfield, and Worcester. All these places were reachable by rail, going through Boston. Some of the games against these teams did not count in the league standings; the newspaper articles made clear which games were league games and which were exhibitions.

The next game produced the first printed criticism of Manager Selee. On June 5, Springfield beat Waltham 8–3 at Waltham. Waltham had 12 errors, Springfield 13. The article in the Waltham paper had this sentence: "The manager probably knows his business, but the men should be kept in regular positions, even in exhibition games as it is hard to expect good play from men who are continually changed around."[15] Waltham's next game, an exhibition 8–7 win on June 8 at home against Tremont, had two unusual features. One was the Waltham center fielder, Selee, who was 1-for-4 at bat with one putout and three errors. Another was the triple play turned by Tremont that was correct under the rules of the day but would not be today.

Waltham had the bases loaded with nobody out. The batter struck out, and the catcher dropped the third strike. The Tremont catcher stepped on home, then threw to third, then on to second for forceouts. The requirement of the catcher to catch a third strike is one of the few rules that has been kept in the rulebook since the first official rules formulated by the Knickerbocker Club in 1845. That rule has changed some, as evidenced by this play. Now, if there is someone on first with less than two outs and the catcher drops the third strike, the batter is out. That was not the case in 1884.[16]

Some things about baseball never change. Waltham lost 6–0 to Worcester at home on June 15, and the report in the newspaper blamed the umpire. Waltham played an exhibition against Lawrence at Hudson, Massachusetts, on the 16th. Selee had arranged this with the understanding that there would be no charge for using the ballpark there. After the game, both teams received a bill for $15 for using the ballpark. They returned home to Waltham for a league game on the June 17 against Holyoake, drawing a crowd of 500 to a 12–10 Waltham win. Players got hurt, and others played different positions. A new third baseman was signed before a June 25 home game against Boston Reserves. This player got hurt in pregame warmup, was unable to play, and contributed by selling tickets. This game started at 4:40 to try to entice factory workers to come after getting off work at 5 p.m. At the end of June, Worcester led the league with a record of 11–3. Waltham was fourth at 7–5, and Lawrence seventh at 3–7.[17]

In the June 30 edition of the *Waltham Daily Tribune*, there was an ad for Fourth of July game in Waltham against the Boston Reserves, featuring many other athletic competitions. No record of this game exists in the July 5 edition. Waltham played at Lynn on July 6. The game was delayed for a relatively common reason in these times: the umpire from Boston assigned to the game had not shown up. The Lynn manager umped the game, under protest from Selee. The protest was forgotten when Waltham won, 8–3. One of Waltham's runs was a home run over the fence by their left fielder, the first such hit noted in any article about this team. Waltham won two more games in the next ten days. On July 18, there was an exhibition game against the American Watch Co., Selee's old employer. Waltham won a five-inning game, 6–3. After the game there were competitions like foot races, long jump, hop skip and jump, and others.

Waltham played one more game, on July 20 at home against Lawrence, winning 15–5. After the game, there was a meeting of the Board of Directors of the Waltham club. The Board went over their financial situation, determined they had a $300 deficit, and voted to disband. The Lynn club made the same determination on the same day. The Board of the Waltham club decided to try and operate the club outside the league. However, the Lawrence club engaged Selee and five players from Waltham to join Lawrence. This was agreed to by all parties, and the new Lawrence employees were present for their first game on July 24.[18]

Lawrence

Lawrence, Massachusetts, is a town about 40 miles north of Boston, on the Merrimack River near the New Hampshire border. In 1884, Lawrence was like Waltham in that both were manufacturing towns. Waltham was where the first large textile mill was built in Massachusetts around 1830. In 1845, a group of industrialists led by Abbott Lawrence purchased the site for the purpose of building some more mills. These mills were built by 1850 and were operating at full capacity in 1884. The mill buildings are still there today in Lawrence.

The Lawrence team had been in this league since the beginning of 1884. The first games played after the arrival of Selee and five players from Waltham were exhibition games. The first one was on July 24 against Haverhill, won by Lawrence, 17–3, at home. The next day Selee released a player from the Lawrence club, the first instance of an action he would have to take many times in his career. By July 26, four teams in this league had disbanded: Waltham, Lynn, Salem, and Worcester. Boston Reserves now topped the standings. Before their next league game, the Lawrences received new uniforms, described as "brown cap trimmed in navy blue, blue shirt with brown L on chest, brown knee trousers with navy blue cord, blue ribbed stockings."[19] Selee's first league game with Lawrence was at home, a 6–5 win over Springfield on July 31. Their next five games were non-league games, two at Lawrence and three at Biddleford. In one of these games, the Lawrence pitcher batted leadoff, and the opposing pitcher batted fifth. Lawrence had league games at home on August 8 and 9. The summer fair was taking place at this time in Lawrence on grounds adjacent to the ballpark. Per space in the *Lawrence Daily American*, the fair was a much bigger deal, especially the horse races.[20] Lawrence won these games. An exhibition was played against a Waltham team of amateurs on August 12 in Lawrence. Selee played center field for Lawrence, going 1-for-3. Their next away game was on August 15 in Springfield. Springfield won, 16–9. The article in the Lawrence paper had a box score and noted, "The Lawrences met a crushing defeat in Springfield yesterday, and evidently were out of sorts. At one point during the game umpire Crawford had to call upon the police for protection."[21] That's the whole article.

The feelings of people about baseball were all over the place, as shown by an item in the Lawrence paper. In the August 16 edition, there was an item saying that "a juvenile base ball club was captured by the police on

Sunday, while engaged in a game, but were released after being given some wholesome advice."[22] That advice was probably about a "Blue Law" which would have forbidden any organized sporting event on a Sunday. Blue Laws affected Selee his entire career. On August 16, Lawrence swept a home doubleheader from Holyoake. On August 17, the Providence National League club played an exhibition at Lawrence, drawing the biggest crowd of the year, between 1600 and 2000. Providence won the toss, batted last, and won 5–4 by scoring the winning run in the bottom of the ninth. Better quality of play prevailed in this game, as Providence had three errors, and Lawrence four.[23]

The rest of the games Lawrence played in August were exhibitions. Most were against town teams. One at Newburyport drew a good crowd of 1,000 on August 20 to witness a 4–0 Lawrence win. The following day, Lawrence played at Lowell. Lawrence won, 4–0, and the Lawrence paper reported, "the umpiring was execrable." On August 25, the paper reported that the Springfield team had disbanded and that the league now consisted of the Boston Reserves and Lawrence. Lawrence had an exhibition game scheduled for the 25th at home against the Detroit National League team, which was canceled due to a rainout in Providence that had to be made up. An actual league game was played on August 29, against the other league team, Boston Reserves. Lawrence won this home game, 9–4, before an estimated crowd of 500. Lawrence won two more home exhibition games on the 30th and 31st. Per the newspaper reports, Lawrence's record since Selee took over on July 21 was 17 wins, two losses, and two ties. Most of these games were exhibitions.[24]

All the remaining games in 1884 would be exhibitions. The league had collapsed, and the only two teams still operating were Lawrence and Boston Reserves. At the time the league shrank to two teams, Boston Reserves had a better record. On September 8, the secretary of the state baseball association told the Boston Reserves to play a best-of-five series against Lawrence to determine the champion. Something came of this, which will be explained below. Lawrence had played four games in September so far, winning all of them. One was at Manchester, New Hampshire, during the New England Fair. This game had to be completed by 4 p.m., so the Lawrence team could catch the 4:20 train to return home. The Board of Directors of the club were pleased enough to announce in the September 7 newspaper that a ball would be held to honor the Lawrence club on September 26. Lawrence played against the Boston National League club at home on September 12, losing 16–0. Lawrence played at Portland, Maine, on September 15. They were winning 6–3 in the seventh inning when their pitcher hurt his ankle running the bases. There was no other pitcher available, so he had to finish the game. Portland scored four runs in the last two innings to win.

The next day, the Lawrence paper announced a three-game series between Lawrence and the Boston Reserves for a prize of $200 to start on the 18th. Lawrence played a warm-up game at Newburyport on the 17th, winning 9–7. The first game of the series with Boston Reserves was played on the 18th in Lawrence. Lawrence won, 6–4, in a game lasting two hours, featuring six errors by each team. A statement in the Lawrence paper on September 20 read, "The Boston Reserves decline to play again for the state pennant." Before the end of their season, Lawrence played the Boston Reserves twice more, splitting two games in Boston on September 25–26. Another game was scheduled for October 18 but was rained out.[25]

There was nothing in the Lawrence paper about who was declared champion of their league by the state association. After their game in Boston on September 26, the Lawrence team returned to Lawrence and attended the ball sponsored by the Board of Directors. Their next game was September 30 in Concord, which Lawrence lost, 13–8. The articles detailing this loss blamed the Lawrence players for carousing continuously since the September 26 ball. On the 30th, Selee signed a player from the Boston Reserves for the rest of the year. The final game was played on October 5. One more was scheduled but was rained out. On October 7, the Lawrence paper published the statistics for the year.[26]

This year was the start of Selee's apprenticeship in baseball management, late 19th-century style. The league he was involved with did not make it to the end of the year, a rather common occurrence. He had to change teams due to one team failing financially. Selee learned about scheduling games, securing good financial terms, and other ways to keep a ball club going. This was off the field. On the field, he was successful in putting together a successful team at this level. The record of the Lawrence team after he took over was 27–7–2. This was against all types of competition, ranging from National League teams to local amateurs. He was learning how to handle the rowdy men who played baseball at this time and learning how to recognize talent.

Selee tells a good story about his time at Lawrence in his article "Twenty-One Years in Baseball."

> I was entirely new in the business at that time and one day a representative of the Sanford [Maine] Club came to Lawrence and arranged with two of our directors, without my consent, for our club to go to Biddeford, Maine, on a Saturday afternoon, which was our best attendance day. On this trip we were to represent Sanford against Biddeford, there being a great rivalry between the two towns. According to the story of the two directors afterwards, we were to get $250 and expenses from Lawrence to Biddeford and return, as they claimed, win or lose. We started down, never doubting but what we would win easily enough, but to make a long story short, they beat our club 15 to 1, and we did not get a cent. I will never forget my meeting the two directors the next morning at Old Orchard Beach, and the hard luck faces which they wore.[27]

The Lawrence papers in 1884 show a trip to Biddeford from August 5–7. Three games were scheduled. Lawrence won two by scores of 21–4 and 29–5, and one was rained out. If the story told by Selee is true, it was not in the Lawrence paper.

Selee's description of the beginning of the 1885 season is as follows: "The next spring Walter Burnham took the Lawrence Club and I was with him a while helping him in a general way."[28] Selee was not the manager of Lawrence at the beginning of the 1885 season and was manager of the Haverhill club by the end of this season, as detailed in the *Haverhill Evening Bulletin* in 1885. At the start of this season, both Haverhill and Lawrence were members of the Eastern New England League. There were supposed to be six teams: Biddeford, Brockton, Gloucester, Haverhill, Lawrence, and Portland. Before the season started, Gloucester dropped out. Haverhill's first league game was on May 7 after playing four exhibition games. The first mention of the manager of Haverhill was made during the story on an exhibition game on May 5, and his name was Price.[29] The Portland team scheduled 50 non-league games for this season. Haverhill played at Biddeford on May 11. The field was so bad that there were 30 errors in the game. Biddeford's next few home games were moved to Lawrence so they could improve the field.[30] When Lawrence played at Haverhill on Saturday May 9, the attendance was 1,500. Four hundred fans came from Lawrence, and six horse railway cars were used to convey fans from the railway station to the ballpark. On May 15, the horse railway cars were insufficient to handle the crowds after a Brockton-Haverhill game in Haverhill. On May 16, during a Biddeford-Portland game at Portland, the umpire was run off the field by the Biddeford team.[31]

Exactly what Selee was doing with the Lawrence team during this time is not clear. The only source that mentions him at all was quoted above. His name first come up in the Haverhill paper in a surprising way. Soon after the May 16 incident involving an umpire, there was an announcement that Frank D. Steele of Waltham had been engaged as an umpire by the Eastern New England League. I am quite sure that this person was the subject of this book.[32] The reason is that the umpire for May 19 Haverhill-Biddeford game was listed in the box score as Selee. The article on the game states, "Frank Selee made a very favorable impression as an umpire, showing good judgement on balls and strikes."[33] By June 9, Selee had umpired five more games for Haverhill, and I suspect a few other games in the league. On that date, there was a report in the Haverhill paper that the Biddeford club decided "that rather than play any more games with Mr. Selee as umpire they would forfeit them."[34] A separate article says that in a recent game "Selee's decisions were all against the Haverhills." On June 16, there was a game between Lawrence and the Philadelphia National League team at Haverhill.

Selee was the umpire. A note in the paper on June 16 says, "Frank G. Selee of Brockton was engaged as manager of the Portlands, but it seems they don't want him now. Mr. Selee will probably sue them for it."[35] This was the last mention of Selee as an active umpire in the *Haverhill Evening Bulletin*.

The Haverhill team's record after July 4 was 14–20, good for third place in this five-team league. Half of their losses were to Brockton, the league leader. On July 6, Haverhill beat Lawrence at home by a score of 6–1. In the next day's paper, under the box score, was a note that "Manager Brackett has been released and Frank G. Selee formerly of Lawrence has been elected Manager."[36] The article is not clear on which person managed the July 6 game. So Selee's first game as Haverhill manager was either on July 6 or July 8.

Haverhill

Selee's own comment on this hiring was "One morning I was very much pleased to get a telegram from William H. Moody, now Justice of the Supreme Court of the United States, asking me if I could come up and manage the Haverhill Club, of which he was president. I did not waste any time in making arrangements but went up there and did well with that club that year."[37] As we have seen above, there was an interval between Selee's employment with Lawrence and Haverhill, which he spent as an umpire. One of the major features of his subsequent career was a relatively tolerant view of umpires. As we will see, the 1890s was the most difficult time in all baseball history to be an umpire. With very rare exceptions, there was one umpire per game. The umpire could not see everything on a baseball field, and players took advantage of this fact. Add in the normal human imperfection, and many calls were missed. This caused arguments which went farther than we are used to in modern baseball, even before replay. There are many instances of a player and umpire exchanging blows. We will see instances of umpires forfeiting games when an ejected player refused to leave the field. These events would not occur when Selee was managing a team. He would complain about bad calls to the press, and his players would argue during the game, but it was very rare that one of his players was ejected or suspended. I think that his short experience as an umpire had something to do with this attitude.

Haverhill, Massachusetts, was at that time another manufacturing town on the Merrimack River. It is located about 10 miles downstream of Lawrence, which translates to about eight miles as the railroad went. Today there are no mill buildings in Haverhill, as there are in Lawrence and Waltham. However, it was a river mill town in 1885. Due to their location,

Lawrence and Haverhill were rivals in the Eastern New England League. In many of the articles about games between the two clubs, it was noted that fans made the trip from Lawrence to Haverhill and vice versa.

The first game I am sure that Selee managed for Haverhill was a 3–2 home win against Portland on July 8. His first game against Lawrence took place in Haverhill on July 9. The result was an 8–4 win in a rain-shortened, seven-inning game. The article reporting this game in the Haverhill paper included the following quotes:

> Frank G. Selee, who ignominiously failed as a New England league umpire, has been engaged to manage the Haverhills, and began his duties yesterday. (*Biddeford Journal*)
>
> Mr. Selee, it is intimated, was hardly a success as an umpire. As a manager of a base ball team he has not an equal in the New England league, as the Biddefords will find before many days. His success the last of last season with the Lawrences, and previous to that with the Walthams is well known. (*Lawrence American*).

This was a good reputation to have as an apprentice manager.[38]

The prediction from the *Lawrence American* that the Biddefords would find the Haverhills difficult was not borne out in their next two games. Biddeford won 5–4 in Boston on July 11, and 5–3 in Haverhill on July 12. This moved Haverhill to fourth in the league. Before July 21, Haverhill went 1–2 in league games and 2–1 in exhibitions. On July 20, it was announced that Biddeford was going out of business. On July 21, it was announced that Biddeford would move to Newburyport and that Lawrence would move to Manchester, New Hampshire. Haverhill's next game was at Newburyport, which Haverhill lost, 10–8. The league now consisted of Brockton, Haverhill, Manchester, Newburyport, and Portland. A new league schedule was printed in the Haverhill paper on July 24. Haverhill finished out the month with an 18–25 record, in third place. Haverhill had a winning record against all the teams in the league except Portland. Its record against Portland was 1–10. An example of the attitude regarding players was shown in the Haverhill paper of July 31: "Rittenhouse of the Brocktons was yesterday suspended for 10 days without pay, with a promise of being blacklisted if he does not do better."[39]

After the announcement that Lawrence was moving to Manchester, the Lawrence team continued to be identified as Lawrence, though a couple of its home games were played at Manchester. On August 3, Selee released two players from Haverhill who were signed by Lawrence later that day and played in Lawrence's game on the August 3. Haverhill and Lawrence played on August 10 in Haverhill and August 12 in Manchester. Haverhill swept those games, which featured a home run hit by Foster of Haverhill that was "the longest ever hit here in Manchester." This left Haverhill in third place behind Portland and Brockton. Brockton played at Haverhill on August 15, resulting in a 4–2 Haverhill win before 1,800 fans. The

Haverhill paper commented, "Umpire Donahue should have fined Cudworth [Brockton 1B] for the contemptible and ungentlemanly epithet he applied to him on Saturday." Haverhill beat Brockton again on the 17th for a five-game winning streak, reaching a .500 record. On August 24, after a loss to Newburyport put Haverhill two games below .500, "Manager Seelye [sic] fined both Hawks and Murphy for careless and indifferent playing at Newburyport yesterday." We tend to think that disclosure of salaries is a recent development in baseball. On August 27, the salaries of the Portland players were printed in the Haverhill paper. Maybe these numbers encouraged the Haverhill players, as they won three games to put themselves one game over .500 by August 31.

On September 2, a rule change by the National League was published. Before this, if someone was released, there was a 10-day waiting period before anyone else could sign him. That waiting period was eliminated. This rule would change back and forth during Selee's career. A player from Newburyport, Jandron, was released in early August and then worked as an umpire in this league. On September 5, Newburyport signed Jandron as a player for the rest of the year. Haverhill continued their good play into September, winning nine straight until a loss at Brockton on September 8. That same day, Selee signed Tommy McCarthy, late of Boston NL. On September 14, the Newburyport board of directors met and decided to finish the season rather than disband immediately. Haverhill continued in third place in the league. On September 21, Haverhill played a home exhibition game against the Boston Resolutes, described in the article as "a colored nine." Selee played four positions in this game, a 22–15 win in front of 150 fans. Haverhill had 27 errors, Boston 29. By the final league game, won by Haverhill 6–4 over Newburyport, the standings of the first three teams were in dispute. Lawrence and Brockton were in first and second, with the order in dispute. Haverhill was in third with a final record of 44–35. Per my calculations, Haverhill's record under Selee in league games was 29–15.

Here are a couple of examples of the things that happened in a low-level league like this during this time. On October , the assets of the Newburyport team were sold at auction. The Haverhill team played a benefit game on September 29, proceeds to be divided up between the players. One of the players, Foster, got his money from the benefit and left town. The Haverhill paper reported that he left behind many unpaid bills. The final standings between Lawrence and Brockton were disputed, mainly because of two rainouts. The league secretary ordered these games to be made up in early October. The first game was scheduled for Lawrence on October 3. One thousand fans showed up, but the Brockton team did not. The umpire declared a forfeit to Lawrence. After some haggling, this result was thrown out. Lawrence won at Brockton on October 11 and at Lawrence on October 15 before 1,500 fans. Lawrence was declared winner of the league.

There was a meeting of the stockholders of the Haverhill club on October 12. It was reported that the team had $407 in the bank, with $90 inunpaid bills. At this meeting it was agreed that Selee would be the manager for the 1886 season. The first mention of the new baseball season in this league was made by Tim Murnane, the baseball writer of the *Boston Globe*, on April 1. He stated, "Judge Moody, President of the New England League, was very competent."[40] The league scheduled a meeting at Haverhill for April 7, requiring a $500 bond from each club in the league to ensure they would finish the season. Before the meeting on April 7, the players in the area from the Lawrence club played Haverhill in an exhibition. Neither team had required their players to report yet. Before the team reported, some business was done for the Haverhill club. An offer to buy the team was referred to a committee. The local railroad company offered to build a separate entrance for ladies at the Haverhill grounds. Per an article on April 17, "Seelye [sic] has 15 men signed, and sold Peter Carrington to Manchester." The players in town had been practicing together, and all players reported by April 19.

Before the start of the season, Haverhill played four exhibition games, winning them all. Two more players were signed, bringing the total to 17. Practice was held every day, weather permitting. Haverhill put season tickets on sale for $15. The league ordered umpires to wear orange and black striped cap and jacket. No illustrations of these survive, but they must have been strange-looking. Opening Day took place at Haverhill on April 30. Two thousand five hundred fans attended an 11–2 win over Lawrence. A notable quote from the Haverhill paper regarding this game read: "The 3rd base line is in most horrible condition." During a Haverhill win on May 4, their starting pitcher, Murphy, was fined $5 for kicking, called a "would-be Kelly" by the *Boston Globe*. The same article said the Haverhill club complained loudly the whole game. The Haverhill paper reported on May 7 that the "baseball club has moved its residence from Hotel Webster to the boarding house of Mrs. Ford." On May 11, the *Boston Globe* said that "Con Murphy, LF and P, is a kicker that ranks with Kelly." These references to Kelly show how famous Mike "King" Kelly of the Chicago National League team was. Kelly was known as the most creative player and kicker in the big leagues. Selee would encounter him later in his career. After a 17–6 loss at Portland on Monday May 17, the Haverhill paper stated why Haverhill lost this game. "Haverhill team was paid on Saturday, partied on Sunday, and this was the result." On May 18, "Manager Seelye [sic] put his team thru a rigid regimen of soda water," resulting in a 9–0 win the next day. A May 26 article stated that the Haverhill club was trying to secure land for a new park, as the old one was insufficient for the crowds being drawn. The league raised umpire salary from $125 to $150 per month. On May 31, Haverhill beat Lawrence, 3–2, at Lawrence before a crowd of 3,690, the biggest they had played before. Haverhill's record was 12–9, in first place on this date.

On June 1, sportswriter Tim Murnane took over the Boston Blues of this league, posting the $500 bond required by the league. Newburyport was back in the league and made the news several times in June. The umpire did not show for a Haverhill game at Newburyport. The managers agreed on a Newburyport player as the umpire for a game that resulted in a 7–4 Haverhill win. "At this game, a Haverhill supporter in the stands flashed the sun in the eyes of the Newburyport batters, with the aid of a pocket mirror. They tried to find him unsuccessfully. But the flashing stopped." On June 8, a pitcher in this league last year, Ledell Titcomb, pitched for the Philadelphia National League team. On June 9, Haverhill hosted the Boston National League team for an 8–1 loss before 1,000 fans. The *Boston Herald* commented after this game about the Haverhill ballpark, "The grounds are not only remote, but are very poor, and the large attendance, especially of ladies, evinces the deep interest that Haverhill people take in base ball and their nine. The diamond is downhill, and the outfield uphill, so that the base runner goes downhill to get to 1st base. The surface of the ground is very sandy, dusty and uneven, and the balls are very hard to judge, so that accurate fielding becomes very difficult, and errors are in most cases excusable."[41] On this day, the Newburyport board of directors were hauled before a Justice of the Peace there and had to swear that the team was not throwing games. During a 12–11 loss at Haverhill, Brockton pitcher and manager McGunnigle was fined three times for a total of $65. Haverhill player McGarr asked for his release on June 25. He had played in every game for Haverhill this year at 3B or SS. His brother was with the Worcester team in the National League, and he wanted to try to catch on there. McGarr was not released at this time. After a June 26 game at Haverhill, this comment was made about a Boston Blues player: "RF for the Boston Blues is McGough, a left handed batter and thrower. His left hand is minus a thumb, and how he manages to throw straight is a mystery." Haverhill ended the month of June with a record of 22–14, tied for first place with Lawrence.

July did not start so well. After a second loss in a row on July 1, the Haverhill paper commented that the last two games "have given the croakers a wonderful chance, and they have exercised it." The next game was a loss at Brockton, which led to this comment: "How would it do for Manager Seelye [*sic*] to read the riot act to his nine?" There were some unusual games in this month. On July 5, Haverhill and Newburyport played a doubleheader, a morning game in Newburyport and an afternoon game in Haverhill. The afternoon game drew a crowd of 3,277, and Haverhill had its first errorless game of the year to complete a sweep. On July 7, Haverhill was scheduled at Portland, and the umpire did not show. Both teams agreed to allow a fan to umpire, whom the Haverhill paper called incompetent. During the 14–7 Portland win, a home run was hit in the seventh inning. Per normal procedures then, the players attempted to get the ball back. A youth secured the ball and ran away from the park. The nearest outfielder chased him down and got the ball, which was returned to the Haverhill pitcher. The pitcher refused to use the old ball and officially protested the game, which was called for darkness after the eighth. A couple of further comments in the Haverhill paper show that Selee was on increasingly thin ice. There was a headline on July 12 of "UNEXPECTED BACKBONE." The story said, "Manager Seelye [sic] has fined Murphy $10 and indefinitely suspended him for 'chinning.' Slattery also fined $5 for the same offence." On the 13th, the article contained this quote: "A stock holder in the Haverhill Athletic Association proposes to call a meeting of his fellow sufferers next week and fire the directors of the association for the defeats suffered by our star aggregation of ball players." On the 15th, there was a board meeting of the Haverhill club. It was reported that the finances of the club were in good shape, and there was a discussion about the performance of the club. Selee sold the club's best player, McGarr, to the Athletics of the American Association on July 16, and signed two new players.

The climax of this activity took place after the July 19 game, a 4–3 win over the Boston Blues at Haverhill. Under the box score was a story starting, "Frank G. Selyee [sic] has been released from the management of the Haverhill team at his own request." After this game, Haverhill's record was 27–23, in third place. After the July 20 game, the reporter stated, "The members of the Haverhill base ball club have agreed to sign the pledge for the remainder of the season, if Manager Seelyee [sic] will return to his position and their proposition will probably be accepted." Their proposition was not accepted. Selee's entire comment on the 1886 season in his article written after his retirement was "In 1886 I started the season with Haverhill but did not finish the season, as one of the directors was insisting on a change."[42] It appears that after the July 19 game, Haverhill was managed by one of the players until a new manager was named. This action was finalized during the July 26 board meeting. The report of this meeting included the statement: "At the meeting of the Directors of the Haverhill Athletic Association, Manager Frank G. Seelye [sic] was released and John Irwin was appointed to fill the vacant position." Irwin had been the fill-in manager and remained player-manager the rest of the year. The standings after the July 26 game were: Haverhill 33–23, Portland 30–25, Brockton 31–27, Lawrence 28–25, Newburyport 30–28, Boston Blues 16–39. The new manager did a good job the rest of the year, with a record of 27–15.

However, it was not enough to win the pennant. Portland won with a record of 66–36, and Haverhill finished second at 60–38. An earlier comment in the Haverhill paper on the occasion of Selee's official release was "And yet Haverhill people are crazy enough to wish to get rid of a good manager right in the middle of the season while the pennant is within their grasp, simply because he is not perfect." Well, the pennant was not won.

Selee himself made no comment on what he did the rest of this baseball season. He tells of his contact with a person from Chicago that led to his next job, but that would not start until March 1887. I presume he returned to Melrose and lived with his parents. These three years in the local minor league consisted of Frank Selee's apprenticeship in baseball management. He learned many basic lessons about putting a team together and managing both the players and the business. Soon, he would have an opportunity to show these skills on a larger stage.

2

The Minors

Oshkosh

Selee stated in his article "Twenty-One Years in Baseball" that "it was at Oshkosh, Wis. in 1887 that I obtained my real start in baseball."[1] Exactly how he secured the job managing the Oshkosh team in the Northwestern League is not clear. The only hint is given by Selee in that article: "I will never forget a young man by the name of Cody, from Chicago, who was the means of my going there; in fact, he secured the position for me. He advised me to leave the East as there was no chance for advancement there at that time. Still without much experience, I followed his advice and took this club, realizing that it would be a good opportunity to learn a lot about the game and how it should be played."[2] Other names came up in the research as people who ran the Oshkosh club in 1887, so the nature of Mr. Cody's connection to the club is not clear.

The game changed slightly in 1887. For this year only, five balls would be required for a walk, and four for a strikeout. One of the leading catchers in the majors, Buck Ewing, said, "The new rules will make catchers work harder than ever because more men will be on base and the catcher will then have to play under the bat longer."[3] New ball-strike indicators were issued to the umpires, reflecting this change. The National League ordered all clubs to erect a wire screen behind the plate to keep balls out of the stands. It was not clear how far this screen was to extend down each baseline, probably left up to each club. Another article in the *Oshkosh Daily Northwestern* detailed the scoring changes to go along with the rule changes.[4] A walk would be counted as a hit. A hit by pitch and balk were scored as errors on the pitcher. Hitters could not call for high or low pitch anymore. Pitchers were not allowed to run up on the pitch, could only take one stride while throwing the pitch.

On April 12, the players under contract to Oshkosh reported for preparation for the season. There was no trip south; spring training took place in Oshkosh until the season started on April 30. Their first practice took place outside on April 15. The *Oshkosh Daily Northwestern* listed the roster in its article on April 16: seven Irish (Cooney, O'Connell, Burns, Doran, Nagle, Roche, and Hillery), three Germans (Gastfield, Krock, and Shafer), and four Americans (Hoy, Ellis, Burdick, and Harkness). The paper predicted that Oshkosh would win the pennant. Five amateurs from Oshkosh joined the team during spring training so they could play intrasquad games. Oshkosh played two exhibition games and four intrasquad games before the season started on April 30.

Of the players inherited by Selee, the most notable was William Hoy. Hoy lost his hearing and voice due to meningitis when he was three, and he became a cobbler. This was a common profession for hearing handicapped people then. Hoy owned his own shop for three years in his hometown of Houcktown, Ohio, playing Sunday ball. He was good enough at baseball that he decided to try that as a profession. Hoy visited several teams during the 1885 season, trying out as a catcher. The Milwaukee club offered him a contract. Hoy asked for $75 a month, and Milwaukee would only go to $60. Hoy went back to Houcktown. He caught on with Oshkosh as an outfielder at the start of the 1886 season. In his words,

> One rainy day in the spring of 1886 the Oshkosh players were assembled in the clubhouse getting ready for opening day. A newspaperman entered to take down the age, height and weight of each player. When it came my time to be interviewed, he omitted me because I was a deaf mute. Also, he had not the time to bother with the necessary use of pad and pencil. When I read his writeup the next day, I found he had me down as twenty years of age. He had made what he considered a good guess. Now in my school days, I had been taught to refrain from correcting my elders. Then, too, he had whiskers! After thinking it over, I decided to let the figures stand. What would you have done in my place?[5]

As Hoy was born in 1862, his baseball age was four years less than his real age. This is another thing that has happened throughout the history of baseball. Hoy was at the beginning of a career that carried him to a 14-year Major League stay. His great assets were his speed and intelligence. At the age of 41, he stole 46 bases in the Pacific Coast League. In the fashion of the times, he was known as Dummy Hoy. He said that, despite his handicap, he never had a serious outfield collision in his career. Hoy lived to throw out the first ball of a 1961 World Series game in Cincinnati, dying later that year at the age of 99.

The regular season started at home on April 30 with a loss to Duluth. The second home series was with Eau Claire. An ad in the *Daily Northwestern* promised a three-game series, with admission of $.25 for each game. The series turned into a two-game sweep for Oshkosh. Selee was learning his players. On May 10, he released Hillery and signed left-handed pitcher Devine. Devine was a graduate of Syracuse University and a law student in the off-season. While Selee would not limit himself to college men, he showed a marked preference for them.

On May 10, Oshkosh turned a triple play on a line drive to first base during a 14–7 loss to Minneapolis. While on the road, Selee wrote a letter to the baseball writer for the *Daily Northwestern*, received and quoted on May 23. Selee stated: (1) Devine is a good pitcher, (2) Umpire in recent loss to LaCrosse was rank, and (3) Oshkosh pitcher Burdick was sick last week, OK now. Burdick pitched on May 23, securing a 3–2 win at Des Moines. There was an interesting story in the May 25 paper about an exhibition game between Eau Claire and Winona, Minnesota. The game was played at Winona in a park adjacent to the Mississippi River. The game was called during the sixth inning after 21 balls had been hit into the river. The Winona team had sent out people to secure balls from nearby residents when they saw what was happening but ran out anyway.

Selee stated in "Twenty-One Years in Baseball," "Oshkosh was one of the most loyal towns I ever saw in baseball. The patrons of the sport there would rather have had us win from Milwaukee than to have won the championship. However, Milwaukee did not do a thing but beat us 14 straight games at the start."[6] The record in the *Daily Northwestern* shows that Oshkosh won the first game at Milwaukee on May 27. Milwaukee won five games from Oshkosh in the next six days. The pay of the Oshkosh players was detailed in the paper on June 2. All players received $200 per month except O'Connell and Cooney, who received $250. Cleveland of the American Association inquired about acquiring pitcher Gus Krock. This was normal in the life of a minor league team then. Remember there was no farm system. Most players were signed to the club that employed them, and they could be traded or sold, as players are today. Selling players to the Major Leagues was a major source of income for minor league teams. A problem that was more common in those days showed up in a game with Des Moines at Oshkosh on June 7. Des Moines won 5–4 after an Oshkosh player was caught off third base on a fake throw on a double steal. The newspaper comment was that "considerable money changed hands on this game." Gambling and reports of gambling were common. After the June 10 games, the standings for the Northwestern League: Milwaukee 20–8, St. Paul 19–9, Des Moines 16–14, Oshkosh 16–14, LaCrosse 14–14, Minneapolis 14–14, Duluth 10–18, Eau Claire 6–24.

Oshkosh continued to improve, moving into third place by themselves by June 24. Selee reports in his article, "About the last of June 1887, Mr. Sawyer, one of the principal backers of the club, went East and bought the release of Lovett and Wilson the Bridgeport club, and Tommy McCarthy of the Philadelphia National League Club."[7] Since Selee was familiar with all these players, having managed Lovett and McCarthy and managed against

Wilson, it is safe to say he was behind these moves. McCarthy first appeared in an Oshkosh box score on June 28, as both RF and P. Lovett and Wilson made their first appearance as a battery on July 12. By this time, Selee had determined a way to aid Dummy Hoy. An 1888 article explained, "Hoy is left-handed, and when he bats a man stands in the captain's box [coaching box] near third base and signals to him decisions of the umpire on balls and strikes by raising his fingers."[8] At this time, umpires shouted out their ball-strike call, but there were no physical indications and no scoreboard notations. The catcher or batter asked for the count and would get a verbal answer. This may have been the first use of ball and strike signals on the baseball field. The raising of the right hand for a strike would not become standard until the 1910s.

Selee states in his article that after McCarthy, Lovett, and Wilson joined him, "Milwaukee never won another game from us that season."[9] After McCarthy arrived on June 28, Milwaukee won three games from Oshkosh. After Lovett and Wilson joined him on July 12, Milwaukee lost all their remaining games with Oshkosh. The Milwaukee team was the leading team of this league. It was owned and managed by James Hart. Some teams in this league complained about beer sales at Milwaukee home games leading to overly rowdy crowds. In a July 5 article, Selee stated that Hart was one of the fairest businessmen he had ever dealt with. Hart and Selee would compete in the same league every year from 1887 to 1901 except 1889. Hart would then hire Selee. James Hart was one of the most important people in Selee's career.

One fact often cited about Selee is that he was one of the few managers who never played baseball professionally. Another was James Hart. Hart was born in Girard, Pennsylvania, and got involved with the local amateur baseball club as secretary at the age of 15. He became involved with the professional Louisville club a few years later, eventually becoming an investor by the time Louisville joined the American Association in 1882. In 1882, Hart was appointed Vice-President and became a member of the Board of Directors. He was the manager of Louisville, after only business experience, for the 1885–1886 seasons. After the 1886 season, he sold his interest in the Louisville club and bought the controlling interest in the Milwaukee club, then in the Northwestern League. We will follow Hart's career, and its effect on Selee, until 1905.[10]

Two of Selee's players were targets of other teams in July. Selee refused to sell either Roche or Shafer. On July 16, an off-day for Oshkosh, Devine and Cooney played for the Neenah, Wisconsin, town team, receiving $50 apiece. Selee announced the next day that Devine would not pitch for a couple of days. On July 18, McCarthy had to pitch the eighth inning in a 19–12 loss at St. Paul. The fact that the starting pitcher (Burdick) was shelled would not cause a pitching change, as we will see in many games managed by Selee. Burdick claimed a sore arm, so McCarthy came in and gave up seven runs. On July 22, the Eau Claire manager picked Oshkosh to win the league after a 20–0 loss. The same day, Selee gave one of his catchers, Nagle, a week off to go fishing. During their final home series of July, Oshkosh won a game from Minneapolis on July 28 by a 9–0 score as a forfeit. The Minneapolis pitcher gave up seven in the first inning, then claimed a sore arm. Minneapolis had no other pitchers, so they forfeited. During this home stand, the *Daily Northwestern* made this characterization of the Oshkosh team: "It is said that the Oshkosh boys are saving their money. One thing is certain, and that is that they are as gentlemanly and orderly a set of ballmen as Oshkosh ever saw." Similar statements about his teams would follow Selee around. For the road trip starting on July 31, Selee took 13 players. After a series at St. Paul, the top of the league standings showed: Milwaukee 48–23, Des Moines 43–27, St. Paul 42–30, Oshkosh 39–31.

Gus Krock started the next game in Minneapolis, was hit by a liner in the second inning, and had to come out. McCarthy finished the game, an 18–10 Minneapolis win. Oshkosh then won six in a row. During the August 8 win at Duluth, McCarthy was fined $10 for disorderly conduct. One of the pitchers left home, Dilworth, was put into a mental hospital in Oshkosh on August 10. Selee was told that Dilworth's mental condition was okay, but his physical condition was not good. On August 12, Selee wrote a letter to the Oshkosh Board of Directors, discussing how to schedule make-up games with Des Moines, and how the team was doing on the current road trip. The road trip ended with a make-up game at Milwaukee, won by Oshkosh 11–2. After this game, Oshkosh had 43 games left, 25 at home. The top of the standings consisted of Milwaukee 52–27, Des Moines 46–30, St. Paul 46–32, Oshkosh 44–34.

After winning the first three games of their home stand, Oshkosh had won five in a row and 12 of their last 16. Selee accounted for the success of the Oshkosh team by stressing the harmony of the players. He released Dilworth on August 20. The home stand ended with three wins against Des Moines, whose manager stated he would not make up the postponed games with Oshkosh. The next road games were at Des Moines, which swept a three-game series. Two negative comments were recorded about Selee at this time. The *Daily Northwestern* blamed the series loss on bad management. *Sporting Life* magazine said that Oshkosh spent $10,000 on players and was 7½ games out.[11] At the end of August, Oshkosh was in fourth place, five games out.

On September 2, one of the Board members said that Oshkosh would have a team next year, with Selee the manager. Selee said he would not announce the battery for any game until just before games the rest of the year. After four straight wins, three against Milwaukee, Oshkosh was in fourth place, 1½ games out. Their pitchers' records at this point: Lovett 14–1, Krock 23–14, Burdick 15–9, Devine 1–10. Manager Hart of Milwaukee said that Des Moines would win the league. Selee signed pitcher Con Murphy on September 9 for the rest of the season. The last-place team, Eau Claire, was in Oshkosh for five games starting September 9. Oshkosh swept these games, going into a tie for first. After this series, Cooney was quoted in the *Daily Northwestern* that Oshkosh would win the pennant. He said that Selee was as good a manager as Hart, even though Selee was a very quiet man.

Selee canceled the remaining exhibition games scheduled during the season due to make-up games. Oshkosh swept a doubleheader from Duluth on September 13. The pitchers were Lovett, who had been with Newburyport last year, and Murphy, who had been with Haverhill. By September 15, Oshkosh had not lost a game all month, winning 11 straight and moving into first place. After losing to St. Paul at home, Oshkosh won four more against both the Twin City teams. Milwaukee did better, and Oshkosh left for Duluth in second place. Three games were scheduled for Duluth. The first was a 10–10 tie, called by darkness. The next two were rained out. The Duluth team agreed to make up these games in Oshkosh, subject to league approval. Standings after September 30: Oshkosh 70–40, Milwaukee 71–43, St. Paul 70–45, Des Moines 68–44.

There was an exhibition game in Milwaukee on October 2 between Oshkosh and Milwaukee. Hart declined to make up any postponed games with Oshkosh. After Oshkosh won two of three at St. Paul, the final series of the year to decide the pennant took place. Oshkosh was at Minneapolis, and Milwaukee at last-place Eau Claire. After a rainout on October 8, Oshkosh won both games of a doubleheader on October 10. Lovett pitched both games, winning 12–1 and 5–1. Times of these games were 1:20 and 1:30. The final standings: Oshkosh 76–41 (.6496), Milwaukee 79–43 (.6475). As winning percentage determined standings, Oshkosh won the league by .0021.

After this game, the Oshkosh team returned via train from Minneapolis. There was a big reception at the train station when they arrived. The Milwaukee paper said that Oshkosh lost $30,000 to win the pennant.

On October 14, Manager Hart of Milwaukee said he would not protest the pennant. An article in Milwaukee on the 15th said that Selee would be replaced in Oshkosh. Selee protested in an article in Oshkosh that it was not true. There was a benefit ball game in Oshkosh on October 22 to raise money to award a medal to the Oshkosh team. Selee said he could get medals for all team members for $200. Tommy McCarthy was signed by St. Louis of the American Association on October 23. At a league meeting on October 24, Oshkosh was awarded a pennant and trophy. An article on October 27 in the *Daily Northwestern* said that Oshkosh lost $20,000 that year.

Selee's comment about this year in his "Twenty-One Years in Baseball" was "I had a very pleasant season there, learned a great deal about the game and won the championship much to the delight of the directors and the best people of the city. I remember one day, Senator Sawyer, father of board member Edward Sawyer, who was interested in the club, came out to see a game, and when several fly balls got away from the outfielders he turned to his son and said 'Edward, why don't you hire more men out there to catch those balls.'"[12]

Tommy McCarthy with St. Louis of the American Association. It appears all team members were issued a sport jacket. St. Louis was McCarthy's next stop after Oshkosh.

Omaha

Selee's performance during the 1887 campaign impressed some people outside of the Northwestern League, to the point that Selee's prediction that he would be in Oshkosh for the 1888 year was overturned. The directors of the Omaha club in the Western Association offered Frank Selee a reported $3,000 salary to bring his Oshkosh team to Omaha and manage them.[13] As we will see, most of the Oshkosh players went along with Selee to Omaha. He had two holes to fill in the outfield after McCarthy went to St. Louis of the American Association and Hoy moved on to Washington of the National League. As Hoy had hit .367 and McCarthy .345 for Oshkosh, these were big holes to fill.

Selee signed Lovett, his leading pitcher from the year before, for a salary of $3,250 for the 1888 season, with a promise to sell him to the Major Leagues after the season. Lovett agreed and was the best pitcher for Selee again in 1888. On the day Omaha players reported for pre-season training, the leading pitcher in the National League, John Clarkson, was sold from Chicago to Boston for $10,000. Clarkson was the second player sold for that much, following Mike Kelly on the same path and the same price. All these prices show that baseball was becoming a more popular sport, considering that the average income for a four-person household in 1888 was around $500.

Omaha players reported for training on April 4 in Omaha. There was no trip south for spring training. The first exhibition game was played in Omaha on April 8. Four exhibition games and one intrasquad games were played before the April 28 Opening Day. Selee recruited three local players to fill out the intrasquad game, as he had 15 players in camp. A major issue in baseball was Sunday ball. When Selee lived in Massachusetts, there was no Sunday ball. Oshkosh did not allow Sunday ball. Omaha did. On Sunday, April 15, St. Paul played at Omaha. Omaha won the exhibition game, 13–2, before a crowd of 2,500. The front page of the *Omaha Daily Herald* featured reports on several sermons preached around town against Sunday ball.

Omaha continued the exhibition season on the road. There was a crowd on 2,000 at Minneapolis on April 18, witnessing a 6–0 Minneapolis victory. Omaha lost four of five games in Minneapolis and St. Paul. There was no Sunday ball in these cities. The road trip ended in Davenport, Iowa. Omaha won two of three, making for a 3–5 record on their first road trip. Davenport complained about one of the Omaha victories. The umpire had not shown up for this game, and the teams agreed upon Selee as the umpire. Omaha won, 10–6, in a game that featured 18 errors (11 by Davenport). Davenport claimed that Selee made bad decisions as the umpire.

The season was scheduled to open at Omaha on April 28, but that game was rained out. One of the pitchers on the Omaha team was unable to pitch due to a sore arm and malaria. Selee signed one of his players from Oshkosh, Ed Gastfield. Omaha swept the two games played with Minneapolis, using two pitchers who played for Oshkosh the previous year, Lovett and Burdick. Omaha won seven games in a row at home to start the season. There was a game scheduled for Sunday, May 6. Religious groups secured an injunction to prohibit Sunday ball before that game. The game was postponed, and the injunction was appealed. A reversal was issued before the next Sunday. On May 13, Omaha lost its first Sunday home game to Des Moines, 1–0, before a crowd of 7,500. Burdick pitched for Omaha, and neither team committed an error. The headline for the story of the game read "The Best Game Ever Seen in This City." Arguments were heard regarding the competing injunctions on April 16, with the court expected to issue a final ruling by the end of April. Omaha completed this home stand with a record of 9–4 before their first road trip of the year. All games except one were pitched by Lovett and Burdick.

The road trip started in Kansas City with Lovett winning a game on May 22. On May 23, a judge in Omaha ruled on Sunday ball, allowing professional baseball games to be played in Omaha on Sunday. On May 24, Omaha beat Kansas City, 2–0, in a game delayed by fans and Kansas City players arguing a call for over five minutes. Soon another pitcher joined the Omaha starting staff. Omaha completed a 5–5 road trip on May 30. All the games were pitched by Lovett, Burdick, and Clarke. The next home stand started on June 2. New pitcher Healy pitched a complete game in an 18–6 loss to Kansas City before 1,500 fans. Clarke pitched the next two games and Lovett played RF due to injuries. On June 7, Selee had his first view of Bobby Lowe, playing left field for Milwaukee. From now until the end of Selee's Major League career in 1905, Lowe would be in the same level of league as Selee. As we will see, Lowe spent most of this time playing for Selee. The short home stand was two games, swept by Omaha, leaving them with a record of 16–9.

The next road trip started with two losses in Milwaukee, managed by James Hart. The next game was an exhibition in Oshkosh. As we have seen, some teams that were in the Northwestern League in 1887 migrated to the Western Association in 1888 (Milwaukee, Minneapolis, St. Paul). The Oshkosh team of 1887 was now playing in Omaha for Selee. A group of Oshkosh baseball lovers formed a new team and played in the Northwestern League. As of this date, the teams in the Western Association were in Omaha, Kansas City, Minneapolis, St. Paul, Des Moines, St. Louis, Milwaukee, and Chicago. This was a bigger stage than the Northwestern League. However, as was common in leagues during this period, these towns were subject to change. By the time this road trip ended on June 24, the St. Louis team had dropped out and transferred to Sioux City. Omaha went 2–10 on this road trip, making its record 18–19. Selee noted that the best player on the Chicago team was a Chicago native, Herman Long.

Omaha started their next home stand with a 25–2 victory over Lafayette, a colored (as they were referred to in the newspaper) team based in Omaha. On this same day, a new schedule was issued by the league, substituting Sioux City for St. Louis. The first Sunday of the home stand featured a 6–2 win over Des Moines before a big crowd. That same week, a judge in Minneapolis denied a request to legalize Sunday ball in the Twin Cities. Selee saw another player who would be very important in his career for the first time on July 6. Lovett, who had been playing outfield as well as pitching, started against Kansas City. The opposing pitcher was an 18-year-old named Charles Nichols. For good reason, he was nicknamed Kid. Nichols and Kansas City won this game, 8–5. Selee had now seen three players in the Western Association that he would take to fame in the National League when they were all a little older. On July 9, Long played LF for Chicago in a 4–3 Omaha win. There was an article in the *Omaha Daily Herald* on the July 10 about the possible dissolution of the Western Association. By

July 18, Long had been traded to Kansas City. In a game in Omaha on that date, Nichols pitched and Long played LF for Kansas City in a 6–3 Kansas City win before a large crowd. The game the following day was played earlier than usual, so Kansas City could catch a train for their required travel. After this game, Kansas City and Omaha were tied for third place in the league behind Milwaukee and St. Paul. The home stand, which had started on June 30, continued until August 7. Omaha played all the other teams in the Western Association during this time. They finished the home stand with a three-game sweep of Milwaukee and went 20–9 on this home stand. By August 7, the Minneapolis franchise had transferred to Davenport, Iowa, and the Chicago team was for sale.

Now Omaha went on the road for 2½ weeks. They won the first game in Des Moines on a player scoring by advancing to third and scoring on a bad throw in a 2–1 game. This put Omaha in second place, their highest position to date that year. After the series in Des Moines, Selee signed pitcher Kennedy, just released by Des Moines. On August 11, the Davenport team did not show up for the advertised game time due to threatening weather. It was not raining, so the umpire forfeited the game to Omaha, who were present. The next day was a Sunday, and there was a game in Davenport, won 3–2 by Omaha. Lovett denied a rumor that he was being sold to Chicago of the National League. Omaha then lost three to first place St. Paul. The losing streak reached five in Milwaukee before Omaha won on August 21, with Clarke pitching. After three games in Chicago, Omaha completed the road trip with a 6–7 record. The last home stand of the year started with a four-game series with first place St. Paul. Omaha won the first three, moving up to third place behind Des Moines and St. Paul. During the first week of this home stand, the Omaha club tried starting games at 1 p.m. This lasted until September 4 and drew crowds of less than 300 per game. The game on September 5 went back to the normal starting time of 4 p.m. and drew a crowd of about 1,000. Their series against Chicago concluded with a game on September 6. The Chicago team was ahead, 10–7, after seven innings and asked to have the game declared complete so they could leave to catch a train. Omaha denied their request, Chicago left anyway, and the umpire declared the game a forfeit win for Omaha. The final series in Omaha was against Milwaukee. Omaha took three of four, resulting in a 10–5 home stand.

All remaining games except three in 1888 were on the road. Omaha was in third place at the start of this road trip, which started at first-place Des Moines. Des Moines won the first two games, Omaha the third, Des Moines the fourth, and the fifth ended in a tie called by darkness. The tie game was played off the next day. The umpire assigned to the series had left for another assignment, so a Des Moines player served as umpire. Omaha won, even though the Omaha paper said this Des Moines player was biased towards his team. Three games with Sioux City were played in Omaha in two days, Omaha winning two. Two games in Kansas City gave Selee his first view of Herman Long playing shortstop in two Kansas City wins. In the second game, the Kansas City pitcher was Kid Nichols. Omaha went to Davenport, winning two of three with the last game on September 30. On the next day, the Davenport team disbanded, not finishing the season. Omaha won three more games in St. Paul, putting Des Moines back into first place. Selee's first season in Omaha ended in Milwaukee against James Hart's team. Two games were split, and the final game of the season ended in a tie. This was probably the last time Selee and Hart met this year, but their relationship must have been flourishing, as will be shown below. The final game of the Western Association season was played on October 9. Des Moines beat Kansas City to win the pennant by a game over St. Paul.

No final standings were printed in the Omaha paper. I could not find final standings on the Internet. Omaha finished with a record of 55–48, in fifth place. Lovett had a fine year, winning 30 games. Selee kept his promise to Lovett, releasing him after the season. Lovett signed with Brooklyn of the American Association. Selee's comment about this year in "Twenty One Years in Baseball" was "We had a strong club in '88 as well as an experienced one. I think I paid Lovett $3250 upon his promise that he would let me get what I could for his release that fall. The best we could do that year was to finish fifth."[14] Selee would make some changes the next year.

Selee made his first public comment on the upcoming 1889 season in a March 31 article in the *Omaha Herald*. "I have got the cream of last season's club, and the new men are in all respects superior to the players they succeeded. If a club of the best all-around players that money could secure is capable of winning the Western League pennant, the pennant will fly over the Omaha grounds next season. The boys are united in a common ambition to be called champions, and no internal wrangling will interfere with their work." The players he was taking about were listed in the article: C.H. Willis P, Elmer Cleveland 3B, Joe Strauss OF, James Cooney C, Jack Crooks 2B, James Canavan OF, J. A. Leighton OF, George Preusser P, Jack Messitt U, Thomas Nagle C, Wally Andrews 1B, Ted Kennedy P, William Clarke P. Five of these players (Cooney, Canavan, Leighton, Kennedy, and Clarke) had been with Omaha the year before. The other players were cheaper. Selee stated, "As a result of the experiences of the season of '88 we decided to establish a salary limit of $12,500 for the '89 season. I had entire charge of the club."[15] One other important point was determined before the start of the season. Selee stated, "I was acting as agent for the Boston National League club that year."[16] I would presume this was on the recommendation of the new Boston manager, James Hart. Hart had sold his interest in the

Milwaukee club and was taking a second try at being a Major League manager. One major rule change was implemented this year. The requirement for walks and strikeouts went back to the numbers that are still familiar: three strikes and four balls.

Omaha held their pre-season workouts in Omaha, with no trip south. Their first exhibition game was with amateurs from the Omaha area and drew a crowd of 1,500. Willis and Kennedy were the pitchers and the umpires. Their first road exhibition game was at Kansas City, which had changed leagues and was now in the American Association. The umpire working that game left in the fourth inning because he was not willing to take the abuse. The league schedule came out the same day, showing Opening Day would be on April 20. Omaha played six more exhibition games, two against Kansas City. Long, Nichols, and McCarthy were on the Kansas City team during the pre-season. Selee signed Walsh, late of Milwaukee, as a shortstop. Soon after Omaha's Opening Day, Kansas City released Nichols, even though he had a 16–2 record in 1888. Selee scooped him up for Omaha.

Omaha started the season with a 12-game home stand against Minneapolis, St. Paul, Milwaukee, and Des Moines. Willis and Clarke started and finished the first eight games as pitchers. Nichols was mixed in after that, pitching two games on the home stand. Omaha finished this opening stretch 9–3, in first place. Omaha went on a road trip to two new cities (Denver, St. Joseph) and one from the prior year (Sioux City). Willis, Clarke, and Nichols pitched all complete games. One game was a 4–4 tie on May 16 at St. Joseph. Omaha went 4–5 on this road trip, returning home with a record of 13–8.

The next home stand was kicked off with a 3–1 win over Sioux City on May 18. Nichols pitched a complete game, and the time of game was 1:15. Selee had signed a fourth pitcher, George Proesser. He made his second start on May 20, with the same result as his first start. In each game, he lost and walked eight men. In the game on May 20, Proesser batted sixth. Willis pitched and won against St. Joseph on May 24, and then played RF and batted third in a win against Denver on May 25. This must have tired him out, as Willis pitched against Denver on May 26. Willis had a shutout through seven innings, then gave up seven in the last two in a 7–6 loss. Until the next time standings were listed in the Omaha paper, all games were pitched by Willis, Clarke, or Nichols. All were complete games except the one on June 7 at St. Paul. Clarke started, went seven innings, and won a 15–10 game. Nichols finished. Second baseman Crooks, a St. Paul native, had five hits and 17 total bases. He was cheered by the St. Paul crowd. After this game, Omaha was 3½ games behind St. Paul.

In Omaha's next game at St. Paul on June 10, the same two pitchers were used again. Clarke started and lost. He was pulled after one inning, and Nichols finished the game, a 12–3 St. Paul win. There had been a couple of rainouts in this series. St. Paul manager Barnes asked Selee to play a make-up game on June 12 before Omaha's next scheduled series. Selee declined due to his pitching situation. Omaha was still in the area, as their next scheduled series was with Minneapolis. Selee's read of his pitching situation was confirmed in the first game, a 12–5 loss. Omaha won the two remaining games in Minneapolis. Both teams then traveled to Omaha, where Omaha won two of three. The only loss came when Willis, playing center field, made an error to allow the winning run in a 6–5 Minneapolis win. St. Paul came to town for three games. Clarke pitched and won the first two on June 21 and 22. The third game was on Sunday, drawing a crowd of 5,000, Omaha's biggest so far this year. Omaha batted first due to losing the coin flip before the game. Omaha scored two runs in the tenth inning to win 10–8 behind a Nichols complete game. After this game, St. Paul's lead over Omaha was reduced to two games. By June 29, Omaha was on an eight-game winning streak and was in first place.

In an example of what can happen when researching information about this age, there was a gap in Omaha newspapers before July 7. On that day, Omaha lost to St. Joseph at home, falling into a tie with St. Paul with a record of 38–16. From May 27 thru July 12, all Omaha games were pitched by either Nichols or Clarke. Willis had moved to center field and was playing every day. Selee signed a new catcher on July 12. Omaha had a one-game lead. It was noted in the Omaha paper that only two players, Willis and Canavan, had been fined so far that year. Fining players for rowdy or inappropriate behavior was very common in baseball in the 1880s, enough so that this was notable. Willis pitched an exhibition game on July 15. He would next pitch in a regular season game on July 29. All games before then were started and completed by Clarke or Nichols. Nichols pitched and won both ends of a doubleheader at Minneapolis on July 27. The split morning-afternoon double header drew over 6,000 fans. Omaha was now four games ahead of St. Paul. The listing of statistics for the American Association showed that the leading base stealer was Herman Long of Kansas City with 53. The final game of the July home stand was won by Omaha against Des Moines. Willis pitched, Nichols played RF, and Crook caught. Omaha was three games up on St. Paul.

St. Paul shaved a game off the lead with a 2–1 series win at St. Paul to start Omaha's road trip. The next series in Milwaukee started with a 7–6 Milwaukee win in 15 innings. Both pitchers (Nichols and Alexander) went the distance. Omaha batted last, scoring two runs in the bottom of the 15th after Milwaukee scored three in the top. Clarke won the two remaining games in Milwaukee before Omaha returned home. Bobby

Lowe played LF for Milwaukee during this series. Most games during this year featured offense. The first game on the Omaha home stand on August 14 did not. Minneapolis won, 1–0, Clarke pitching again for Omaha. Omaha's best chance to score was on a wild pitch. The runner was tagged out at the plate by the pitcher, who was spiked severely enough that a doctor had to be called out of the stands. The Minneapolis pitcher was carried off on the stretcher. Minneapolis scored on a suicide squeeze in the bottom of the ninth. The next series with St. Paul started on August 16. On the 15th, the Omaha club held a five-inning benefit game for Selee. Many St. Paul players participated. Selee pitched for one team and batted for the other. There were athletic contests between the players, such as a 100-yard dash, long-distance throwing, competitive running around the bases, and rifle shooting. Omaha won two of three against St. Paul and went up by 4½ games. The umpire for this series was Tim Hurst, whom Selee would see for many more years in the National League. On August 21 against Des Moines, Selee started Willis at pitcher and Clarke in the outfield. With the score tied in the fifth inning, those two switched positions. Omaha won, 18–7. Omaha finished the home stand with a nine-game winning streak.

Omaha continued winning on the road. The winning streak reached 20 before Denver beat Omaha on September 13. After this game, Omaha had a 10½ game lead over St. Paul. Stories in the Omaha paper were headlined "Omaha's Champions." When asked what he would do after the season, Selee said he would "return to Melrose, Mass. and borrow a chair in the office of my brother, who is a real estate broker there." Asked the same thing, Kid Nichols said he would "hibernate in Kansas City, where he will attend to the wants of those who patronize his pool room." The rest of the season was a triumphal progress. Even though their record was 7–7, Omaha had no concerns about being caught. There was an unusual story about making up games in this league on September 15. That was the day of the last game scheduled in St. Joseph for the Sioux City team. Due to rainouts, those two teams played four games that date. The first three were five innings long, the final one seven innings. Sioux City swept. Selee was trying to arrange an exhibition game after the season with any Major League team. An article on September 20 stated that Omaha would play at Detroit in October, but no date was set. The same article stated that Selee had been offered the job as manager for the Boston National League team, but that he would return to Omaha. On September 22, Selee was quoted as saying, "We are in a position where we don't care what happens or how they come" during a game while sitting in the stands.

The final standings read: Omaha 83–38, St. Paul 77–46, Minneapolis 66–53, Sioux City 60–61, Milwaukee 57–62, Denver 50–71, St. Joseph 42–69, Des Moines 40–75. Omaha's 83–38 record and .686 winning percentage were the best in organized baseball that year. Kid Nichols posted an excellent 39–8 record. Before Nichols returned to Kansas City, he was signed to a contract with Boston of the National League. The director of the Boston team who signed Nichols, William Connant, had a mission on his return to Boston. He persuaded the other two directors to hire Selee as well. The negotiation was easy, as Selee had returned to Melrose by this time. By late 1889, the Boston manager from 1889, James Hart, had accepted a job offer from Albert Spalding, so the position was open. Selee was named manager in late 1889 (no exact date given).

Selee's five years in the minors had been his education in baseball. He had been the agent for the Boston club for 1889 on the recommendation of Hart. The main result of this was the signing of Nichols for 1890. Selee now had the reputation of someone who could recognize talent and let it bloom under his management. He had formed his style. Even though this was an era of hard-drinking, hard-living players, Selee went in another direction. The son of a minister, he was not a drinker. Selee was soft-spoken, relying on preparation to lead his players. There is one famous quote that appears in everything I have read about Selee, which indicates that he was a players' manager. He said, "If I make things pleasant for the players, they reciprocate. I want them to be temperate and live properly. I do not believe that men who are engaged in such exhilarating exercise should be kept in strait jackets all the time, but I expect them to be in condition to play. I do not want a man who cannot appreciate such treatment."[17] There were very few reports of harsh discipline by Selee during his minor league career. He would soon find out how this worked in the National League.

3

Boston:
The First Seven Years

Getting Settled

The first professional baseball league was founded in 1871. That league, the National Association of Base Ball Players, had a team in Boston. That franchise lasted the entire life of the National Association. The manager was Harry Wright, who had invented the job of managing a professional team over the prior two years with the Cincinnati Reds. Harry Wright brought some of the players from the Reds to Boston. After finishing second in 1871 with a record of 22–10, Boston won the pennant the next four years. As we have seen in the leagues Selee was involved in from 1884 to 1889, teams dropped out and new ones entered over the course of the five-year life of the National Association. Over the winter of 1875–1876, the owner of the Chicago franchise, William Hulbert, rebelled against the National Association by forming a new league, the National League. Hulbert laid the groundwork for this move by signing four of the best players from Boston to contracts for 1876 in July 1875. Those players (Al Spalding, Cal McVey, Deacon White, and Ross Barnes) finished out the 1875 season with Boston but played for Chicago in 1876. The new league included six teams from the National Association. Two new franchises joined the National League. Seven teams from the old National Association folded.

The Boston franchise had been called the Red Stockings from 1871 to 1874. In 1875, the name was changed to the Red Caps and remained so until the 1883 season. In 1883, the team was called the Beaneaters. As we will see, team nicknames during this era changed quite a bit. They could change from newspaper to newspaper. The Boston franchise that started in 1871 is the only franchise from that initial professional baseball league that still exists. It is the Atlanta Braves today.

One year after the start of the National League, the Boston franchise was sold. The buyers were referred to as "The Triumvirate" in the Boston papers for the entire time they owned the team, until 1906. We met one of the three at the end of the last chapter. William Connant was a businessman in Boston and bought a piece of the team in 1877. Another businessman, J. B. Billings, bought a piece of the team in 1877. These two were directors, and the junior partners in the Triumvirate.

The senior member had been involved with the Boston franchise from the start in 1871. Arthur Soden started a roofing business in 1867 after serving in the Civil War as a hospital steward. He ran the roofing business for 50 years as his main source of income. He was a minority owner of the Boston franchise from 1871 through 1876, watching the majority owner operate the team. Soden, Connant, and Billings bought a majority share in 1877. Soden would be the member of the Triumvirate most involved in the day to day running of the team. Soden became a power in the National League. After the death of Hulbert in 1882, Soden was interim president of the League until a permanent president was named in 1884.

The National League had a rival in the late 1870s. The International Association operated from 1877 to 1879, trying and failing to establish itself as an equal of the National League. During the skirmish with the International League, Arthur Soden concocted a clause to put into a contract with the players on his team. The National League approved this clause at a meeting on September 29, 1879. That very day, the International Association collapsed. The clause was the Reserve Clause, a major factor in the development of how baseball teams operated until it was voided in December 1975.[1]

Soden was a leader in dealing with the American Association and Union League. The Union League was the effort of a St. Louis millionaire to start another Major League. It failed after one year (1884). I agree with Bill James that the Union League was not a Major League.[2] The American Association was different. The AA started in 1883 and was still operating in 1890. The AA and NL had co-operated in standardizing the rules over the past couple of years. The teams played exhibition games against teams from the other league. The teams from each league accepted the reserve clause in the contracts from the other league, after a four-year fight. Soden was known as someone who was careful with the dollar.

But the Boston team had done well under the ownership of the Triumvirate. Harry Wright won the pennant as manager of Boston in 1877 as a result of the collapse of the Louisville club. This led to an investigation of Louisville and the worst gambling scandal in baseball until the Black Sox.[3] In 1878 the Boston club repeated. This was a team of iron men. Their final record was 41–19, and the team consisted of 10 men. Tommy Bond pitched all but 11 innings, which were pitched by Jack Manning, the right fielder.[4] The only substitute played in two games. Wright remained manager until

1881. John Morrill, a regular on the Boston team since 1876, managed from 1881–1888. The Triumvirate established their reputation as cheap during the first years of Morrill's term. But they got tired of finishing around .500. After the 1886 season, Boston acquired the most famous player of the day, Mike "King" Kelly, from Chicago for $10,000. After finishing fifth in 1887, Boston acquired the best pitcher from Chicago, John Clarkson, for $10,000. These were the largest prices paid to acquire players up to this time. This led to a fourth-place finish in 1888.

One of Soden's maneuvers from the 1887 season paid off in 1889. The Detroit franchise had the best team in 1887, but Detroit's attendance was too small to generate the income at home to meet payroll. The Detroit owner expected to make up the difference on the road. Soden and Chicago owner A. G. Spalding forced through a rule allowing the home team to keep a larger share of the gate, depriving Detroit of necessary income. Detroit hung on for one more year, but the franchise died after the 1888 season. Soden secured four fine players from this wreckage: 2B Hardy Richardson, 1B Dan Brouthers, C Charlie Bennett, and U Charlie Ganzel.[5] The Boston team was much-improved for its new manager, James Hart. The record improved from 70–64 in 1888 to 83–45 in 1889. Boston finished one game out of first because they lost two more games than New York, who finished with a record of 83–43. It was rumored that King Kelly had undermined Hart's authority.

Soden's invention, the reserve clause, was extended to the minor leagues in 1888. By this time, all players in professional baseball were reserved. After the 1888 season, A. G. Spalding led a team of all-star players on a world tour. Spalding's sporting goods company was by now his main source of income, and he was trying to expand his market. The first serious effort to form a players union had started in the mid–1880s. The leader of the Players Brotherhood by 1888 was the shortstop of the New York Giants, John Montgomery Ward, an outstanding player who was also a lawyer. Ward was a member of Spalding's touring team and was out of the country with this team in late 1888. The National League owners (usually referred to as magnates in the newspapers of the day) met and determined to impose a salary limitation on the players.

When Ward heard of this policy, he asked to be released from the touring team. He was released and returned to confront the owners on behalf of the players. The owners ignored Ward's pleas. However, earlier in the tour the players had discussed putting together a league of their own. These plans went on the front burner when the 1889 season started. The 1889 season was played under the contracts signed before that season, and there were no fights about the reserve clause that year. During the season, Ward was putting together plans and contacting investors to start the Players' League for the 1890 season.[6]

This was the biggest revolution in the history of organized team sports in the U. S. After the players were more in control of their contracts under the National Association, owners took control under the National League and American Association. The relationship we are used to today was formed during these years (1876–1890). While there have been many adjustments to this relationship, we still have the owners owning a franchise, signing players to play, and controlling when, where, and how much the players make. Of course, there has always been negotiation involved in this, but most would agree that the owners had the upper hand until the elimination of the Reserve Clause. In 1890, to use Communist terminology, the workers tried to seize the means of production. In the Players' League, players largely owned and operated the franchises. There was no Reserve Clause. A player could not be traded without his consent. Before a manager could release a player, the board of directors on his team had to give their consent. The Players' League made other changes to the game to make it more attractive. National League baseballs were supplied by Spalding, and American Association baseballs were supplied by ex-player Al Reach. Active player Tim Keefe supplied the baseballs for the Players' League, and these balls were livelier than the Spalding or Reach balls. The PL used two umpires for all games. The pitching distance was increased from 56 feet 6 inches to 57 feet.[7]

Ward was a very persuasive person. Most of the best players from the National League and American Association left the security of contracts to give the Players' League a try. Of the three major leagues in 1890, the Players' League had the best players and the highest quality of play. But as the *New York Sun* pointed out before the season started: "The Brotherhood of Ball Players have one great difficulty to contend with: the trust or combination against them which they are seeking to overthrow is composed of eight or ten members. The one they would like to form is composed of nearly 150 members. That is much more difficult to handle than the other. They will need not only loyalty but enthusiasm all along the line."[8] With the best of intentions, the bottom line would determine the fate of the Players' League.

Selee stepped into this maelstrom after he became manager of the Boston NL team. The Triumvirate was known to be economical in paying players. This led most of the important players on the 1889 Boston team to sign with the Players' League. A list of the top 12 players on the 1889 team reads: Dick Johnston, Hardy Richardson, King Kelly, Dan Brouthers, Billy Nash, Joe Quinn, Tom Brown, Charlie Ganzel, John Clarkson, Charlie Bennett, Hoss Radbourn, and Kid Madden. Of these players, only Clarkson, Ganzel, and Bennett were on the 1890 team. The Triumvirs were realistic enough to offer King Kelly a large pay raise to $10,000 over the winter. Kelly had already promised to go to the Players' League. After due consideration,

Kelly said, "I'll stick with the boys." He became the player-manager of the Boston team in the Players' League. Kelly brought many of his 1889 Boston NL teammates along: Hardy Richardson, Dan Brouthers, Billy Nash, Joe Quinn, Tom Brown, Hoss Radbourn, and Kid Madden. The Players' League profits were to be shared equally with all members of the Players Association who jumped. The Players' League initiated three lawsuits contesting the Reserve Clause during the 1890 season and won all of them.[9]

By the time the 1890 season started, there were 25 teams in the three leagues. Selee had to fill out a roster in competition with these teams. As stated above, only three regulars carried over from 1889. One substitute, Pop Smith, stayed with the National League team. As the normal roster size was around 16 during this era, Selee had to find 10–12 new players. Three were the result of Selee's experience in the Western Association. Kid Nichols had been purchased by Boston, on Selee's recommendation, before Selee was hired. Selee recommended the purchase of Bobby Lowe from Milwaukee. That was executed for $700 over the winter. Selee had seen Herman Long during the 1888 season. Long played for Kansas City of the American Association in 1889, having a good rookie year with a .275 average. That franchise was selling its assets before disbanding. Boston purchased Long. Acquiring three talented, very young players was a good start for Selee. This showed his eye for talent. One other player who came from the minors became a regular, Steve Brodie. Other players who were not regulars came from minor leagues.

The rest of the regulars had played in one of the Major Leagues in 1889. Tommy Tucker led the American Association in batting average in 1889 for Baltimore, becoming the first switch-hitter to lead any major league in that category. Soden was aggressive in signing AA players and secured Tucker even though Baltimore remained in business. The Indianapolis franchise of the NL played its final season in 1889, selling off its players. Boston acquired three. Marty Sullivan and Paul Hines were outfielders and comprised two-thirds of Boston's outfield in 1890 at the beginning of the year. Charlie Getzein had been on the outstanding Detroit team in 1887. He was picked up by Indianapolis in 1889, then by Boston in 1890. By the time all these moves shook out, a starting roster was in shape. The Boston NL team started the 1890 exhibition season with this lineup: Tucker 1B, Brodie RF, Sullivan LF, Lowe 3B, Smith 2B, Long SS, Bennett C, Ganzel C, Nichols P, Clarkson P, Getzein P. Selee and the Triumvirs had put together a representative team from the shambles.

The Triumvirs had more to do with putting this team together than Selee, who was not familiar with the players in the Major Leagues and allowed himself to be guided in the composition of his initial team. The most talented young players on this team would shake out this season. This would be Selee's first Major League test as a talent selector and manager.

The 1890 version of the Boston NL team did not go south for spring training. Between April 3 and 18, Boston played 11 exhibition games and was rained out four times. Nichols, Getzein, and Clarkson did most of the pitching. Selee tried Lowe at various positions. Long was cited by the reporter covering the team as the outstanding newcomer, both in the field and at the bat. In an article on April 14, Selee was complimented as an even-tempered leader.[10] The *Boston Herald* covered both Boston teams equally, and usually the story about the Players' League team was in the paper earlier than the NL story. The PL team was expected to win their league, and nobody was sure of what to expect from the NL team.

Boston opened the 1890 season at home against Brooklyn on April 19. The lineup read: Long SS, Donovan CF, Sullivan LF, Tucker 1B, Ganzel RF, Lowe 3B, Smith 2B, Bennett C, Clarkson P. Ganzel was the captain of the Boston team. Clarkson won a 15–9 game before 3,200 fans. Boston committed 13 errors, Brooklyn 19. The Players' League opened the same day in Boston with the same matchup, Brooklyn vs. Boston. More fans attended the PL game. Tim Murnane, the leading sportswriter in Boston, wrote an article on April 21 discussing the Players' League rebellion. He concluded that the PL had the players, but the NL and AA had the money. He was not picking a winner.[11]

Boston was home through April 28. Ganzel got hurt on April 21, replaced by Brodie. Boston won a forfeited game on April 24 when New York argued about a call too long. The umpire gave them a specific time to stop and forfeited to Boston when New York continued. Selee postponed a game scheduled for April 25 due to rain at 1 p.m., 2½ hours before game time. In a 3–1 loss to New York on April 26, Boston turned an unusual triple play. New York had men on second and third with none out. On a grounder to SS, Long looked the runner back to third, then threw the batter out at first. Both runners ran on the throw. Tucker threw home to Bennett, who tagged both runners out at the plate. On every home date that conflicted with the Players' League, the Boston NL team was outdrawn by a significant amount. By the end of the home stand, the NL was considering changing their schedule to avoid conflicts with the PL in towns where each league had a team. Boston finished the home stand with a record of 5–2.

As we will see throughout this book, the National League was informally split between eastern and western teams. For the 1890–1891 seasons, this split was Boston, Brooklyn, New York, and Philadelphia, eastern teams; Pittsburgh, Cleveland, Cincinnati, and Chicago, western teams. During Selee's Major League career, road trips and home stands would consist of games against either fellow eastern teams, or western teams, or all the league. The home stand just concluded was against eastern teams, and the upcoming road trip would be limited to the east. The news on April 29 was that Selee was trying to acquire Chippy McGarr, who had played for Selee in Lawrence and Haverhill. John Taber pitched a complete game on April 30, losing 8–7 to a Brooklyn walk-off. McGarr was acquired, to report on May 1. After a rainout on May 1, McGarr started in RF in a 15–2 Nichols win. This put the pitching back to normal.

After a loss in Philadelphia on May 5, Boston's transportation back to the hotel was not at the ballpark after the game. An attorney in the crowd offered to take Selee and his team back with the two tally-ho horsecarts he had. Selee accepted, and the entire Boston party crowded onto these carts, including the writers covering the team. A new signing, Tony Von Fricken, pitched on May 9 in New York. New York won, 16–3, and that was the only game Von Fricken pitched for Boston. The New York stay provided some interesting games. Two umpires worked a 3–2 Boston win on May 10. May 12 featured the first match ever of two youngsters who would be leading pitchers throughout the 1890s. Kid Nichols faced Amos Rusie. The game lived up to expectations. New York won, 1–0, in 13 innings. A new ball was put into play in the top of the 13th and put out of play with a home run by Mike Tiernan of NY. Boston could not score in the last of the 13th. There were 21 strikeouts in a game lasting 2:15. New pitcher Al Lawson pitched the final game of the New York series, losing 7–2. He was then sent to the minors, just like Von Fricken. The starts by Taber, Von Fricken and Lawson on this trip were aberrations. The rest of the games in the 1890 season were started by Clarkson, Nichols, and Getzein. Taber would pitch once more in relief.

Boston returned home to face Philadelphia and then all the western teams. In the first game against Philadelphia, the writer who was doubling as official scorer noted an incident between the umpire and Bennett. Bennett took four balls in one at-bat and started to first. The umpire called him back, stating the count stood at three balls. Bennett argued and got back in the box, eventually making out. This is a reminder that there were no scoreboards keeping track of balls, strikes, and outs in the ballparks of this era. Boston's record was 8–11 after this game, in last place. Chicago won two of three, with Clarkson losing in his first game back from a brief interruption due to injury. In the first game of the Cleveland series, Nichols won 1–0 in 10 innings. Long scored in the top of the 10th on a squeeze bunt. The game coverage stated, "The Boston club made no mistake when it signed Nichols." Clarkson won later in the series to give Boston two out of three against Cleveland. In the first game against Cincinnati, Brodie made an error that allowed the winning runs to score. Cincinnati took two of three against Boston, Nichols winning the final game, 1–0. The home stand ended with three games against Pittsburgh. Boston won three straight to move to a 15–16 record before its next road trip.

John Clarkson was the best pitcher in baseball during the 1889 season. My main reference book[12] for 19th century baseball lists 11 statistical categories for pitcher performance each year. When a pitcher led the league, the statistic is printed in boldface. Clarkson's statistics for 1889 are boldface for nine of 11 categories.[13] He led the league in games, innings pitched, games started, complete games, wins, strikeouts, walks, shutouts, and ERA. Clarkson was known for an erratic temperament, but his team put up with it due to his outstanding performance. Selee had planned for Getzein to start the game on June 3 in Philadelphia. Clarkson asked to pitch, and Selee let him. This resulted in a loss by Clarkson and a loss by Getzein on the June 4. Even though Nichols, Clarkson and Getzein started all but three games for Boston this year, that was not the only contribution they made. Each played the outfield at least once during this season. That was the consequence of the roster size, which was usually 16, and injuries. This happened all over baseball. A good example came in the Boston game against New York on June 6. Clarkson was opposed by Jesse Burkett on the mound. Jesse Burkett was an outfielder and one of the best hitters in the game. Burkett batted fifth and went 3-for-3. Pitcher Amos Rusie played RF for New York in a 10–3 Boston win. The next , Getzein started for Boston, shut out New York for seven innings, then gave up nine runs in the last two innings in a 9–3 loss. Boston had won the coin toss before the game and chose to bat last.

The point of mentioning these games is to show that Selee was managing a game of baseball that was quite different from today's game. One thing that has not changed is hyperbole. The article about the June 11 game with Brooklyn started: "Charley Getzein made a solemn vow that he would jump off [the]Brooklyn Bridge if he did not pitch Selee's men to victory."[14] Getzein pitched a shutout and survived. That was the final game of this eastern road swing. Boston had two more series at home before their first western road trip. This home stand featured three doubleheaders in four days (the day without a game was a Sunday). All innings were pitched by Nichols, Clarkson, and Getzein. Getzein pitched complete games on both June 16 and 17. Boston went 5–2 on this home stand and left town with a record of 22–20.

Boston started the western swing by taking three of four games from first-place Cincinnati. During this series, Paul Hines reported and started in CF. Selee had acquired Hines from Pittsburgh, probably at the urging of the Triumvirs. Hines wasn't a bad player, but he was at the end of a distinguished career. Hines had been in the Major Leagues since 1872. He was a great player during the late 1870s–early 1880s.[15] Now he was 39 years old and on his last legs. But any player could be dangerous, as Hines proved by driving in the winning runs in the top of the ninth on June 27. This was part of a four-game sweep by Boston in Pittsburgh. A rainout on the first date in

3. Boston: The First Seven Years

John Clarkson in 1888, when he was the undisputed ace of the Boston staff.

Cleveland resulted in three games in two days. Boston swept all three from Cleveland. The final game was on June 3. Boston was ahead 8–0 after the fifth inning. They then stopped trying to get any more hits, so they could make the train to Chicago after the game.

The first day in Chicago was July 4, so there was a morning-afternoon doubleheader. Boston saw the largest crowds they had seen so far this year. Attendance at the morning game was 4,673. After this game, Long was given a silver pitcher by friends from his hometown of Chicago. The afternoon game had 7,820 fans in attendance, watching Boston finish off a sweep. Boston won one more game in Chicago, which made 12 straight wins. After the game, Chicago manager Cap Anson said Chicago would win the pennant and that Boston had only one pitcher (Getzein). Boston returned home to face all the western teams. The largest crowd of the year so far (5,327) attended the July 12 game against Chicago, a 3–2 Chicago win. One of the first comments about Selee's style was made in the *Boston Globe* on July 18. "[Cincinnati manager] Tom Loftus coaches his men from the bench. Selee never does that, but he gets there just the same."[16] Boston went 11–2 against the western teams at home, and 23–5 over the road trip and home stand. Boston was in third place, three games out.

There had been several newspaper stories that summer about the finances of the teams involved in the baseball war. National League establishment figures said the Players' League was running out of money. Players in the PL said the National League was running out of money. The American Association was suffering the most at the gate. The truth was that all parties were suffering. More stories would come out while Boston was on its next road trip, another western swing. Their first stop was in Pittsburgh. The Pittsburgh team was playing better now that their pay had caught up after a missed monthly paycheck. The Pittsburgh ownership would not have taken heart after drawing a crowd of 74 to their game with Boston on July 25. On Boston's trip from Pittsburgh to Cincinnati on July 27, their train was delayed for five hours due to a wreck on the line. That same day, the *Boston Globe* printed attendance figures for the Boston PL team, which was averaging 4,442 per game. The average attendance for all PL games so far was 2,782, and for all NL games 1,913.[17] It was known that the lead Triumvir, Arthur Soden, loaned the Boston club $6,000 to make payroll that season.

Unlike the New England League during Selee's time, no teams folded in the three major leagues this year. Boston started the road trip going 5–1. On July 29, Charley Getzein lost his first game after 10 straight wins. Getzein won his next start in Chicago, going 3-for-3 at bat. After playing all the western teams, the road trip concluded with two games at Brooklyn and one at Philadelphia. In an example of the fluid situation among the leagues, this Brooklyn franchise had played in the American Association in 1889. Brooklyn won the pennant in the AA in 1889 and was contending for the NL pennant in August 1890. Boston finished the trip with a 10–5 record and was in second place.

One way that baseball was different from our time was the length of home stands and road trips. Up until now in the 1890 season, none of the home stands or road trips for Boston had been over 2½ weeks. The end of the road trip cited above was August 9. Boston would be at home, playing all the other teams in the NL, until September 4. Then Boston would spend the rest of the season visiting all the other teams.

At the start of this home stand, Boston was three games behind Brooklyn, in second place. Boston won two games from Philadelphia before welcoming Brooklyn for a three-game series. Brooklyn won two of three, even though Boston got Ganzel and Lowe back from injuries. The first game of the Brooklyn series featured something that was noted often in the 1880s and 1890s. Boston's battery was Getzein and Ganzel. There were a few batteries in baseball that featured two players of German descent. Whenever it happened, someone would note that a "Pretzel Battery" was performing. Brooklyn won two of three from Boston and left town ahead by three games. Boston concluded their home schedule against eastern teams by taking three of four games from New York. By this time, the average attendance for Boston NL home games was up to 2,201.

During the next series with Cleveland, Boston had its first look at a rookie pitcher, Cy Young. Young won the second game of the scheduled three-game series. The final game was canceled "due to the poor conditions of the grounds." The grounds were okay the next day, when Pittsburgh came in for four games. Boston swept these games in three days. The month of August concluded with a three-game series against Cincinnati. Cincinnati won two of three. The biggest takeaway by the reporter covering the series was the talking of Arlie Latham. Latham had been a star with the St. Louis team of the American Association in the 1880s. He was a sub with Cincinnati. There were no coaches in major league baseball during Selee's career. There was no one in the coach's boxes if there was no one on base. If someone got on, a player who was not playing or not scheduled to bat soon would become the coach. Latham was famous for his mouth, as reflected in this nickname: "The Freshest Man on Earth." He had not played in Boston since 1880 because he had been in the American Association. The writer was surprised by his antics.[18] The home stand ended with two doubleheaders against Chicago. Chicago won three of four. At the end of the home stand, Boston was in second place, 5½ games behind Brooklyn. As of this date (September 3), average Players' League attendance in Boston was 2,680. Average National League attendance was 2,116. The average attendance for the Boston National League team in 1889 was 4,659. Boston would play three more home games in the middle of their next road trip, making up games with Philadelphia and Brooklyn.

The east coast portion of the remaining schedule went from September 3 thru 16. Brooklyn swept two games, one in Brooklyn and one in

Boston. Injuries played a role in the rest of the season. In Philadelphia on September 4, Nichols pitched and Clarkson played RF. On September 6, Clarkson pitched and Getzein played RF. Boston went 4–5 before heading west, still 5½ games back of Brooklyn.

Boston's record against the four western teams had been very good up until now. After two rainouts in Cleveland, the story in the *Boston Globe* was about all the players who had signed for next year (all on the roster except Getzein, McGarr, Taber, and Hardie), and the fact that the Boston team thought the pennant was out of reach and were trying for second place. This western swing got off to a bad start with a four-game sweep by Cleveland. Pittsburgh won the first game there, leaving Boston with an eight-game losing streak. Boston won the final game in Pittsburgh and left town in fourth place, with a record of 75–52. Chicago swept Boston, and Cincinnati won the first game of the final series. The final two games were split, leaving Boston with a 76–55 record in fifth place. Brooklyn won the pennant, the only instance of the same franchise winning the pennant in a different major league in consecutive years.

The Boston Players' League team won the pennant, led by player-manager King Kelly. Final attendance figures showed that the Boston Players' League team averaged 2,703, and the Boston National League team averaged 2,202. Total attendance for the Boston National League team was 147,539. Most of the stories about baseball during the remainder of October were about the financial bath that all parties took in this war.

This was a unique environment for Selee to make his debut in as a Major League manager. The team he took over lost most of their good players. Most of the new players were players he was not familiar with, as they had been in the majors while he was in the minors. He had four players on the Boston roster at the end of the year that he knew before 1890. Two performed well. Kid Nichols had 48 starts and 47 complete games with a 27–19 record. Herman Long played 101 games at shortstop, hitting .251 and drawing many compliments throughout the year on his fielding prowess. Bobby Lowe had injury problems and never became a regular even though he hit .280. Chippy McGarr played 121 games and hit .236. The best hitters on the team were Tommy Tucker and Steve Brodie. Neither player fit Selee's style. Both fit what was becoming the 1890s style of play, which was dirty. There were many comments in the coverage of the Boston team during the 1890 season that they did not fight or argue as much as other teams. When someone was arguing, it was usually Tucker or Brodie.

Looking through the statistics in all three leagues for 1890 reveals that Boston was the team that relied on three pitchers to the greatest extent. Most teams featured three main starters. Only Boston had three pitchers start 98 percent of their games. Nichols, Clarkson, and Getzein started all but three games. Clarkson started and completed 44 games, while Getzein started 40 and completed 39. Clarkson was 26–18 and Getzein was 23–17. Selee was going through a National League season for the first time and processed all this information. The Triumvirs indicated that Selee would return for the 1891 season. All would have to await the shakeout from a season with three leagues.

The Class of the National League

All three major leagues had serious financial problems. It was likely that none of the teams made any profit during the 1890 season. Several teams in the Players' League had trouble meeting payroll by the end of the season, and that also happened in the National League and American Association. The National League did a better job of hiding its problems. The committee that ran the Players' League, led by John Montgomery Ward, talked a good game until January 14, 1891. They decided to terminate on that date. Negotiations between all three leagues resulted in a revised two league structure. The Players' League disbanded. The National League continued with the same eight teams. The American Association continued with nine teams, the same number as in 1890. The teams changed around some in the AA. As part of this agreement, all players in the PL who had been subject to the reserve clause at the end of the 1889 season were to return to their former clubs. This agreement was broken immediately by a new team in the AA, the Boston Reds. Most of the players from the Boston PL team moved over to the Boston Reds of the AA. This included three top players who were reserved by the Boston NL team (Hardy Richardson, Tom Brown, and Dan Brouthers). Hence, Selee would have to deal with another major league team in Boston and do without three players who theoretically should have reverted to the Boston NL team.

The Boston NL team secured three players from the Players' League. Two were reserved from the 1889 season. Billy Nash played third base for Boston NL from 1885 to 1889. Joe Quinn played second base for Boston NL in 1888 and shortstop in 1889. Both had played for Boston PL in 1890. Both returned to Boston NL under the agreement concluded with the Players' League. At some point during the winter, Selee became aware that a top outfielder from the Players' League, Harry Stovey, was a free agent due to a paperwork mistake by the team that could reserve him, the Philadelphia Athletics of the AA. Boston claimed Stovey, and the dispute went to a board consisting of one NL owner, one AA owner, and the new AA president. To everyone's surprise, the AA president sided with the NL owner, and Stovey was awarded to Boston. As a result of this decision, the AA withdrew from their agreement with the NL. This meant the two leagues were at war again.

By the time spring practice began in Boston on April 1, the Boston NL team had a new look. Of the players from 1890, Selee had released Chippy McGarr 3B, Pop Smith 2B, Paul Hines CF, and Lew Hardie U. The expected roster for the Boston NL team: Herman Long SS, Tommy Tucker 1B, Harry Stovey RF, Billy Nash 3B, Steve Brodie CF, Joe Quinn 2B, Marty Sullivan LF, Charlie Bennett C, Charlie Ganzel C, Bobby Lowe U, Kid Nichols P, John Clarkson P, Charlie Getzein P. This was the core. New players could emerge in spring practice. The first exhibition game took place at Boston's home ground on April 2 against the defending champion, Brooklyn. It was a nice day, and a crowd of 6,155 saw a 13–2 Boston win. Throughout the exhibition season, Selee stressed sacrifice bunts in his practices. All innings in exhibition games were pitched by Nichols, Clarkson, Getzein, and Jim Sullivan. Nash and Long missed some time during the exhibition games but were ready to go by Opening Day. Nash was named team captain.

The role of a captain on any major league team was much more important during this time. Selee as manager in the majors never wore a uniform and never came out on the field to argue with an umpire or change pitchers. Selee sat on the bench or in the stands in a suit and tie. The captain performed these tasks. Reviewing the articles covering Selee's major league managing career, it seems the responsibility for running the game fell to the captain. Obviously Selee and the captain could talk when the captain was on the bench. Selee could signal to the captain if he wanted to change a pitcher or move fielders around. The newspaper coverage of Selee's teams indicates that the captain made these decisions during the game. I'm sure that Selee told the captain how he wanted to play the game. But it seems Selee let the captain run the game. This was common at the time. The best short discussion of the role of a captain came from Harry Davis, captain for Connie Mack's Philadelphia A's from 1905 to 1911.

> Placing players in the field correctly according to the batter and the pitcher. The captain calls the player who is to take a fly ball. Must watch his pitcher closely to see when the time is ripe for a change, or when the twirler needs a moment or two to collect himself. He should create opportunities for the men to pull themselves together when they have become confused. He must be able to anticipate the wishes of the manager in order that valuable time not be lost and valuable point given to the opposition by his running to the bench to receive information. The captain must also watch the play of his opponents in the field in order to impart to his players any weakness he may discover or to the umpire any infringement of the rules by opposing players. The captain should be on the coaching lines as much as possible to give his player the benefit of his knowledge and observation.[19]

It may be that Connie Mack, both as a captain and as a manager, learned this style from playing against Selee's teams in the National League. Mack was the captain of Pittsburgh from 1891 until he was named player-manager in September 1894. He remained player-manager of Pittsburgh until he was fired in September 1896.

Billy Nash was from Richmond, Virginia. He started playing professional baseball in his hometown in 1884 at the age of 18. This team, the Richmond Virginians, was in the Eastern League until August 2, 1884. The Washington Senators of the American Association disbanded on that date. The American Association brought the Richmond Virginians in the AA to complete Washington's schedule. Hence, Billy Nash played 45 games in the AA at the age of 19. He was overmatched, hitting .199. Nash remained with Richmond for the start of the 1885 season. He was sold to Boston NL in August 1885. Nash was a sub for the rest of the 1885 season. He became a starter in 1886, playing 109 of 118 games for Boston, hitting .281. He was the regular third baseman through the 1889 season, hitting .283 over those three years. Nash went to the Boston PL team for the 1890 season. He played 129 of 130 games on this championship team, hitting .266. Nash was thought to be the best third baseman in the National League from around 1888 until the mid–1890s. He was a fiery leader and handled the arguments with umpires. Very often during his time as captain, the reporters writing the daily stories about the Boston PL team said that Nash made the strategic moves during the games, and that the players were trying to win for Nash.[20]

After their game with Brooklyn on April 2, the rest of Boston's exhibition games were against minor league or college teams. All took place in New England. Boston won them all. Clarkson, Getzein, Nichols, and Sullivan did all the pitching. They ventured out of New England on Opening Day in New York. Amos Rusie faced John Clarkson in a matchup of future Hall of Famers before a crowd of 17,000. Boston won the toss and chose to bat last. NY went one run up in the ninth inning. Boston walked off this way: Nash walk, Bennett single, Clarkson out, and Long hit deep fly ball to the center fielder, who dropped it, scoring both runners.

Boston swept a four-game series before starting their home season on April 28. Clarkson started against Philadelphia on April 28 and led 11–2 after eight innings. Selee put Sullivan in to start the ninth. He gave up four runs, got one out, and Nichols finished up. This was the only pitching appearance in the majors for Jim Sullivan until 1895. Boston's home crowd of 7,500 was reasonable compared to the crowd for Opening Day in New York. Nichols started the next day and gave up 11 runs in the first two innings. He completed a 13–9 loss, recording no strikeouts. Boston went to Brooklyn and split four games. Selee confessed to sportswriter

Tim Murnane (main baseball writer for the *Boston Globe*) that his team's pitching needed improvement. Murnane's opinion was that Boston NL was strong in the infield, okay at bat, but poor in pitching. Selee tried rookie John Kiley against New York on May 7. Kiley lost his only game for Boston, 9–3, and never pitched in the Major Leagues again. By the end of their eastern games, Boston was 9–4, and it was clear they did not have any pitchers beyond Clarkson, Getzen, and Nichols. Selee skipped their train trip to Chicago to scout the Harvard-Yale game.[21]

Chicago had been the gold standard in the National League in the 1880s. Owned by A. G. Spalding and managed by Cap Anson, Chicago had won pennants in 1880, 1881, 1882, 1885, and 1886. Anson was a great first baseman and a very tough man. He ruled the Chicago team as a dictator and did not like to be crossed. He wanted to control everything. However, the best player on his team from 1880 through 1886 was uncontrollable. Everything about King Kelly set Anson off, except the fact that Kelly was a great ballplayer. Anson had most of the prejudices of a person from the Midwest during this era. He did not like Irishmen, and Kelly was flamboyantly Irish. Anson did not like drinkers, and Kelly was a notorious drinker. Anson did not like players who ran around, and Kelly ran around when he was not at the ballpark. After the 1886 season, Anson told Spalding he did not need Kelly anymore. Spalding complied, selling Kelly to Boston. The best pitcher on the Chicago team for 1885–1888 was John Clarkson. Anson had a hard time handling Clarkson, who needed to be encouraged to pitch his best. Anson recommended selling Clarkson as well, and he was sold to Boston after the 1888 season. Several other fine players from the Chicago pennant winners had left by 1891. Spalding had sold a minority ownership share to Anson and James Hart after the 1890 season. Spalding kept control of the franchise but put Hart in charge of the business side of the team. Spalding had signed Anson to a 10-year contract after the 1887 season, so Anson and Hart were stuck with each other. The only starters remaining from Anson's last championship team were Anson and second baseman Fred Pfeffer. Anson had a new team and thought he was ready to reclaim the pennant in 1891.[22]

By the time of their second game at Chicago, the Boston RF was George Rooks, a local Chicago player used due to injuries. He played the next five games, hitting .125 before Selee moved Lowe into LF and put Stovey back in RF. The two teams split a four-game series, leaving Chicago one game ahead of Boston. Cincinnati won three of four on the next stop. Tucker had to finish pitching the last game. Cleveland won three of four on the next stop. Selee fined Long $25 for talking back, and Selee criticized his team by saying, "These high-priced men should know something about the game." By the time the team got to Pittsburgh, Selee was desperate enough to sign a pitcher recommended by second baseman Joe Quinn. The pitcher started the first game in Pittsburgh and gave up six runs in the first inning in a 10–1 Pittsburgh win. This was the only game Charlie "Tod" Brynan pitched in the majors in 1891. The Boston regular lineup was back together on May 27, when Boston won the final game of the road trip. They returned home after a 3–9 trip.

Selee had a new pitcher when they returned home. This pitcher ended the failed experiments looking for a new arm. Harry Staley was acquired from Pittsburgh at the end of the road trip. Staley had been playing in Pittsburgh since the middle of the 1888 season. His record for the Pittsburgh NL team was 37–43. He moved to the PL for the 1890 season, going 21–25. Staley was experienced and had shown the durability to be a starting pitcher. He made his first start for Boston on Decoration Day, winning the second game of a doubleheader sweep against Cincinnati before 10,000 fans. During this series, Tim Murnane said the acquisition of Staley made the Boston club strong enough to make a good fight for first place. Nine days later, Murnane criticized Selee and the team severely after a loss to Chicago. The team was 19–21 on June 9, in sixth place. Boston won the next six games against Chicago and Pittsburgh. That ended the western portion of the homestand.

Boston won their next three against Brooklyn for a nine-game streak. On June 19, an article in the *Boston Globe* showed the public standing of an ex-Boston player. This article said the NL was trying to get King Kelly back. Kelly had led the Boston PL team to the pennant in 1890. In 1891, the AA put a franchise in Cincinnati and got Kelly to be the player-manager, even naming the team Cincinnati Kelly's Killers. That was where Kelly played in June 1891. The Boston public and press were still longing for him. No comment came from Selee on whether he wanted Kelly. Boston lost the final game to Brooklyn before heading out on the road.

This road trip started on June 22 and would see them visit every team in the league. Philadelphia took three of four games on the first stop. Getzein pitched one of the losses, his first start since Staley joined the team. Boston had two games in New York, on a Saturday and Monday. Clarkson pitched both games, splitting the decisions. Boston won two of three in Brooklyn. The final game was on July 2. The Boston and Brooklyn teams got on a train to Philadelphia. The Philadelphia and New York teams joined the train there so all of them could get to their games on July 4. All had doubleheaders starting a western swing. Boston had the shortest trip, getting off in Pittsburgh. Boston won four games in Pittsburgh and two in Cleveland before losing. Boston was in third place, two games out of first. Cy Young stopped the winning streak, beating Getzein. Boston won two of three against Cincinnati. This series was notable in that Hoss Radbourn pitched all the innings for Cincinnati and had started the game prior to this series. The trip ended with three games against first-place Chicago. Chicago swept this series. The last two games were won in walk-off fashion in extra innings. Boston returned home with a 38–32 record in third place.

Boston came home on July 18 and stayed home until August 15 except for a two-day trip to Philadelphia. The first nine games were against eastern teams. By this time, Bobby Lowe had worked his way into the starting lineup in left field. Most players stayed healthy the rest of the year, so the lineup would be: Long SS, Tucker 1B, Stovey RF, Nash 3B, Brodie CF, Quinn 2B, Lowe LF, Bennett or Ganzel C, Nichols, Clarkson or Staley P. Lowe went 5-for-5 in the first game in Philadelphia. Boston was 45–34 at that point, still in third place behind Chicago and New York. The second game in Philly was won in walk-off fashion by Boston on an error. Staley threw a shutout. Boston returned home to face all the western teams. After taking two of three from Cincinnati, Chicago came to town with a 1½-game lead. The series was very tight. Chicago won the first two in extra innings. Nichols lost in the 13th by hitting a batter with the bases loaded. Clarkson lost in the 10th on a wild pitch. Staley won the finale before a crowd of 8,619, biggest since Opening Day. The home stand finished with a three-game sweep of Pittsburgh and a two-game split with Cleveland. The doubleheader scheduled for August 15 was rained out. Boston would now be on the road until September 7.

The trip started in New York. Selee had Boston stay at the same hotel for six nights, which covered all their games with New York and Brooklyn. Boston won the first game even though Long, Lowe, and Clarkson had to wear New York uniforms. Their uniforms had not made it to the ballpark. Boston won four of six from these two teams before heading west. About the time Boston left on this road trip, the Cincinnati team in the AA folded. King Kelly was assigned to the Boston AA team, played four games there, then jumped to Boston NL. Kelly joined the team in Pittsburgh. Kelly signed a contract with Boston NL calling for $25,000 total for the rest of 1891 and 1892. This was much more money than any other player on the Boston team would get. Selee acquiesced to this move but did not initiate it. The Triumvirs knew Kelly from his past service with Boston NL and thought he might make the difference in a pennant run. While Selee was not a severe taskmaster, he expected his players to stay sober and not run around. He would have a major test with Kelly on the team. Boston lost two of three games to Pittsburgh. Kelly played his first game on August 27 in Cleveland. He caught his old battery mate, Clarkson, in a 12–2 Boston win. Boston won three of four games in this series. After an August 31 win in Cincinnati, Boston was 2½ games behind first place Chicago. Boston lost the last two games in Cincinnati before heading to Chicago. Chicago won two of three, leaving Boston six games behind heading home. Tim Murnane made this comment in the story of the last game of the road trip: "Anson will find the Eastern Teams in pretty good condition for a fight and the chances are both Boston and New York will be close to him when he leaves for the West in 2 weeks" (after Chicago completed its eastern trip).

The home stand started with two doubleheaders against Cleveland. Boston won three of the four games. Cy Young started one game each day for Cleveland, losing both. After this series, the *Boston Globe* stated that the Boston NL team had signed Tom McCarthy and Jack Stivetts from the St. Louis AA team for the 1892 season. King Kelly supposedly handled this transaction. Boston swept three from Cincinnati, putting

Mike "King" Kelly, the most famous player of the 1880s. He basically finished his career with Boston in 1891 and 1892, playing part time on two pennant winners.

Boston four games behind Chicago. By this date (September 14) the Boston AA team had a large enough lead in that pennant race that it was considered done. Chicago won two of three games, beating Clarkson and Staley. Nichols won the final game. Chicago left town five games up.

However, the final game of the Chicago series was the start of one of the greatest stretch drives in baseball history. There were 16 games remaining on Boston's home stand. Boston won all of them. As was true of every team before the development of the infield tarpaulin in 1908, there were quite a few doubleheaders in September to compensate for rainouts and postponements due to wet grounds. Add in the fact that tie games were replayed in full, and all teams had games to make up at the end of a season. Boston swept doubleheaders against Pittsburgh on September 19, Brooklyn on September 23, and New York on September 29 and 30. That ended the home stand. Boston left for their final series in Philadelphia ½-game up on Chicago. Boston won the first two games in Philadelphia to clinch the pennant with an 18-game winning streak. After losing the final game, Boston's record was 87–51 to Chicago's 82–53. All innings during the winning streak were pitched by Nichols, Clarkson, and Staley. Kelly played some, but his final average for Boston was .231. He may have given the Boston players and fans a jump start, but not on the field. The regulars won the pennant.

As was common in this era, Chicago complained that some teams laid down for Boston. Chicago business manager James Hart filed a protest that New York did not try in their series in Boston. New York lost five in a row to Boston from September 28–30. Nothing came of the protest. The Boston pennant was the product of the fine play of nine regular field players, four pitchers, and some help at the end from Kelly. The nine regulars all had reasonable years at the bat. The averages ranged from .282 (Long) to .215 (Bennett). The Boston team led the league in runs scored and walks. Stovey led the league in triples (20), home runs (16), and slugging (.498). After a so-so start, the pitching staff came on strong. Getzein had 11 starts through June, with a 4–5 record. After the acquisition of Staley, the threesome of Nichols, Clarkson and Staley pitched every inning from June 24 until the pennant was clinched. Their final records: Clarkson 33–19, Nichols 30–17, Staley 20–8. Selee had built a pennant winner in his second year at the helm. His major contributions after the season started were the acquisition of Staley and moving Lowe into the regular lineup. Home attendance for this season was 184,472.

This was Selee's first success on the Major League level. His philosophy of team building had worked in the minors to the tune of two pennants. He stated about his Boston experience, "It was my good fortune to be surrounded by a lot of good, clean fellows who got along finely together. To tell the truth, I would not have anyone on a team who was not congenial."[23] King Kelly was certainly congenial but did not fit the rest of Selee's description. Kelly was most congenial in a bar, and his behavior was not to Selee's liking. But Kelly was not a major player on this team. By the time Kelly arrived, Selee was in control of the team.

The first article written by Tim Murnane after the Beaneaters' season ended was about the baseball war. Tim Murnane was very familiar with baseball wars. Of the five leagues that claimed Major League status before 1891, Murnane had played in three of them: the National Association, National League and Union League, and he managed in the Union League. After this career, he became the baseball writer for the *Boston Globe*. During Selee's tenure in Boston, Murnane was the only writer in Boston whose name appeared as part of his reporting. Most stories in newspapers in the 1890s did not have bylines. His name appeared at the end, not the beginning, of his articles. He had a good relationship with the Triumvirs, having played for them at the beginning of their tenure as owners in Boston. Murnane was named the outstanding sportswriter of the 1890s by Bill

3. Boston: The First Seven Years

James in his *New Historical Baseball Abstract*.[24] The Triumvirs were familiar with baseball wars as well. They had owned the Boston NL franchise since 1877 and had outlasted the Union League and Players League. The only remaining obstacle to a Major League monopoly was the American Association.

That obstacle was eliminated on December 18, 1891. The two leagues merged into one, officially called "The National League and American Association of Base Ball Clubs." This name was only used on official correspondence. All eight National League teams survived. One American Association team folded during the 1891 season (Milwaukee).[25] Four American Association teams (St. Louis, Louisville, Baltimore, and Washington) joined. The other four teams from the AA disbanded. The new league bought out these four teams for a total of $135,000. Each team in the new league was to contribute 10 percent of its gate receipts to a fund until this amount was paid off.

The American Association continued to have an influence on baseball after its demise. The survivors, called the League in all the papers, adopted several of the AA's founding principles. NL teams could now charge a minimum of $.25 for a ticket, down from $.50. Each club was given the right to decide whether to sell alcoholic beverages at their home park. NL teams had not played on Sunday up to now. The AA had. Now teams made their own decision but could not force their opponent to play. All the clubs that could immediately adopted Sunday ball for the coming season. Most eastern cities still prohibited Sunday ball. The Boston franchise decided not to play any Sunday games, home or road. The geographical division in the National League was now (East) Boston, Baltimore, Washington, New York, Brooklyn, Philadelphia, (West) Pittsburgh, Cleveland, Cincinnati, Louisville, Chicago, St. Louis.

As had been written in the *Boston Globe* in September 1891, Tommy McCarthy and Jack Stivetts of the St. Louis AA team came over to Boston for the 1892 season. One other player was acquired from the AA. Hugh Duffy was the right fielder for the AA champion Boston Reds in 1891. Adding these three to a champion team, Boston was the favorite to repeat as NL champions. The League decided before the season to split the season into two halves. They were worried that it would be hard to sell tickets for teams in the lower depths of the standings without any hope. This required a league championship series, which would be the only one in the Majors until 1969.

Another adjustment made in the 1892 season was to player pay. The players had an advantage since the formation of the AA in 1882. Players could jump leagues, even though there was an agreement between the NL and AA. The Players' League had added to the players' clout. Now the NL owners could enforce salary restrictions. We will see this throughout the rest of the 1890s. Arthur Soden, the lead Triumvir, was known to be a hardliner on salaries when he could be. He would now exercise that power.

The only regular from 1891 not with Boston in 1892 was Steve Brodie. He went to St. Louis as compensation for Stivetts and McCarthy. All except Stivetts were present when Boston opened spring training in Charlottesville, Virginia, on March 23. This was the first spring training for Selee in a warmer climate. They stayed in Virginia until April 3. All days except March 28 consisted of workouts at the University of Virginia. Boston played UVA once, winning 22–0. Boston went north to play exhibitions against minor league and college teams, starting April 4. A game against Yale on April 6 featured three umpires, unlike the normal one. Selee saw Brown University catcher Fred Tenney for the first time in a game on April 9. He would remember Tenney. By Opening Day in Washington, the lineup was Long SS, Duffy CF, Stovey LF, McCarthy RF, Nash 3B (Captain), Quinn 2B, Kelly C. Ganzel, Bennett and Lowe were the bench players. Nichols, Clarkson, and Staley would start off as pitchers. Stivetts had finally reported just before Opening Day. Selee said he was not ready to pitch yet and would be held out for a while.

Before Opening Day in Washington, Selee had a reunion with another player from his Oshkosh 1887 Northwestern League champions. Tommy McCarthy was the left fielder, and Dummy Hoy the center fielder from that Oshkosh team. McCarthy was now on Boston, and Hoy was on Washington. Hoy had spent the last four years on three different teams in three different Major Leagues, never crossing paths with Selee until April 12, 1892. Opening Day was the only game played in Washington, with the next two rained out. After a Boston win, there was a scheduled off-day. Boston had a practice in the morning. In the afternoon, Stovey and Nichols tried to teach the other players how to use a new kind of vehicle, the bicycle. Long fell off into a hitching post but escaped injury.

The rest of the road trip to Baltimore and Philadelphia resulted in a 3–1 record and two rainouts. In Baltimore, a fan stole Tucker's ring, wallet, and diamond pin during a game. Tucker received all these back on April 22, Opening Day in Boston. Baltimore was the opponent, and the story did not say who gave Tucker his property back. Opening Day was rained out, Boston's fourth rainout so far. There was a doubleheader the next day. Stivetts made his first appearance, securing a complete game victory in the first game. After a five-minute break, the second game resulted in another Boston win. The short break was because the first game started at 2 p.m. Total time of the doubleheader, including the break, was 4:08. Boston swept two games at New York, then went to Washington to make up the two games rained out there. Boston swept that doubleheader as well. Boston batted last in the final game in Washington. Duffy delivered a walk-off single in the ninth inning. Ganzel caught both games. Before heading on its first western trip, Boston had given the league notice with a 10–1 start to the season.

Their first series in the west was with St. Louis. This was the franchise that had been the bellwether of the American Association, the St. Louis Browns. When the National League started in 1876, two of their main tenets were $.50 admission and banning alcoholic beverages from parks. The AA changed both of those, earning the nickname of "the beer and whiskey league." The St. Louis Browns were the most successful team in the ten-year history of the AA. They finished first four times, second three times, and third once. The Browns were owned by Chris Von Der Ahe. Von Der Ahe was a brewer and saloon owner, and for good business reasons encouraged alcohol consumption at his ballpark and neighboring saloon. Crowds at St. Louis were notably rowdy as a result. The Browns were successful on the field when Von Der Ahe left the running of the ball club to his manager, Charles Comiskey. Comiskey led the team to all their pennants, 1885–1888. Comiskey went to the Players' League in 1890 and returned to the Browns in 1891. He got tired of Von Der Ahe's increasing interference and went to manage Cincinnati in 1892. Comiskey was proved right during the 1892 season. Von Der Ahe went through five managers, resulting in an 11th-place finish. The St. Louis team remained bad until the 1899 season. Von Der Ahe was eventually forced out after serious financial reverses.

After splitting two games in St. Louis, Boston headed to Chicago. Selee told Murnane a few things about the team on their train trip. He said too many of his players were smoking and he would try to get them to lay off. Lowe would be the utility man, even though he had been playing well in place of Stovey, who had been injured. Kelly had been ill and was not yet in shape.[26] These were not major concerns on a team with an 11–2 record. Boston won two in Chicago and Louisville. Stivetts pitched the final game in Louisville, hitting a walk-off double in the bottom of the ninth. The next game in Cincinnati resulted in a 14-inning, 0–0 tie. The old Chicago battery of Clarkson and Kelly played for Boston. This game took 2:20 to play before being called for darkness. Boston won the final game in Cincinnati for a six-game winning streak. The final stops on this trip were Cleveland and Pittsburgh. Cleveland won two, with Cy Young breaking the Boston winning streak. Boston won two in Pittsburgh. Boston returned home with a record of 17–5. Brooklyn was in second place at 13–6.

A crowd of 6,920 welcomed the Beaneaters home on May 15. The team rewarded the crowd with an 8–7 win in 10 innings. Boston won another game before heading to Brooklyn for three. Brooklyn swept that series. This short trip concluded with two scheduled games in Washington. Both were rained out. So far, Boston had been using four pitchers: Nichols, Clarkson, Staley, and Stivetts. Boston returned home on May 23.

This home stand would last until June 22, and Boston would face every NL team except Baltimore. Selee postponed the game against New York on the 23rd due to wet grounds, scheduling a doubleheader for the 24th. Boston had another sweep on the 24th. The doubleheader started at 2 p.m. (two hours before the regular game time) and featured a five-minute break between games. The decision of the first game involved two future Hall of Famers. Nichols pitched for Boston, Amos Rusie for New York. Boston walked off on an RBI single by Herman Long. New York won the next day on a walk-off error by Tucker. The next six series were against western teams. By the end of May, the top four teams in the standings were: Boston 27–9, Chicago 22–13, Brooklyn 21–13, Cincinnati 21–16.

Selee had to take unusual action in the June 2 game against St. Louis. The weather had finally warmed up, and the battery of Clarkson and Kelly were taken out after five innings due to the heat. Stivetts and Bennett came in together. This move did not work, as Stivetts gave up three runs in the eighth inning in a 7–6 loss. In a listing of the top hitters in the NL on June 5, Stivetts was 11th with a .302 average. After the game on June 8, Tim Murnane made the first mention of what would become the franchise nickname. In his story, Murnane called the Boston team "Selee's Braves."[27] Clarkson pitched on June 7. He lost a 7–0 lead and the game, 8–7. Clarkson would not pitch again until June 20. Clarkson won the second game of a doubleheader that day. On June 20, Selee released Stovey, moving Lowe to LF. On that same date, Clarkson was given a choice between a pay cut and his release. After the final game of the home stand, Clarkson agreed to the pay cut. Boston's record was 39–17.

The rest of the first half of this split season was spent on the road. When Boston left on this road trip, Selee took 12 men. These were the seven regulars behind the pitcher, two catchers, and three pitchers. Staley stayed behind and would join the team on the second stop in Cleveland. Kelly was injured during the July 1 game, leaving Bennett the only healthy catcher. Staley rejoined the team and pitched the next day, beating Cy Young in Cleveland. Bennett caught both games of the July 4 doubleheader in Cincinnati. That split doubleheader drew crowds of 7,200 and 8,900. The next game was on July 5 in St. Louis. Staley started and was pulled after walking four batters in the first three innings. Murnane said that Staley had a "yellow streak" and that Captain Nash made the decision to change pitchers. Nichols finished, getting the win. Boston won 12 of the first 15 games on this trip, clinching the first-half title on July 8 in Louisville.

The next day in Chicago, the lineup was strange due to injuries. Staley pitched a 2–1 win with Stivetts in LF, Long in CF, Lowe at SS, and Duffy at

3B. Kelly was back for the final game in Chicago. He sold Selee on the idea of playing in "antique" uniforms and wearing beards and mustaches. Selee secured the uniforms and fake facial hair from a theatrical costumer, and the game was played that way on July 11. The final game of the first half was in Pittsburgh. Stivetts started, lasted three innings, and lost, as Kelly finished. The final standings for the first half were Boston 55–22, Brooklyn 51–26, Philadelphia 46–30. Per the way they listed batting averages in 1892, Stivetts was leading the league in BA with a .387 average. Under modern rules, he would not have had enough plate appearances to qualify. In the first half, Boston ranked seventh in batting average and 8th in fielding average. Per Murnane, Boston won because "they were strong in the scientific points of play: team work, sacrifice hitting and base running."[28]

By this time, Clarkson had changed his mind and asked for his release. Cleveland picked him up. The second half of the season started for Boston with a long home stand. All the western teams and Philadelphia, New York, and Baltimore visited. The team may have been celebrating their first half victory because they lost the first game to ninth-place St. Louis, 20–3. Clarkson pitched for Cleveland in Boston on July 20. Staley opposed him in a 3–2 Boston win where Clarkson made the final out with the tying run on third. Cy Young beat the Beaneaters the next day. After the next game against Chicago, Murnane said that umpire Tim Hurst had been poor the entire home stand. It was normal for one umpire only to work an entire home stand. After the next game against Chicago, Murnane said, "two years of a 12-club league would kill base ball in this city."[29]

Boston finished the portion of this homestand against western teams 6–6. For the last week, Bennett and Ganzel had been injured, Kelly was the only catcher, and he was playing through an injury. Bennett came back on August 2 in a 6–6 tie called by darkness against New York. Boston won two games against Baltimore to end the home stand 11–6, winning all the games against the eastern teams except the tie with New York. After the game on August 4, both Boston and Baltimore took the boat to New York. On the trip, Baltimore outfielder Jocko Halligan punched Baltimore captain Cub Stricker, breaking Stricker's jaw. Halligan was suspended by Baltimore manager Ned Hanlon. Stovey had been picked up by Baltimore, and John McGraw made his National League debut with this team.

This road trip lasted through September 4 and covered all the western cities after visits to Brooklyn, Washington, and Philadelphia. The first game in Brooklyn featured a triple play by Boston and some bat use that was legal then but not now. The triple play came with the bases loaded and went 5–2–3–2. The final out was tagging out the runner from second at the plate. Nichols pitched all 12 innings of a 2–0 win. Stivetts played LF. Stivetts used a flat bat the first two times up, then switched to a round bat.

Stivetts won the game with a two-run, inside-the-park home run in the top of the 12th. Stivetts pitched the next day, when the headline read "Mighty Brooklyn Sluggers Shut Out Without a Hit." A game like this was not called a no-hitter, but something like this headline or a line in the story would acknowledge the feat. Nichols played LF in this game. Boston finished the eastern portion of the trip 3–4.

A play was noted in one of the games in Philadelphia that seems unusual to a modern reader. In a sacrifice situation, the Philadelphia batter (who was using a flat bat) bunted to third. The first baseman was off the bag, but the right fielder covered first. The bunter was safe.

After the last game in Philadelphia, Stivetts left the team for the funeral of his brother. The first western stop was with first-place Cleveland. Cleveland won two of three games, putting Boston in sixth place in the second-half standings. The next series in Pittsburgh was missed by the regular umpire. A local umpire was pulled out of the stands for the first game. The final two games had one player from each team as an umpire. Pittsburgh won two of three. Before their upcoming trip to play St. Louis, Selee agreed with St. Louis owner Chris Von Der Ahe to move the games to Kansas City. There was a Knights of Pythias convention in Kansas City, and Von Der Ahe thought he could draw more fans. This was to be a three-game series, and there were disputes about which games would count and which was an exhibition after the teams played two consecutive doubleheaders following a rainout. They finally agreed that the first three games would count, with Boston winning two of three. Nichols pitched one game each day before the home folks, winning both.

Stivetts had not yet returned from the funeral, notifying Selee that he would join the team in Cincinnati. Selee signed another pitcher to use in Louisville. Leon Viau, who had pitched for Cincinnati, Cleveland, and Louisville over the last five years, pitched his final game in the major leagues on August 27 for Boston, winning 8–1. When Stivetts showed up in Cincinnati, Viau was released.

In Cincinnati, Boston exhibited a tame form of the rowdy behavior that was developing in 1890s baseball. Long was on second base when an attempted pickoff throw got away from the second baseman. Long went to third, where the throw got away from the third baseman. Duffy, coaching third, grabbed Long and boosted him toward home. Long was safe at home but was sent back to third by the umpire due to coach's interference. Duffy was thrown out of the game later for arguing. The next day, Stivetts made his first start on his return from the funeral. Kelly was the catcher, and he could not handle Stivetts' pitches. Kelly convinced Captain Nash to change pitchers, bringing in Staley. Stivetts got the loss. Stivetts pitched the next game, throwing a complete-game victory to Ganzel. The road trip ended with Boston taking two of three in Chicago. Boston ended the road trip two2 games under .500, in second place behind Cleveland.

The remainder of Boston's games against the western teams were played on the next home stand. Boston started with a doubleheader sweep of St. Louis. Stivetts pitched a total of 20 innings to win both games. The Boston victory on September 7 was not the headline news in the *Boston Globe* on September 8. The only other sporting event that could outshine baseball occurred on the September 7. Boston native John L. Sullivan lost the heavyweight boxing championship to James J. Corbett in New Orleans. That was the biggest story. Stivetts pitched the final game against St. Louis on September 8 after two days' rest. The team had just received their paychecks, and Stivetts discovered that his pay had been docked for the games he missed in August. Stivetts pitched poorly in a 7–1 loss. Cleveland came to town seven games ahead of Boston in the second-half standings. The teams split two games.

One of the directors of the Boston team asked Selee to get some new pitching, advice which Selee ignored. Boston swept two games from Pittsburgh, passing Pittsburgh in the standings. Due to rain, the next two-game series with Chicago was played as a doubleheader, which Boston swept. The second game was called after 6½ innings so Chicago could catch a train to Baltimore. Murnane blamed Boston's first-game loss to Cincinnati on the umpire. He said Nichols had Bid McPhee struck out in the sixth inning, but the umpire called a ball. McPhee hit a game-winning home run on the next pitch. Bennett was called out for leaving third base early on a sacrifice fly in the eighth. There were lots of arguments with the umpire. Selee was not involved in these arguments, leaving it to the players and captain. Boston won the final game of the home stand against Cincinnati, ending the stand with a 9–3 record. The rest of the regular season would be against eastern teams.

Nash stayed at home to heal an injury at the start of the next road trip. He missed two Boston wins in Baltimore and joined the team in New York. Boston went 3–3 against New York and Brooklyn on this New York visit. The next game against Washington at home called for severe comment from Murnane. One big difference in newspaper stories about ballgames in the 1890s was the emphasis placed on good and bad fielding plays. Considering that these were the only eyewitness accounts of a game that most of the readers would see, this makes sense. Boston won their September 29 game, 12–8. Boston committed 14 errors, Washington nine. Only two field players made it through the game without an error. Murnane called this the worst fielding game of the season. Even with all the runs and errors, the time of the game was 1:53. The two games remaining in this series were split. Cleveland was seven games ahead of Boston for the second half.

With 11 games left, the league held a vote on how to determine the champion. As a result of a 10–2 vote, there would be a six-game series between Boston and Cleveland after the season ended on October 15. Boston voted against this series. After this vote, Boston won seven in a row. Cleveland had clinched by this time. Even with that, Boston lost only one game the rest of the year. The final second-half standings were: Cleveland 53–22, Boston 50–26.

Boston had to travel from Washington to Cleveland for the first game on October 17. The game started at the normal time of 3:30 p.m. Young and Stivetts both pitched 11 shutout innings. The game was called by darkness at that point. Remember there was no daylight savings time. Boston won the next two games in Cleveland, both by one run. Staley beat Clarkson, and Stivetts won the rematch with Young. The final three games were played in Boston. Boston won these games by scores of 4–0, 12–7, and 8–3. All the pitchers completed their starts for both teams. Stivetts and Nichols won two games, and Staley won the other. Duffy led the way with a .429 average and nine RBI. Selee's judgment on Clarkson was borne out. Clarkson had the worst series of any of the pitchers, losing both his starts with a 5.29 ERA.

If the 1892 season was considered as one season instead of a split season, the same pennant winner would have resulted. Boston became the first team to win over 100 games in a major league campaign, finishing with a 102–48 record. Cleveland was second-best at 93–56. In the listing of league leaders for 1892, two Boston hitters show up. Duffy was third in hits and runs, and fifth in total bases. Long was fifth in hits. The only statistic that Boston led the league in was shutouts with 15. Nichols, Stivetts, and Staley finished third, fourth, and fifth in the league in winning percentage. Nichols and Stivetts were both 35–16, Staley was 22–10, and Clarkson was 8–6 with Boston. Bill James named this pitching

Charles "Kid" Nichols, the best pitcher of the 1890s in the National League.

staff the best staff of the 1890s.³⁰ This was a very well-balanced team, strong in all areas. Duffy led the way with a .301 average. Stivetts was second with a .296 average. Tucker and Long were the only other players over .280. The team hit .250. The split season experiment did not work as far as attendance in Boston was concerned. Home attendance sank to 146,421.

This off-season would bring a significant change to the game, like the previous off-season. However, this time it was to the game as played, not off the field. The magnates of the National League thought the poor attendance for the 1892 season was due to games being too low-scoring. They took drastic action by changing a lot about pitching. The most noticeable change was pitching distance. As of 1887, pitchers had to start their motion with their back foot on a line 55'6" from home plate on a flat area. In 1893, this distance was changed to 60'6". The back line was changed to a white rubber plate 12" by 4". The pitcher was required to keep one foot on this rubber while delivering the pitch. The pitching area could be elevated if the home team so chose. Flat-sided bats were banned. It would literally be a new ball game, particularly for pitchers, in 1893.

Selee made one change to the team over the winter. He traded 2B Joe Quinn to St. Louis for OF Cliff Carroll. The main impetus behind this move was to put Bobby Lowe at 2B. Lowe had played all over the place in 1892 (90 games in OF, 14 at 3B, 13 at SS, 10 at 2B). Selee wanted him in the lineup and sought an improved double play combo. As the double play combo of Long and Lowe would be together until 1901, Selee succeeded.

Herman Long was born in Chicago in 1866 to German immigrants. He spoke German fluently. He started pro ball in Milwaukee in 1887. Selee saw Long as an opposing player for the first two years of Long's career. The Kansas City team of the AA purchased Long in 1889, and he played that year in the AA. When Selee moved to Boston for the 1890 season, he inquired about getting Long and acquired him, one of his best moves. Long played in Boston until 1902. Long and Hughie Jennings were thought to be the best shortstops of the 1890s. During the early part of his career, Long was called "the Flying Dutchman" before this nickname was given to Honus Wagner. Long was known as one of the great fielders of this time. Selee told the story of one play Long made in the Reach Guide for 1894:

> The most remarkable play I ever saw was made by Herman Long, of the Boston team, in 1892, on the Boston grounds. With a base runner on first, the batsman hit a hard ground ball to Long's left, directly over second base. He made a great effort, but seeing he could not reach the ball he threw out his left foot and caught the ball on the point of his shoe enough to bring the ball in the air, and by a great left hand catch he was able to get the ball to Joe Quinn in time to catch the base runner at second; all this was done while he was moving at the top of his speed, and the audience went wild over the phenomenal play.³¹

I did not find that exact play described. However, many times the writer extolled Long's excellent fielding. Long's reputation was not even hurt when he had a bad fielding year in 1893. Two shortstops in the NL, Herman Long of Boston and Joe Sullivan of Washington, were the last shortstops in major league history to make more than 100 errors in one season, in 1893. Both made 102 errors. There was never any desire on the part of Selee to move Long off shortstop.[32]

Bobby Lowe was born in New Castle, Pennsylvania, in 1868. He was working as a machinist and playing on the local ball team when he was signed as a pro in 1887. Lowe was in the same league as Selee from 1887–1889, playing in Eau Claire and Milwaukee. Lowe had no regular position in the minors. No one else was interested in Lowe after the 1889 season. Selee bought his contract for $700 and brought him to Boston. John McGraw, who saw Long and Lowe for eight years in the NL, called them the best double play combo he ever saw. Lowe was known as the stronger hitter of the two, Long the better fielder. Lowe would be with Selee for even longer than Long. Long, Lowe, and Nichols were the three players who were on the Boston Beaneaters the entire managerial term of Selee.[33]

Bobby Lowe gave this summary of Selee as a manager: "He was a good judge of players. He didn't bother with a lot of signals, but let his players figure out their own plays. He didn't blame them if they took a chance that failed. He believed in place-hitting, sacrifice-hitting, and stealing bases. He was wonderful with young players."[34] All this would be tested in Boston's run for a third consecutive pennant in 1893.

Players were to report to Boston for spring training on April 1. Nash signed on March 31. That left only McCarthy and Duffy unsigned. They both signed on April 2. The policy of Arthur Soden to keep salaries down was working. Selee earned $3,500, and none of the players earned more than $3,000. Boston did not go south at the beginning of spring training. Exhibition games were played against Ivy League schools for a week. At a game against Harvard in Hartford on April 11, the Boston pitchers used the new distance of 60'6", and the Harvard pitchers used the old distance. Boston won anyway. After playing at Princeton, Boston went south to Virginia for a few exhibition games. Boston won all 14 exhibition games, nine against college teams and five against minor league teams. Selee selected 13 players for the roster on Opening Day: Duffy CF, Long SS, Lowe 2B, Tucker 1B, Nash 3B (Captain), McCarthy LF, Carroll RF, Ganzel and Bennett C, Nichols P, Stivetts P, Staley P, Jim Garry P. Kelly had been released over the winter, helping Soden to hold down salaries. Even though Kelly and Selee had co-existed for more than one season, it was clear that Kelly was not Selee's type of player. Kelly signed with New York. In an article before the season, Tim Murnane went through the history of major league baseball. He

3. Boston: The First Seven Years 65

Bobby Lowe, at the end of his playing career with Detroit of the AL. Lowe spent the most time playing for Selee of any player (1890–1903).

stated that the only people still in the majors that had been in the National Association in 1871 were Harry Wright and Cap Anson.[35]

Boston opened in New York. The length of the season had been reduced from 154 to 140 games. Hence Opening Day was April 27. That was rained out, even though the rain had stopped by the 3 p.m. game time. The grounds were too wet to play on. Boston split the two games in New York. In the second game in Philadelphia, Garry got his chance to pitch. Stivetts was supposed to start but did not show for the game. Staley started, was shelled, and was pulled after 2⅓ innings. Garry came in and gave up several runs in a 2⅔-inning stint. Nichols finished an 11–7 loss. Stivetts returned the next day, with no fine mentioned in the newspaper. The next game in Baltimore showed Selee willing to admit and fix two mistakes. He released Garry, leaving the team with three pitchers for the moment. Selee had used Lowe at SS and Long at 2B in spring training and for the first four games. Long and Lowe switched positions in the second game at Baltimore and remained that way for the rest of their Boston careers when healthy. Per the newspaper, Nash convinced Selee to make this change. This opening road trip lasted until May 14. Boston finished the trip to all the other eastern teams with a 6–7 record.

Between May 15 and June 25, all the other teams in the league would visit Boston. Nichols won the opening game in Boston against New York before a crowd of 8,000. Boston swept the three-game series, scoring eight, 10, and 16 runs. Boston swept three games from Brooklyn to start the home stand 6–0. Bennett hit a three-run home run to win the final game against Brooklyn. During the next series, where Boston took two of three games against Philadelphia, Murnane made his first complaint about the new rules. Discussing an 18–6 win by Boston on May 23 that featured four home runs, Murnane said, "The game proved one thing conclusively, and that is that the South End grounds are not large enough to play the game as it should be played under the new rules." The South End Grounds ballpark was known as the best hitter's park in the National League during the 1890s due to short porches in both left and right field. Center field was very deep. Selee had signed a utility man, Bill Merritt, after the first road trip. Merritt hit two home runs in the game Murnane complained about. While Washington was in town, Selee left to look for a pitcher. Nash ran the team in his absence. Washington took two of three games, and Selee signed pitcher Frank Sexton from Brown University. Sexton went to the minors and would not appear with Boston until 1895. Other than Garry's short relief outing, all pitching so far had been done by Nichols, Stivetts, and Staley.

Boston got its first look at the western teams starting May 29. Three games were played against Chicago in two days, the second date being Decoration Day. The split doubleheader on May 30 drew 4,713 for the first game, 11,500 for the second. Boston won two of three. Boston won five straight against Louisville and Cleveland before losing the final game against Cleveland. In the final game of the winning streak, Boston hit three home runs. Murnane described it this way: "McCarthy, Long and Lowe lost 3 balls by putting them into the old junk pile near the round house." There was a railroad yard just over the left field fence at the South End Grounds.

As an example of how the new rules were working to increase offense, the scores in the Cleveland-Boston series were 9–6, 12–10, and 13–11. As an example of the type of behavior that was taking over baseball in the 1890s, Patsy Tebeau of Cleveland was ejected by the umpire for throwing dirt in Long's eyes while Tebeau was on base. Boston split the next six games against Cincinnati and Pittsburgh. In the final game against Pittsburgh, Long collided with catcher Connie Mack at home. Long was able to continue, but Mack was seriously hurt. He was able to play in the majors until 1896, but he was never the same player after this collision.[36] Long was too sore to play the next day. McCarthy played SS and had a walk-off hit against St. Louis. St. Louis was short of outfielders and signed Massachusetts native Jimmy Bannon on Selee's recommendation. Bannon played two of the three games for St. Louis. St. Louis was the final visitor from the West. Boston went 13–5 against the western teams. Brooklyn visited again for three games, Boston taking two. The only NL team not to appear so far in Boston came next. Only one game was played with Baltimore due to rain. Boston won it to go into a tie with Philadelphia for the league lead.

The upcoming road trip was a western swing ending with a series in New York. It started with Boston taking two of three from Louisville. A sweep of three games in St. Louis put Boston in first place by itself for the first time in 1893. Boston swept three games from Chicago in two days. The second date was July 4. The morning-afternoon doubleheader drew a total of 15,500. Nichols pitched two complete game victories over these two days. Stivetts started the other game and had to come out after a collision on the bases with Cap Anson. Turnabout was fair play, as Boston was swept by Pittsburgh in their next series. Selee protested the first loss due to the incompetence of the umpire. Selee tried a new pitcher in the final game of this series. Bill Coyle, a Pittsburgh native recently signed, started and lasted three innings in a 13–0 loss. Nichols, Staley, and Stivetts all pitched in this game. This was Coyle's last appearance in the National League.

While in Cleveland, Selee received a letter from Arthur Soden regarding poor play in Pittsburgh. Selee said he was trying to sign recently released pitcher Hank Gastright. Gastright was signed while Boston was in Cleveland. Boston won two of three in Cleveland and ended the western portion of the trip by sweeping Cincinnati. Gastright won the second game in Cincinnati. This was the first game won by any pitcher other than Nichols, Staley, or Stivetts for Boston in 1893. The road trip ended with New York taking three of four games. Gastright won the only Boston victory in New York. After this 14–8 road trip, Boston was 1½ games behind Philadelphia.

Both teams took the boat to Boston for the start of the next Boston home stand. Boston swept three games from New York. Gastright pitched the first game of the next series against Washington, making his home debut. He lasted eight innings and left with a three-run lead. Nichols gave up five runs in the ninth to make the final score 17–15 in favor of Washington. Nichols won the final game of the series, hitting a home run in a 5–2 win. Baltimore visited next. Boston swept five games over three days. The first two days of this series were doubleheaders. In the four games over these two days, the pitching went like this: Nichols CG after CG the day before, Stivetts CG, Nichols CG, Stivetts started, Staley pitched last three innings. Gastright pitched the final game. The day after this series was a Sunday. On his day off, Bobby Lowe went to Marblehead, Massachusetts. At a gathering there, several people made large wagers on whether Lowe could throw a ball 400 feet. Lowe said he could, and he did. The next day was the start of a series with second-place Philadelphia. Boston won the first two behind Nichols and Stivetts. Staley lost the final game of the home stand. Boston went into first place for good after this 12–2 home stand. Boston was 55–28, Philadelphia 49–30, and Pittsburgh 48–33.

The next road trip was against four eastern teams. Boston swept three games in Brooklyn. Nichols pitched the first game, then had three days off. He must have been relieved. Nichols started and won the first game in Washington. The only reason Boston visited Washington at this point in the season was on the insistence of Arthur Soden. Per Tim Murnane: "Washington team has been transferring games from this city to other places. Since the season opener, the Wagners [Washington owners] have transferred every Saturday and 22 other contests."[37] Soden refused to transfer these games. Boston won all three games and was rewarded by total attendance for the three games in Washington of 3253. The attendance for the last game in Brooklyn was 10,612. Remember that paid attendance was the biggest portion of income for any professional baseball team during this era. They might have received some income from concessions, but other modern sources of income (parking, TV and radio rights, T-shirts, and other accessories) did not exist.

Washington was not the only franchise to transfer some home games. The schedule for 1893 called for 132 games, 66 at home and 66 on the road. Louisville played 52 games at home, 73 on the road. Washington played 48 at home, 81 on the road. Boston moved on to Baltimore. The umpire was late for the first game there, so a local umpire was called out of the stands. He worked one inning before the regular umpire showed up. Boston swept the three games. In the second game, Baltimore pitcher McMahon got upset when a foul ball in the fourth inning could not be found in the stands. A new ball was put into play, and Boston scored six runs to go ahead. In the final game, Murnane said, Boston delayed the game by their incessant kicking. Staley started this game, replaced by Nichols in the seventh inning. Murnane said Captain Nash made the change. The road trip ended with four games in Philadelphia. Philadelphia outfielder Billy Hamilton missed the series with typhoid fever. The *Boston Globe* had a quote: "Before the season opened, Manager Selee of Boston wanted to release McCarthy and Duffy, which would have been the hight [sic] of folly. So it can be seen that as great a manager as Selee can made mistakes."[38] Selee had no comment about this. Boston took three of four games from Philadelphia, returning home with an eight-game lead in the standings.

Boston returned home on August 18. This was their final home stand of the year, lasting until September 8. Then there would be one final western swing. Pittsburgh came in town for three games. Only one was completed before they had to leave town. Boston won the one game finished. The final game ended in a 5–5 tie due to darkness. The doubleheader the next day was rained out. Boston won the first two games against Cincinnati to take an 11-game lead. The *Boston Globe* declared, "the race is over." Cincinnati won the final game of the series. Boston took two of three against Cleveland. Chicago was swept in a three-game series. In the final game of the Chicago series, the umpire did not show up. John Flynn, an ex-Chicago pitcher attending the game, umpired. Cap Anson had a big argument with him.

Boston swept a three-game series from both St. Louis and Louisville to finish their home season. On September 5 against St. Louis, the umpire did not appear and a local substitute was used. A recent signing, Bill Quarles, pitched and won. Bill Merritt, the utility man, suffered a broken wrist in this game. Even though Boston was comfortably in the lead, there was still criticism. In the article on September 8, Murnane wrote: "The Boston team use small bats and their hitting is light in consequence. Duffy could handle a bat double the weight of his present outfit."[39] Hugh Duffy was in the process of hitting .363, good for fourth in the league. Boston finished its home schedule with a record of 49–15–1. This was the best percentage of any home team in 1893. However, Pittsburgh won more home games, because Washington and Louisville home games were transferred to Pittsburgh. Boston played only its scheduled home games. The home attendance for Boston increased to 193,300.

Boston took to the road with a 12-game lead. During the final game in the first stop, Chicago, McCarthy slid into third base and broke two toes. Boston lost two of three games at second-place Pittsburgh, closing the lead to 10 games. In their final game in Cleveland on September 19, Boston won, while Pittsburgh lost. Boston clinched the pennant. The team celebrated on the train to Cincinnati.

Before the game the next day, there was a contretemps on the bench (this was before dugouts). Selee felt Tucker was not ready to play and told him to sit. Tucker and Duffy protested, vociferously enough that the local police wanted to arrest Tucker. Cincinnati manager Comiskey intervened and escorted Tucker to the clubhouse. The article covering these events in the *Boston Globe* stated that Tucker, Duffy, Stivetts and Staley overindulged. The article quoted Selee: "Let Tom down easy; this is the 1st time I have ever had any trouble with him and he is not responsible for his actions now. Tomorrow he will be sorry for this." The same article quoted Tucker: "Either Selee or I will have to leave Boston for this."[40] After this tempest, Cincinnati won the game with Nichols playing RF for Duffy and Ganzel playing 1B for Tucker. Duffy and Tucker apologized to Selee the next day. As the game was rained out the day of the apology, the story in the *Globe* was entirely about that incident. Tucker and Stivetts had scheduled a fight at the hotel the night before at 9 p.m. Tucker showed up, but Stivetts thought better of it. Selee summed it up this way:

> There are three or four men with very hot tempers on the Boston team. I believe that I have gotten as good work out of them as any manager in the land could have done. The Bostons of today are 25 percent stronger than they were last season. The secret of their success has been temperance in the players, good, honest and intelligent playing of all points of the game. There are league teams that are their superiors in hitting and their equals in fielding, but I really think that in intelligence Boston has a shade the best of any of them. No excuse can be offered for that scene on the field yesterday, but I think the story was exaggerated and the offenders given the worst of it. Certainly it was unjust to drag Harry Staley into it. In the four years I have had the club, Tucker has performed very well. He keenly feels the position in which he has placed himself. This is

the first time in all his career as a ball player that he has been guilty of any such escapade. Without shielding either Duffy or Tucker from just criticism, it is only fair to say they are far from being loafers. Tis said that both Duffy and Tucker have vowed that never again will they look upon the lager when it foameth.[41]

The next day, Cincinnati pitcher Icebox Chamberlin no-hit Boston in the second game of a doubleheader. This game lasted seven innings due to darkness, and the no-hitter was not specially mentioned. The article on September 27 stated that Selee, Nash, Duffy, and McCarthy had signed for next year. The article also mentioned that Selee was offered the chance to buy the Milwaukee franchise in the Western League and turned it down. There was a note in the article on September 28 that "several clubs will try at the next league meeting to pass a rule compelling the umpire to stand back of home plate all the time during the game." The season wound down in St. Louis on September 30. Boston finished 86–43 to Pittsburgh's 81–48.

A big part of Boston's success over the last two years was an entity named the "Heavenly Twins." Both Hugh Duffy and Tommy McCarthy had been acquired by the Boston NL team after the death of the American Association. Sometime during the 1892–1893 pennant-winning seasons, a newspaperman in Boston gave them the nickname. Both were known for their hit-and-run ability. Per many observers at the time, this Boston team originated the hit-and-run play as we now know it. During the 1893 season, John Montgomery Ward stated, "I have never, in my twelve years' experience on the diamond, seen such skillful playing. The Boston players use more head-work and private signals than any other team in the country."[42]

Bill James stated that he thought Selee was the first manager ever to give the hit-and-run signal.[43] I respectfully disagree. I have no doubt Selee was involved in the development of this play. There are several mentions in newspaper articles about the Boston team practicing this play under Selee's direction. But it seems to me from Lowe's comment quoted above and other statements from players that Selee let the players call their own games. By all accounts, Duffy and McCarthy were excellent at this play. Both were known as good outfielders as well.

Hugh Duffy was from Providence, Rhode Island. He turned pro in 1886 at the age of 19. Tim Murnane recommended Duffy to Cap Anson, who gave him a chance in 1887. When Duffy reported to Chicago, Anson told him that the Chicago team already had a bat boy, not being impressed with Duffy's 5'7", 150-pound stature. But as Duffy was there, Anson let him play a few times. Duffy stuck in Chicago through the 1889 season, jumping to the Players' League in 1890 and the AA in 1891. Duffy was part of the Boston AA champions in 1891, hitting .335 and leading that league with 110 RBI. Both Selee and Duffy were happy Duffy could stay in Boston after the death of the AA. Duffy hit .301 in 1892 and .363 in 1893, leading the outfielders in games played. Duffy remained in baseball until his death in 1954. Duffy named Selee as his all-time great manager. Duffy has a record shared by no one else. He had a career batting average over .300 in four different major leagues: .336 in the AA, .326 in the NL, .320 in the PL, and .302 in the AL. Duffy was elected to the Hall of Fame in 1945.[44]

Tommy McCarthy was a son of South Boston, born in 1863. While working in a clothing factory, he played sandlot ball around town until 1884. Again, Tim Murnane was involved in getting him into pro ball. Murnane was the manager of the Boston entry in the Union League in 1884. He gave McCarthy a tryout and signed him to that team. McCarthy was a pitcher and outfielder and did not impress at either position. The Boston NL team signed him in 1885. A .182 average led to his release during the season. Selee picked him up to play for Haverhill for the rest of 1885. McCarthy had 1½ mediocre seasons with Philadelphia in the NL before Selee picked him up for Oshkosh, as discussed in Chapter 2. That earned McCarthy another chance in the majors, and this time he stuck. McCarthy played very well for St. Louis in the AA for the next four years. St. Louis won the AA title in 1888 and finished second in 89. McCarthy was named manager at the start of the 1890 season after the prior manager left for the PL. McCarthy lasted 24 games before reverting to just playing. He remained in St. Louis until the club folded after the 1891 season. McCarthy led the AA in at bats in 1889, stolen bases in 1890, and hit .350 in 1890.

McCarthy was a major contributor to Boston's success in 1892 and 93. His offensive statistics were not great in 1892 but improved significantly in 1893 to the tune of a .346 average and leading the team with 46 stolen bases. McCarthy was the originator of a play that led to a rule change. When a fly ball was hit to him in a sacrifice fly situation, he would bobble the ball while running in toward the infield. According to the rule then, the runner could not advance until the fielder totally controlled the ball. After McCarthy got away with this a few times, the rule was changed to allow the runner to leave when the fielder touched the ball. McCarthy was elected to the Hall of Fame in 1946. Many consider him the worst ballplayer elected to the HOF. We will see how the rest of McCarthy's career with Boston played out.[45]

Selee, Duffy, and McCarthy were involved in businesses in the Boston area after the 1893 season. Selee and Sid Farrar (ex–Philadelphia NL first baseman) opened a haberdashery shop in Melrose after the 1891 season that was still going strong. Duffy and McCarthy opened a bowling alley in Boston after the 1893 season. McCarthy liked to work there and swap baseball stories at the bar. He started to gain weight, which would show up next season. The other outfielder in 1893, Cliff Carroll, had not worked out. Carroll hit .220 in a year of big offense, and Selee released him at the end of the season. On October 3, Selee signed Jimmy Bannon, the player he had recommended to St. Louis, to replace Carroll.

Selee had an impressive start to his major league career. After dealing with the Players' League war in 1890, he built a three-time champion. His original signings of Nichols, Long, and Lowe had worked out great. The death of the PL and AA had made Nash, Duffy, McCarthy, and Stivetts available. All were acquired by Selee. He had built one great team. How long would this last?

Rebuilding

Selee expected the Boston team to continue its championship ways. Before March 4, 1894, Selee had signed Nash, Duffy, Long, McCarthy, and Lowe from the 1893 team. He had also signed four new players: catcher John Ryan, utility man Frank Connaughton, outfielder Jimmy Bannon, and pitcher Henry Lampe. Selee said in March that he expected all reserved players from last year's team to sign and that he would hold Stivetts out for a while due to a sore arm. The reason Selee signed John Ryan was due to a personal tragedy. While on a hunting trip in Kansas in January 1894, Charlie Bennett tried to board a moving train. He fell under the train, which ran over his legs. Both legs had to be amputated. Bennett survived, but his baseball career was over. Bennett had a very distinguished career, starting in 1881 after six years in the minors. During his first year in the majors, Bennett and his wife developed a new type of chest protector. This piece of equipment was very successful. Bennett led National League catchers in fielding for 10 seasons during his 14-year career. Three major pieces of catcher's equipment were invented during Bennett's career: mask, glove, and chest protector. After this accident, Bennett returned to Detroit and acquired artificial legs. He opened a newsstand/tobacco store near the Detroit ballpark and ran it the rest of his life. When the ballpark burned down and was rebuilt, the Detroit owner ran a contest to name the new park. The winner was Bennett Park. Charlie Bennett died in 1926.[46]

Boston players were to report April 1 to Boston for the start of spring training. On March 11, Harry Staley wrote Selee, asking for a contract. Selee went to the Triumvirs, who were against re-signing Staley at this point. On April 1, everyone who had signed reported to Boston except Duffy. Duffy's wife had recently died, so he was excused. Stivetts, Tucker, and Merritt were holding out, and Nichols had not yet signed. By the first exhibition game in Boston on April 4, all players had reported. Negotiations were ongoing with the unsigned players. One of the new pitchers in camp this year was an old discovery of Selee's. Tom Lovett had been on Selee's team in Lawrence.

Lovett got a chance with Philadelphia in the AA in 1885, then returned to the minors. Lovett was with Brooklyn from 1889 to 1893, missing the 1892 season with a sore arm. Selee had decided that Hank Gastright would not be with the team this year, with Lovett and Henry Lampe possible replacements. Boston played exhibition games until April 18, all in New England. A game in Princeton was rained out. Nash asked if the team could go south to Charlottesville like last year. Selee told him all the games were arranged. Nichols was the last player to sign on April 18. During spring training, Selee cited two players on opposing teams he was interested in: Fred Tenney at Brown University, and Fred Klobendanz at Fall River.

The season opened in Boston on April 19. Contrary to his earlier comment, Selee started Stivetts on Opening Day. Staley was at the game, but not in uniform. Boston played an exhibition game in Providence on the April 20 before heading to Brooklyn for their Opening Day on the 22nd. Nichols threw a 3–0 shutout before the largest crowd ever in Brooklyn, 19,200. Boston left Brooklyn with a 3–0 record. The lineup was in place: Lowe 2B, Long SS, Duffy CF, McCarthy LF, Nash 3B, Tucker 1B, Bannon RF, Ganzel and Ryan C. The main pitchers were Nichols, Stivetts, Staley, and Lovett.

The next stop was Baltimore. Boston got a whiff of what was to come in the first game in Baltimore. Boston won the toss and batted last. Boston was up, 3–1, going to the ninth inning with Stivetts pitching. The Baltimore players and crowd got very rowdy, intimidating umpire Tim Hurst. Baltimore started the ninth with four walks and a hit. Nichols came in and was shelled. Baltimore won the game, 18–3.[47] Nichols showed no effect the next day, winning 6–3. Boston won the final game to take the series.

The next day, Boston played an exhibition game against Allentown, Pennsylvania. Allentown was run by King Kelly. Kelly had tried to play for New York in 1893, lasting only 20 games. The 1894 season was the first without Kelly in the majors since 1877. Kelly would continue his lifestyle of wine, women, song, and fine clothes until he died of pneumonia in late 1894. Kelly made a lot of money by the standard of the day and spent all of it. The road trip continued until May 9, covering all the eastern cities. In Philadelphia, Harry Wright had been replaced as manager. That left Cap Anson as the only participant in the first year of the National Association still involved on the field in the National League. Boston finished the road trip 9–6.

Boston started their home stand with a two-game split with Brooklyn. On May 14, a doubleheader was scheduled against Baltimore. Baltimore won the first game and was losing 5–3 in the top of the third in the second game. Per the *Boston Globe*, a fire started below the left field bleachers at the South End Grounds due to a dropped, lit cigarette. The game was stopped as the fire spread around the neighborhood. Two hundred buildings were destroyed, 1,900 people were left homeless, and there were no fatalities. After a day off, Boston arranged to play at the Congress Street Grounds, the old Players' League and American Association park. There were promises from the Triumvirs to rebuild the park at South End Grounds and get back into it by the summer. Boston won the final game of this series at Congress Street Grounds.

The homestand was broken up with a three-game series in Philadelphia. Boston won two of three. Boston returned home until June 20. After taking two of three against New York, Selee released Merritt and started looking for another catcher. Boston won three straight from Washington. This led to a Decoration Day morning-afternoon doubleheader with Cincinnati. Boston swept, 13–10 and 20–11. There were no pitching changes in either game for either team. Boston won the first game by scoring nine runs in the eighth inning. Bobby Lowe had a remarkable day. Lowe went 0-for-6 in the first game. He went 5-for-6 in the second, hitting home runs in his first four at-bats. That record has yet to be exceeded in the majors. Lowe had 17 total bases in that game, another record that stood for a long time. Boston played the rest of the western teams, achieving an 18–7 record on the home stand before Baltimore visited. During this good stretch, Boston's team batting average rose from .258 to .300. It would rise still more.

Selee used pitchers Tom Smith and Henry Lampe for the entire game against Pittsburgh on June 6, losing 27–11. Murnane was very critical of this move. On June 9, Murnane said, "It is even money that Baltimore fails to get as good as fifth place." Cap Anson told the *Globe* that Baltimore was a real good team, and that Boston would miss Bennett.[48] The home stand ended with a four-game split with Baltimore. Murnane was outraged by Baltimore, saying, "The Orioles are playing the dirtiest ball ever seen in this country." Examples he cited: diving into the first baseman long after the runner was out, throwing the catcher's mask into the path of a runner, and catching men by their clothes at third base.[49] Boston would head on the road in second place: Baltimore 30–12, Boston 32–17, Philadelphia 28–16.

The trip started with three games in Washington. Boston took two of three. Stivetts pitched a complete game in the final contest in 97-degree heat. Boston took two from Louisville. During this series, the *Cleveland Plain Dealer* said, "It looks as if the Boston players had not forgotten these salary cuts yet."[50] In the first game in St. Louis, Boston was down 10–7 in the bottom of the ninth. With two on and two out, Stivetts pinch-hit for Nichols and hit a game-tying home run. Stivetts allowed a run in the top of the 10th. But Duffy led off with a single, scored on McCarthy's double, and McCarthy came around to score the winning run on a bad throw. Boston won the next game even though a triple play was turned by St. Louis. The final game of the series was a St. Louis win. The scores in the three games were 12–10, 13–4, 10–9. As we will see, offensive production in 1894 was even better than in 1893. Selee signed pitcher Frank West while in St. Louis.

During the next series in Pittsburgh, Boston played an exhibition game on Sunday in Sharon, Pennsylvania. West pitched that exhibition. Boston took two of three games in Pittsburgh. During a three-game sweep in Cleveland, Boston scored 22, 19, and 16 runs. Boston lost the first game in Chicago, 13–11. On this date (July 9) 10 of the 12 teams in the National League scored at least 10 runs. The desire of the magnates for more offense was being fulfilled. Selee released Tom Lovett on July 10. Nichols, Stivetts, and Staley were doing all the pitching. At their final western stop in Cincinnati, the hotel manager of the hotel they were booked into kicked the Boston team out after they changed at the hotel and went into a carriage to go to the ballpark. The hotel manager said they could stay if they changed at the ballpark. As there was no clubhouse at the ballpark, Selee moved the team to another hotel.[51] Boston took two of three in Cincinnati, going 12–5 on the western portion of the road trip.

The trip concluded in Philadelphia. The first game was a routine Philadelphia victory. In the second game, Boston was up, 2–1, after six innings under a threatening sky. Philly scored seven runs in the top of the seventh, at which point Boston stopped trying to get any outs, hoping for the rain to come and the score to revert to the end of the sixth inning. The umpire put up with this for about 20 minutes, then declared the game forfeited to Philly. Fans came on the field and Tucker was punched in the face. Boston won the final game before a crowd of 10,350. On the ride to the hotel after the game, Tucker was hit by a tomato thrown by a fan and got into a fight with another fan. Boston's record on the road trip was 15–8, and they remained in second place.

Boston returned home to a rebuilt South End Grounds. The ballpark was built with the same dimensions, but fewer seats. As with all ballparks up to 1908, the park was built of wood, and construction went quickly. The team celebrated by taking three games from New York. By the end of this series, Duffy was hitting .431 and leading the league. Selee signed Brown University catcher Fred Tenney and released Charlie Ganzel. Releases in 1894 took effect 10 days after they were initiated, so Ganzel caught the first game of the doubleheader against Brooklyn the next day. Tenney (a left-handed-throwing catcher) started the next two games. Brooklyn won two of three. The next series was in Baltimore. The National League must have received many complaints about Baltimore's style of play. For the first time in my review of box scores since 1890, two regular umpires worked this series. Usually one umpire worked alone. There were times when a regular umpire would not appear for the game, and each team would nominate one player to work as a two-umpire team. The assignment of two regular umpires seemed to be an effort by the National League to control dirty play. Every game Baltimore played the rest of the year had two umpires. This seems to have hurt Baltimore, which lost three games to Boston giving Baltimore a seven-game losing streak. Boston left Baltimore with a four-game lead in the standings.

This short road trip finished with a win and a tie in New York. The final two home series against eastern teams were played against Washington and Philadelphia. There was a fire at the Chicago ballpark during a game on August 5. The Philadelphia ballpark burned down on August 6, and new stands were constructed by August 18. Boston went 3–2 on this short home stand. The final games against an eastern team were at Brooklyn, which won two of three. Duffy remained in Boston with a minor injury, and Tenney played center field. The final game in Brooklyn was pitched and lost by George Hodson, who replaced Staley the rest of the year.

The final home stand started on August 14. This would be against western teams only and lasted until September 6. Boston was still in first place on August 14. Ganzel's release had been revoked, and he was still with the team. During the second game of a three-game sweep of Pittsburgh, Boston turned an unusual triple play. Pittsburgh had runners on first and second with no outs in the ninth inning of a tie game. The batter lifted a short fly to center. McCarthy, playing center field, yelled, "I got it," caught the ball on one bounce, and quickly threw to Lowe at second base. Lowe tagged out the runner who was off the bag and then tagged second for a force out of the runner on first. Lowe threw the ball to Nash at third base, who unnecessarily tagged third. The batter had touched first and returned to home plate. Nash ran to first and touched it. The umpire correctly made no call on that. McCarthy got the ball from Nash and ran in to tag the batter out. Ganzel scored the winning run in the bottom of the 11th.

Boston lost the first game of the next series to Cincinnati. Baltimore won and moved into first place. Boston won the next four games against Cincinnati and Cleveland. Baltimore had a bad stretch, and Boston was back in first place. Charlie Bennett returned to Boston for a benefit game, an exhibition on August 27 that drew a crowd of 8,157. Bennett sat on the bench for the next couple of games. St. Louis took two of three games from Boston to end August. On August 30, the standings were Boston 69–37, Baltimore 68–36. Boston won two of three games from Chicago while Baltimore was winning four. Both played morning-afternoon doubleheaders on September 3. Both swept. Boston attendance was 8,123, Baltimore's 24,450. The home stand ended with Boston taking two of games from last-place Louisville. Murnane printed a remark from Arthur Soden: "Wanted—Two Pitchers."[52] This was Boston's last home game of the year. Their home record was 44–19. All the remaining games this year would be played in the west, as all the eastern teams were done at home. Baltimore had a home record of 52–15. New York's was 49–17. After the games of September 6, the standings were: Baltimore 75–36, New York 74–39, Boston 73–40. These three teams would finish the season on the road.

Baltimore left for their road trip with a 14-game winning streak. They finally lost on September 16, after winning 18 in a row. Boston went 4–2 in Chicago and Cleveland, falling five games behind. One interesting thing occurred on this western trip. Boston did not play any Sunday games, home or road. When Boston was out west, another team would come into the home team's city and play one game on Sunday. On Sunday, September 9, Boston was in Chicago. As they would not play, Cleveland traveled to Chicago for one game. After Boston lost three games at St. Louis, Murnane said Boston had lost heart. By the end of the next series in Louisville, Boston was six out with six to play. The total attendance for the first two games in Louisville was 645. The final two stops on the trip were in Cincinnati and Pittsburgh. Cincinnati took two of three games. The final games were a doubleheader. Boston asked that the second game of the doubleheader end after five innings so they could catch a train to Pittsburgh. This was the day Baltimore clinched the pennant in Cleveland. Boston won two of three in Pittsburgh to end the season on September 29.

After the 1893 season, the president of the second-place Pittsburgh franchise thought there should be a post-season series to determine the champion of the National League. Coincidently, Pittsburgh finished second in 1893. Hence, his proposal was that there should be a best-of-seven series between the first- and second-place teams. William Temple commissioned an $800 cup from a New York jeweler, and his plan was implemented after the 1894 season. The Temple Cup series took place during the first week of October 1894. The Baltimore players sabotaged it. The rules for the series called for a 65–35 split of the players' share, the larger percentage going to the winning team, who would be declared the league champion. The Baltimore players felt they had earned the pennant outright. They made private arrangements with the New York players to split the money 50–50. Baltimore treated the series as an exhibition and lost four straight lopsided games. The Temple Cup concept never recovered from this travesty.

Even though this was the best offensive team Selee ever had, Baltimore was too much. Boston led the league in several team offensive categories: runs, doubles, home runs, RBI, and slugging percentage. Their team batting average was .331, which was third in the league. Hugh Duffy led the league in hits, doubles, home runs, RBI, batting average, and slugging percentage. All this offensive firepower led to a third-place finish. Baltimore was 89–39, New York 88–44, Boston 83–49. The six eastern teams were in the top six except for Washington (11th); the six western teams were in the bottom six except for Cleveland (sixth). As was stated by Arthur Soden, the lead Triumvir, Boston was short on pitching. In 1894, Nichols and Stivetts were the only reliable pitchers. In the most prolific offensive season of the 1890s, Nichols led the league with three shutouts. Nichols was 32–13 and Stivetts was 26–14. The rest of the staff was 25–22. Staley had been released and would hang on for one more year in St. Louis. Lovett was released and never pitched in the majors again. None of the other pitchers tried in 1894 would be on the Boston roster in 1895. Selee had some work to do to catch Baltimore. Attendance suffered due to the fire at South End Grounds. The total home attendance for 1894 was 152,800.

If one considers the decade of the 1890s to run from 1891 to 1900, only two managers won the National League pennant in the 1890s. Selee had won from 1891–1893. Ned Hanlon was the manager of Baltimore for 1894. Edward "Ned" Hanlon was born in 1857. He turned pro in 1877 and made the majors in 1880 with Cleveland. He moved on to Detroit in 1882. Hanlon was the captain of the Detroit NL champions in 1887 and played in Detroit until the end of the 1888 season. He was the player-manager for Pittsburgh NL in 1889, Pittsburgh PL in 1890, and Pittsburgh NL in 1891. Seventy-eight games into the 1891 season, Hanlon was fired as manager of Pittsburgh, but he finished out the season there as a player. By this time, Hanlon was about through as a player. He joined Baltimore as a sub for the 1892 season. When Baltimore started the season 3–16 under two different managers, Hanlon was named manager. His record in 1892 wasn't much better (43–85). Only three of the players on the Baltimore team Hanlon inherited were members of the 1894 Orioles. He made over the roster except for pitcher John "Sadie" McMahon, catcher Wilbert Robinson, and third baseman John McGraw. Before the 1893 season, trades were uncommon in the majors. The climate was changing, and Hanlon built his first great team mostly through trades. Before the start of the 1894 season, he acquired outfielders Joe Kelley, Willie Keeler, and Steve Brodie; infielders Hughie Jennings and Dan Brouthers; and pitchers George Hemming and Kid Gleason via trades. Second baseman Heinie Reitz came up from the minors. Hanlon was a teacher, not a screamer. He taught his players to play rough and look for any edge they could on the field, legal or not. His leadership style was remote. He let the players lead. As we will see over the next couple of years, he had plenty of leaders on this team.[53]

Selee was not convinced that his team had fallen behind. He consulted with the Triumvirs and convinced them not to tear his team apart but to give it one more chance. The regular lineup stayed the same in 1895. Three new pitchers were added: Cozy Dolan, Jim Sullivan, and Zeke Wilson. By March 10, all players had signed except Nash, Duffy, Nichols, and Tenney. Nash and Duffy signed and were on the train heading to Charleston,

3. Boston: The First Seven Years

South Carolina, on March 15. Nichols was still holding out over $500. The March 25 *Boston Globe* reported that Soden offered Nichols the extra $500 if he pitched out of turn. Nichols refused that but said he would pitch when called upon. That was agreed. Nichols reported on March 27. By this date, Baltimore had several players holding out. Nichols pitched in a couple of games before April 5, when Soden wired Selee not to pitch Nichols as he had not yet signed. Fred Tenney had returned to Brown University and had not yet signed. Nichols and Tenney signed before the start of the season. The team played exhibition games, working their way north from March 26 to April 17. At the end of this trip, Selee decided on his roster: Long SS, Duffy CF, Nash 3B, Jimmy Collins RF, Tucker 1B, McCarthy LF, Lowe 2B, Ganzel and Ryan C, Tenney and Warner U, and a pitching staff of Nichols, Stivetts, Dolan, Sullivan, George Hodson, and Wilson. Selee had spotted Jimmy Collins in 1894 during an exhibition game in Buffalo, Collins' hometown. Collins was very young, but Selee had great hopes for him. Jimmy Bannon had been expected to take over in right field.

The season opened in Boston on April 19. Stivetts pitched a Boston win over Washington before a crowd of 15,000. As we have seen in the last couple of years, Boston played their first game in Boston, then went on the road for three series. The next day was Opening Day in Washington. The game started at 4:35 p.m. Nine innings were completed, and the report on the game said it was too dark to play after seven. A great crowd for Washington of 8,575 attended. McCarthy and Long played through injuries. Collins' errors cost Boston one of the games in Washington. Bannon agreed to report on April 26 with the promise of a raise if he became a regular by June 1. Bannon signed for the lower amount on April 28, with nothing in writing about his raise. After splitting two games in New York, Selee released Hodson. The entire three-game series in Baltimore was rained out.

Boston returned home for a three-game sweep of Washington. The middle game on May 3 was an exaggerated version of what baseball had become after the change in pitching distance. Boston won, 27–11. McCarthy hit a grand slam after Duffy was intentionally walked. Boston had 20 hits. Lowe had five, McCarthy and Collins three each. The final two games of the Washington series were pitched by Sullivan, Dolan, and Wilson for Boston. After the last game, Boston departed on their first western trip. The team took the longest train trip needed in the majors, from Boston to St. Louis. Boston would get to St. Louis at 3 p.m. on May 6 for a 4 p.m. game. Ryan and Tenney were left home for this trip, with Ganzel the only catcher travelling with the team.

Selee was greeted in St. Louis with the news that Arthur Soden had told the *Boston Globe* that Selee did not have the right to release players.[54] Selee kept releasing players, but subject to the approval of the Triumvirs.

Boston showed no ill effects of the train trip, winning the first game in St. Louis. Staley beat his old team in the second game. Boston left for Chicago after winning two of three. Bannon pitched the final two innings of the second game in Chicago, a 14–1 blowout loss. Sullivan won the final game to salvage one win in Chicago. Bannon was playing right field regularly. After two rainouts in Cleveland, a double header was split. On the train trip to Louisville, McCarthy and Stivetts got into an altercation in the dining car. McCarthy allegedly hit Stivetts in the jaw. The *Boston Globe* reported that McCarthy stayed out all night their first night in Louisville, making sure he did not run into Stivetts. Selee called both on the carpet before the game and said the trouble was cleared up.

Boston swept two games in Louisville and headed to Cincinnati on May 18. Since May 19 was a Sunday, Boston was off. Washington came to Cincinnati and played. The crowd in Cincinnati that Sunday was 11,885, which was too much for one of the grandstands. The grandstand did not fall, but it weakened enough that three people were injured. The game on May 20 was rained out. Selee sold Collins to Louisville with the understanding that Boston had first rights to Collins when they wanted him back. Ryan joined the team to replace Collins. On this rainout day, the *Cincinnati Enquirer* reported that there was a religious split on the Beaneaters, that Protestants Stivetts, and Lowe did not get along with Catholics Duffy, McCarthy, and Tucker. Tim Murnane said this was nonsense.[55] Cincinnati swept two games from Boston, moving into first place after their 10th straight win. The final stop on the road trip was Pittsburgh. Boston lost three straight to the Pirates, making for a five-game losing streak. On May 23, Louisville forfeited their home game to Brooklyn due to running out of balls. Boston lost the final game in Pittsburgh, 1–0. Nichols pitched great but gave up one run in the sixth inning on a walk, a stolen base, and an RBI single. Pittsburgh moved into first place. Boston was seventh with a record of 12–12.

Boston would be home from May 28 to June 28. All the western clubs would visit. The fans were ready. Twenty thousand showed up for the first three games against St. Louis. Boston swept these games, walking off on homers in the first two. Exhibition games were played the days before and after the St. Louis games. Sullivan, Dolan, and Wilson pitched the exhibition games. Selee signed infielder Charlie Nyce, with both Long and Lowe nursing injuries. Boston swept two games from Cincinnati. In the second game, a 12–5 win, Boston hit four home runs (Bannon, Duffy, Nash, and Nyce). The home winning streak ended at nine on June 5 with a loss to Pittsburgh. Boston won the next six at home against Pittsburgh, Louisville, and Chicago before losing to Chicago on June 14. Boston took three of four games from Cleveland to end the western portion of this home stand. The doubleheader in the Cleveland series drew 10,000.

A new pitcher, Frank Sexton, was signed before the next series. The homestand would conclude with the New York teams and Philadelphia. Boston took two of three from Brooklyn. Sullivan lost his first game of the year, and Sexton won his first start. Boston swept three games from New York. Philadelphia came in for three games, but two were rained out. Boston won the only game played. Boston's home record to this point was 24–5 as they moved into first place. The top four records in the league: Boston 32–17, Baltimore 29–19, Pittsburgh 32–22, Chicago 34–24. Selee said he would take five pitchers on the upcoming road trip: Nichols, Stivetts, Dolan, Sullivan, and Sexton. Boston would not return home until July 30.

Boston started the road trip on a sour note, losing five in a row in Philadelphia and Brooklyn. This losing streak put Baltimore in first place. After the last game in Brooklyn, Boston headed west. Selee told the newspapers, "Our luck will change soon, and then we will win a few games."[56] Boston won two of three games in Pittsburgh, a doubleheader. Boston won the first game, 3–2, with Sexton getting the win and Nichols pitching the ninth inning. Nichols pitched a complete game victory in the nightcap. Louisville won two of three in a four-game series featuring a 2–2 tie that was called after 16 innings. Dolan pitched a complete game for Boston. This series was not a good sign for Boston. After the series, Louisville was in last place with 12 wins, two of which came in this series. The next series in Cincinnati was worse. Cincinnati took three of four. Boston lost the first game in Chicago in a matchup of future Hall of Famers. Clark Griffith defeated Kid Nichols, 2–1. Boston took the remaining two games in Chicago. By this time, Baltimore was in first place and on a similar road trip to the west. On July 19, John McGraw said that if Baltimore went home in first place, it would all be over but the shouting. Boston finished the road trip by sweeping St. Louis and taking one of three from Cleveland. Cleveland was the team that most resembled Baltimore in their attitude and dirty play. The road trip ended on July 28 with these standings: Cleveland 52–33, Pittsburgh 47–30, Baltimore 43–31, Boston 42–31. Nine teams were at .500 or better, with only Washington, St. Louis and Louisville having losing records.

As we can see from simple math, Boston had played the fewest games so far, due to many rainouts and games canceled because of wet grounds. The first date of the home stand with Baltimore was rained out. Baltimore won the two games that were played. In the first game, Baltimore bunted five times to make Stivetts field the ball in a 7–1 win. After the second game, Captain Nash noted, "Boston should recall Collins from Louisville at once; that his phenomenal fielding beat Boston two of the games at Louisville." This was a bit of a death wish, as Collins played the same position as Nash. It was noted in the same article that Selee was the only man now handling a major league team who never had a practical baseball education. The losing was not sitting well with the players or the writers.[57]

During the next series with Philadelphia, Selee replaced Bannon in right field with Tenney due to Bannon's slump. Boston took three of four games from Philadelphia. On the off-day before the next series, Selee had a long conversation on the record with Tim Murnane. Selee made numerous points: (1) Boston is not as good as some of the other teams in the league and needs breaks to beat them; (2) hitters that hit in one direction will fail more than those that use the whole field; (3) he will get Collins back to Boston by the beginning of next year; (4) there will be three new men outside of the pitchers on the Boston team next year; (5) he is not convinced that Bannon is the answer in right field; (6) he will not give even money that Boston will win the pennant this year; and (7) the umpiring in the National League this year is terrible.[58] In the first game of the Brooklyn series, the umpiring was so bad that the crowd almost came on the field. Boston took two of three games from Brooklyn. Boston ended the home stand by sweeping three games from Washington. Selee said Boston needed to take five of eight and three of five in Baltimore on the upcoming road trip.

After the first four games of the Baltimore stop, Selee gave up the ghost of a pennant chance. Baltimore won the first three games. The final day in Baltimore was to be the second doubleheader of the series. The only game played went 15 innings. Both Sullivan for Boston and Dad Clarkson (John's younger brother) for Baltimore went the distance. Baltimore walked off on a single by Keeler, an error by Bannon, and an RBI double by Jennings. Selee told Hanlon after the game that Baltimore would win the pennant, even though Baltimore was in a tie for first with Cleveland after this series. The entire Selee quote was reported by the *Boston Globe*:

> Our club seems to me to be standing still when it is pitted against Baltimore. There is no use in denying the fact that Hanlon has called together the best club in the league. Because they were the best club last year they won the pennant, and because they are the best club this year I believe they will fly the flag again. We seem to be able to best every other club in the league, but it has been demonstrated this year that we are no match for the Orioles. Cleveland is playing good ball just now, but its work is not to be compared with that of Hanlon's men. The Spiders will surely fall down when they come east, and I believe that Baltimore in the long series on the home grounds will forge to the front and finish a comparatively easy winner. I am willing to back my opinion at even money, too. Baseball clubs come and go. There was a certain club I knew of was the strongest in the league. It was in a class by itself, but time deals with ball players as with everyone else. A man who never was fast on his feet will not become faster as he grows older. Meanwhile the youngsters are coming up. They develop and improve, while the older players, though they may be today just as good as the youth, are going back. The club I know of that used to be the best is no longer so. Baltimore, with its

youth and dash and energy, is today the premier club of the land. It is now in a class by itself, and the club that expects to beat the champions out in the race this year will have to play ball beyond its gait today.[59]

Selee also said he had won several bets with his players at the end of the 1894 season regarding where Baltimore would finish.

A couple of points should be made about what Selee said. He clearly had made up his mind by this point that he had to rebuild the Boston team. He intended to do this with youth. The other point is about betting. A couple of his comments seem strange to us today. Not the fact that players and managers bet among themselves, which is acknowledged, but that the bets were about places in the standings. There were no rules against this behavior at the time. These quotes show the language of the time in figuring out how strongly someone felt about a team. Boston ended this short road trip before three big crowds in Philadelphia totaling 29,966. Philadelphia won two of games, and Boston returned home in seventh place.

When Boston returned home, Selee replaced Sexton with new pitcher Otis Stockdale. The first home date was a doubleheader sweep by Boston over Louisville. Between games, there was an exhibition of trick bicycle riding. Stockdale won the second game. Boston won six straight against Louisville and Pittsburgh. In the final game against Pittsburgh, Lowe suffered a serious leg injury.

During the Pittsburgh series, Murnane wrote an article about Selee's status. He said Selee was wounded by the criticism this year and did not have the authority to go out and get players like Hanlon. Murnane also said that Selee had been offered a three-year contract to go to New York as manager. The Triumvirs and Selee responded to this by announcing three days later that Selee had signed to be the manager for 1896, at the same $3,500 salary. This was during a series with Cleveland in which Cleveland won two of three games. Selee announced that Jimmy Collins had been re-acquired for the beginning of next year. Collins would play out the year in Louisville. Boston remained home, playing the western teams until September 10. In the last series at home, St. Louis took two of three games from Boston while Baltimore took two of three from Cleveland. Boston had seven games remaining at home. Standings after this long home stand: Baltimore 73–38, Cleveland 74–45, Philadelphia 69–46, Boston and Brooklyn 63–50. Boston was fifth at 62-30.

A short road trip to New York and Baltimore was next, and lost all three games. After one game in New York, there was a doubleheader the next day in Baltimore. After losing two games, the omnibus the Boston team was taking to the train station was hit by a cable car. Joe Harrington, a utility man on Boston, was injured in the accident and would miss the rest of the year. Not a very good trip to Baltimore. The final seven home games were against these two teams. Boston took all three games from New York. Boston and Baltimore split four games. The first game of a doubleheader on September 17 drew the comment from Murnane that Baltimore won this game due to dirty play. The examples he gave were continual kicking that intimidated the umpire, and the second baseman holding a runner by the belt, preventing him from scoring on a double.[60] Boston won the nightcap in five innings when the game was called by darkness. Selee announced that catcher Marty Bergen of Kansas City had been signed for next year. Selee missed the September 19 game against New York to go to Springfield, Massachusetts, to scout a player. The game in Springfield was canceled. The season concluded with a trip to Brooklyn and Washington. Boston won three of four games. During one of the games in Brooklyn, Selee missed the game to meet with New York president Andrew Freedman.

The final first-division standings showed Baltimore 87–43, Cleveland 84–46, Philadelphia 78–53, Chicago 72–58, and Boston and Brooklyn 71–60. The Temple Cup rules had been changed to a best-of-seven series. Baltimore went to Cleveland for the first three games. The Cleveland crowd treated Baltimore like the Baltimore crowd had treated road teams, by pelting them with fruit and vegetables. Cleveland won all three home games. Baltimore won the next game but lost the fifth. This was the second year in a row that Baltimore did not take the Temple Cup seriously and lost badly. All concerned except the winner of the Temple Cup series felt that the pennant determined the real champion, same as last year.

The Boston club performed in 1895 like it did in 1894. The offense was pretty good but not at the level of 1894. Duffy led the team with a .353 average, followed by Bannon at .347 and Long at .315. McCarthy had a big drop to .290. Selee thought McCarthy was out of shape for much of the season and started looking for a replacement. Beyond Nichols, the pitching was a problem. Stivetts had a down year both offensively and as a pitcher, finishing with a .190 average and a 17–17 record. Dolan and Sullivan appeared to be competent major league pitchers, but not pitchers on an outstanding staff. Dolan was 10–7 and Sullivan 11–9. Selee had some work to do to catch the teams ahead of him. Even though the team struggled in 1895, the fans came out in Boston. Total home attendance increased to 242,000.

Selee started the work over the winter. He traded Billy Nash to Philadelphia straight-up for outfielder Billy Hamilton. Nash had been the captain of the Beaneaters after his return from the Players' League. He performed well all four years he played for Selee. According to the reporting of the *Boston Globe,* most moves made in-game, including pitching changes, were credited to Nash. But Selee wanted the team to get younger and had an alternative in Jimmy Collins. Nash was 30, Collins 25. After making this trade, Selee released Tommy McCarthy. McCarthy was 32, but

Selee thought he had lost a step. Selee thought Billy Hamilton would be an improvement over McCarthy.

Hamilton was 28. He had come up to the majors in the American Association in 1888 and had been with Philadelphia in the National League since 1890. Philadelphia had the best hitting outfield in the NL all the years Hamilton was there. Hamilton was a classic lead-off man. His on-base percentages with Philadelphia were .423, .452, .398, .470, .510 and .464. His stolen base totals with Philadelphia were 102, 111, 57, 43, 98, and 97. For this skill, he was known as "Sliding Billy." Hamilton was an obvious offensive upgrade over Nash, and Selee hoped he would help the outfield defense by taking center field, allowing Duffy to move to left.[61] Selee had already announced that Marty Bergen would come from Kansas City to shore up the catching. The only pitcher he signed over the winter was Willard Mains.

The team left Boston for Charlottesville and spring training on March 18 with 18 players under contract. Fifteen appeared in Charlottesville on May 19. Jimmy Collins and another player missed their connection in Jersey City with the team. Kid Nichols had permission to report on April 1. On March 24, their workout was snowed out in Charlottesville. On March 28, Bergen was out with a sore arm and Tenney was deemed poor at first base. Selee stressed to a reporter that the team should be improved but would not promise competing for the pennant. Tommy McCarthy stopped by on March 31 on his way to report to the Brooklyn club. Even though earlier stories stated that all players had signed, it was reported on April 2 that Collins signed for $1,800. Boston played exhibition games against college and minor league teams until April 14, traveling north from Charlottesville to Boston. Tim Murnane predicted that the pennant race would come down to Baltimore, Cleveland, and Boston in 1896.

Unlike the prior years, Boston did not play the first game in Boston and then go on the road. The first three games were in Philadelphia. Boston and Philadelphia drew a crowd of 23,000, and the total league attendance on Opening Day was 77,000 for six games. Philadelphia won two of three games. All four Boston pitchers threw in the series. Boston had its own Opening Day against Baltimore on April 20. Boston got 27 hits and won, 21–6, behind Nichols. Both teams traveled to Baltimore for a series starting the next day. Each took a ship to New York, and both ships ran into fog trouble near Long Island. Boston made it to Harlem and made the train at Jersey City in plenty of time. The ship carrying the Baltimore team was stymied by fog before getting to New York. The team had to be ferried to Long Island, where they caught a train into New York, then took a ferry to Jersey City. The Baltimore team just made the same train the Boston team was on. Even with those travel troubles, Baltimore beat Boston two of three games in Baltimore. Boston swept three games in New York before returning home.

Selee told the *Globe* that he wanted to sign pitcher Jesse Tannehill from Richmond. He recommended this to the Triumvirs, and it was up to them. After the final game in New York, Boston stopped in Fall River, Massachusetts, to play an exhibition game. Fall River beat Boston. The pitcher for Fall River was Fred Klobedanz. Selee said after the game that Klobedanz was impressive. The final two games before the first western trip of the season were in Boston against Baltimore. Boston walked off as victors in both. In the first, Long singled in Hamilton in the bottom of the ninth for a 5–4 win for Nichols. In the second, seven errors were committed over 10 innings. All were committed by the shortstops (Long four, Jennings three). Boston walked off on Jennings error in the 10th. Stivetts got the win and had three hits. During this stretch of games, Boston survived injuries to Bergen, Ganzel, and Collins to emerge with an 8–4 record.

The trip to all the western league cities started on May 4 in Cincinnati. Cincinnati took two of three games there, Stivetts winning the middle game. Boston swept three games in Louisville, which was a mess. The owner fined each player $50 after Boston won the first game of the series, 17–1. He probably needed the money because the total attendance for the series was 1,250. Louisville's record after this series was 2–17, and to no one's surprise the manager was fired. Chicago won the first two games of the next series. The final game was tied 4–4 Until Boston scored three runs in the top of the 11th inning. Chicago stalled so blatantly trying to get the game called for darkness that the umpire declared it a forfeit victory for Boston. Cap Anson had already protested the game due to alleged interference with a baserunner by Tucker. The forfeit held, and the protest was thrown out.

Boston took two of three games in Pittsburgh. After the first game, pitched by Dolan and Sullivan, Tim Murnane said that Selee needed another pitcher behind Nichols and Stivetts. Right on cue, Nichols and Stivetts won the next two games in Pittsburgh. Two games were played in St. Louis, and another was rained out. Nichols and Stivetts pitched those two games, and Boston won them both. On the rainout day, John Ryan was released. He had caught eight games in 1896. Now Bergen and Ganzel would be the main catchers, backed up by Tenney. Nichols had been sent ahead to Cleveland to rest for the first game of the next series. That backfired as Nichols lost the first game and Stivetts lost the last game of the Cleveland series. The only game won in Cleveland was started by a new pitcher, Willard Mains, and finished by Sullivan. Boston's record on the road trip was 10–7, and they returned home in third place.

After a rainout, Boston split two games with Pittsburgh. The final game of this series was a 7–7 tie in 12 innings. Nichols pitched 10 innings and

Stivetts two in this game. The next day was Decoration Day. All the teams in the league played doubleheaders. Sullivan won the morning game against Cleveland. Both Nichols and Stivetts pitched in the afternoon game, a 14–7 Cleveland victory. This was the best attendance day since Opening Day. Six thousand came to the morning game, 11,000 to the afternoon game. After a Sunday off, Stivetts beat Louisville. Boston lost the second game to Louisville before winning the final game. Chicago took two of three games from Boston, beating Nichols and Stivetts.

During this series, Tim Murnane asked Cap Anson his opinion of Boston's chances this year. Anson replied, "They're not in it. At one time I thought the Bostons would be in the race but now I see they are not stayers. The only catcher they have is old stiff-backed Ganzel. Bergen is no good and Tenney is too erratic. The club is very weak in the box, and the hitting is poor. I'll bet several hundred dollars that Chicago will beat Boston out, and I don't consider we have done much at that."[62] Like most older ballplayers, (Anson was 42) he said his pennant-winning team of the early 1880s was better than any team around in 1896. Later in the article, Murnane made some excuses due to injury for the Boston team and said they would rebound later in the year. Boston finished playing western teams on this home stand by taking one game from St. Louis and two of three from Cincinnati. Now they would play all the eastern teams except Baltimore before going on the road again.

Boston won two games against New York. On the morning before the June 17 game in Boston, the Boston team played an exhibition against a team in Everett, Massachusetts. The Boston team won the real game in the afternoon, but the writer thought the players looked tired. The coverage of the New York series centered on the dispute between New York owner Andrew Freedman and New York pitcher Amos Rusie. Rusie had not yet signed his contract or reported to New York in a dispute over fines taken out of his salary in 1895. Virtually all parties supported Rusie in this dispute, but Freedman would not give in. This was not helping his team any, as Rusie was by far the best pitcher on New York. Two games with Washington were split. Boston swept three games from Brooklyn. In the second game, Boston was down two runs going into the bottom of the ninth. Captain Duffy hit a two-run home run to tie it, and Tenney drove in the winning run later in the inning. The home stand ended with three games against Philadelphia. Nash was cheered in his return to Boston. It was clear by each person's performance that Boston had gotten the better of the deal for Hamilton. Boston won two of three. The standings on June 29: Baltimore 36–19, Cleveland 34–18, Cincinnati 39–22, Boston 33–22. Now came a four-week road trip.

The trip started in Washington with more injuries. Collins was out, and in the first game of the trip the utility man filling in for him, Joe

Harrington, got hurt. Bannon played third base in the second game, Stivetts in the third game. Boston won two of three. The last stop in the east was in Brooklyn, where Boston won two of three. In the first game of a July 4 doubleheader, Stivetts pitched a 3–2 win and was involved in all three Boston runs. In June, Selee had sold Willard Mains to a minor league club, and he was performing poorly there. Selee signed pitcher Ted Lewis in June 1896. Lewis had just graduated from Williams College. He made his professional debut in Louisville on July 6, losing 5–2. No umpire appeared, so a substitute from the stands was used. The *Boston Globe* said Lewis pitched well. Boston took the final two games of the Louisville series. Boston split four games at St. Louis, Lewis and Stivetts losing. At the time of these series, St. Louis was in 11th place, Louisville in 12th.

In the story after the final game of this series, Murnane said Boston could win the pennant this year, had a splendid basis, but needed new blood. Boston took two of three games in Pittsburgh. Lewis lost his third straight decision. Long was out, and Bannon played shortstop with Tenney in right field. Long came back in Cleveland, but Lowe broke his collarbone in pregame practice on July 17. Bannon moved to second base, with Stivetts in right field when not pitching. Boston won one of three games, winning the game Nichols pitched. Boston took Sunday July 19 off, per its policy.

On July 19, Baltimore beat Cincinnati at Cincinnati to go into first-place, one game ahead of the Reds. This game drew a crowd of 24,944. Chicago swept Boston in a three-game series. Lewis lost his fourth straight. Chicago went past Boston into fourth place. During a two-day rain in Cincinnati that canceled both games, Selee met with the manager of the Kansas City minor league club. He was trying to get players. No results came from this meeting. Cincinnati beat both Nichols and Stivetts in the doubleheader played on the last date of the road trip against a major league team. Before returning to Boston in sixth place, Boston stopped to play an exhibition

Jimmy Collins in 1899. John McGraw, a fine third baseman himself, said Collins was the best third baseman he ever saw.

3. Boston: The First Seven Years 89

WILLIAM R. HAMILTON, Center Fielder.
BOSTON, 1900.

Billy Hamilton in 1900. Along with John McGraw, he was the best leadoff man of the 1890s. Hamilton and Collins were two additions to the everyday lineup for the 2nd championship run in Boston.

game on July 27 in Providence, Rhode Island. Lewis pitched and won.

Baltimore had fallen behind Cincinnati. Boston helped Baltimore out by losing two of three games in Boston. Collins and Ganzel returned from injuries. Sullivan pitched the Boston victory. Boston took three straight from Philadelphia in a series where the *Boston Globe* described Long as "brilliant in the field." Lewis pitched another exhibition game in Brockton before the next series with Washington. Boston took two of three from Washington, walking off on a Bergen RBI single in the second game. During this series, the story came out that Philadelphia was trying to acquire Stivetts to play first base. Selee wasn't going to trade his second-best pitcher.[63] The Beaneaters made a one-day trip to Philadelphia for a make-up game, Nichols winning it on August 10. Boston would play nothing but home games until September 9.

Boston played four games against New York in three days. Nichols pitched all three days. He lost the first game in relief. He started, pitched four innings, and lost the second game of a doubleheader the next day. He pitched a shutout win in the final game. Earlier in the year, Selee had recommended Fred Klobedanz to the Triumvirs. One of the Triumvirs went to Providence and scouted Klobedanz on August 14. On August 16, Boston purchased Klobedanz. Boston's final games at home against an eastern team were with Brooklyn. Brooklyn won two of three. The rest of the games on this home stand would be against western teams.

First-place Cincinnati came for three games, and Boston won two. Klobedanz won his major league debut on August 20 before a larger-than-average crowd of 4,000. Cincinnati left town in second place. Pittsburgh split four games with Boston, Klobedanz getting his first loss. Chicago came to town with its top two catchers out. Forty-two-year-old player-manager Cap Anson caught the entire three-game series. Chicago won two of three, and Boston had no stolen bases in the series. Klobedanz got the win and hit a home run in the game he started. Then the two worst teams in the league, Louisville and St. Louis, came to town. Boston won seven of eight games from them. The home season concluded with two doubleheaders against Cleveland. A crowd of 5,000 came out for a two-for-one admission doubleheader split on September 5. The final home games were played on Labor Day, a morning-afternoon doubleheader. The total crowd for the two games was 13,500. Klobedanz lost the final home game to Cy Young. That same day, Baltimore played three games at home against Louisville, winning them all. Standings before Boston's final road trip of the year: Baltimore 80–34, Cincinnati 72–44, Cleveland 71–45, Boston 67–52, Chicago 65–53.

After starting the final road trip with three losses in New York, Boston went to Baltimore. The Baltimore team did not consider Boston much of a threat. The first scheduled game on September 15 was rained out. That evening, the Baltimore players and manager took the Boston players and managers to the theater. Boston returned that favor by taking two of three games in the series. Boston then made it even in New York on this trip, taking three from Brooklyn. Lewis got his first win on September 22. The season ended in Washington. Where Boston took two of three to end up with a record of 74–57, in fourth place. The teams ahead of them were Baltimore 90–39, Cleveland 80–48, and Cincinnati 77–50. Baltimore and Cleveland played the Temple Cup series for the second year in a row. Baltimore took it more seriously this year, sweeping the series 4–0. The winners share was about $200 and the losers share was $117 per man. None of the players were very excited about this series in October weather.

Even though their place in the standings improved from fifth to fourth and the Boston team won six more games, Selee knew some changes had to be made. He had changed over the catching staff and was satisfied with them. Selee was hopeful that adding Klobedanz and Lewis to his old reliables, Nichols and Stivetts, would fix the pitching. Nichols had another fine year in 1896 with a 30–14 record, leading the league in wins. Stivetts bounced back with a 22–14 record. Jim Sullivan was the third pitcher most of the year. Selee hoped Klobedanz and Lewis would be better than Sullivan's 11–12 record in 1896. Hamilton had proven a fine acquisition, hitting .365 with 83 stolen bases. Duffy had a bit of an adjustment to the added duties of captain. His batting average slumped to .300, but Selee still had confidence in him. The third outfielder, Bannon, was a disappointment. In the infield, Long, Lowe and Collins all performed well. Tucker had a decent year at first base, hitting .304. But during the time Lowe was out with a broken collarbone, Fred Tenney had stepped up. Playing 88 games, Tenney hit

.336 with 18 stolen bases. As Tenney was eight years younger than Tucker, moving Tenney to first base was an option. As Selee had shown with Nash and McCarthy, he could get rid of a veteran if he had a better option. The fans of Boston liked what they saw. Home attendance held steady at 240,000.

4

Boston: The Last Five Years

Back-to-Back Pennants

On March 20, 1897, the big story in baseball was the continuing dispute between Amos Rusie and the owner of the New York Giants, Andrew Freedman. Rusie had held out all of 1896. Negotiations were ongoing to either trade Rusie or bring the two parties together. The Boston team left for spring training on March 20. This trip was by ship, to Savannah, Georgia. Selee had signed two new players to compete for the right field spot. Bannon had been released. Charles "Chick" Stahl was from Indiana. He turned pro in 1890 at the age of 17. Selee had been told about him, and signed Stahl for the 1897 season. The other competitor was James "Jimmy" Slagle. He turned pro in 1895 at the age of 21. Slagle had joined the Boston team for the last road trip in 1896 but did not get into any games. On top of that competition, Selee said that he would try Tenney and Stivetts at first base. Tucker was still on the team.

The team hotel in Savannah was one mile from the practice diamond. The team jogged there and back before and after practice. After a week in the hotel, the team complained to Selee and asked him to find another hotel. This took place at a meeting in Selee's room on March 29. The manager and players also discussed trick plays and signals. The hotel problems were ironed out by March 31. Boston played a team of Savannah amateurs on April 3. All five main Boston pitchers pitched; Nichols, Klobedanz, and Stivetts for Savannah, Lewis and Sullivan for Boston. After that game, Tim Murnane declared Stahl the star of the spring. Murnane published Selee's rules for the team in 1897: (1) Players to wake at 8:30 a.m., go to bed by 11:30 p.m. on the road; (2) To come to the ballpark by 10:30 a.m. for home games; (3) Report to the manager's room by 11 a.m. for road games; (4) No player shall take a stimulating drink of any kind before the game.[1] Boston started north on April 4. The first game of this trip in Charleston, South Carolina, featured a lineup of Hamilton CF, Tenney RF, Long SS, Duffy LF, Collins 3B, Lowe 2B, Tucker 1B, Bergen C. The other position players (Stahl, Ganzel, George Yeager, and Stivetts) played for the opposition. By the time Boston finished this trip in Springfield, Massachusetts, on April 17, the roster was set. The April 18 *Boston Globe* listed the roster as: Nichols, Sullivan, Klobedanz, Stivetts, Lewis, Dolan, pitchers; Tucker, Lowe, Long, Collins, infield; Duffy, Hamilton, Tenney, Stahl, outfield; Bergen, Ganzel, Yeager, catchers.

The schedule reverted to the most common start for the Beaneaters. Opening Day was in Boston on April 19, then the team went on the road until May 3. Nichols pitched Opening Day against Philadelphia before a crowd of 12,000. Philadelphia's new first baseman, Napoleon Lajoie, hit a three-run homer in the top of the ninth inning to give the Phillies a 6–0 lead. Boston came back in the bottom of the ninth, scoring five runs. The final three scored on Tucker's double. Ganzel made the final out with Tucker on second. The first stop on the road was Baltimore. In the first game, the writer for the *Globe* said Jennings was up to his old tricks for Baltimore. Jennings claimed he was hit by a pitch that was a strike and got away with it. Boston lost all three games of this series.

After this series, Selee said he would take Tucker out and put Tenney in at first base with Stahl taking over for Tenney in RF. Stivetts had tried first base as well but hurt his arm. In the article disclosing all these changes, Murnane said, "the word goes forth that Sir Thomas Tucker, the big-hearted Holyoake cyclone, must now handle the pasteboard tickets at the turnstile, while hustling Fred Tenney is getting a first-class trying out at the initial bag and young Mr. Stahl is demonstrating his ability to make base hits when they count and field like the wonder he is said to be."[2] Murnane was not kidding about taking tickets. That was a duty of players not in the lineup when the team was at home. After six games, Boston was 0–5 with one tie. Boston finally won on April 28 in Philadelphia. After two games in Washington ending the road trip, Boston's record was 1–6 with two ties and two rainouts. On the trip home from Washington, Selee stopped in New York to explore trade possibilities with the New York owner.

The first game of the home stand featured more rain. Boston won the two remaining games against Philadelphia. The short home stand ended with two more wins and a loss against Washington. Boston then went on its first western trip of the season. Klobedanz had pitched in the final game against Washington. He walked nine men in six innings but did not take the loss. When Boston arrived in Pittsburgh, Klobedanz was not on the train. Selee informed President Soden of this by letter. Klobedanz left the train in Fall River, his hometown. Klobedanz thought he had been treated poorly when Treasurer Billings (one of the Triumvirs) denied his request for a $75 advance on his salary. Klobedanz returned to the team in Pittsburgh. Boston won the two games in Pittsburgh, Lewis and Klobedanz pitching.

The first game in Cleveland featured the best continuing pitching matchup of the 1890s, Nichols against Young. Nichols won this one, 4–1. Cleveland got four hits, two by their new Native American outfielder, Louis Sockalexis. In the article about this game, the Cleveland team was called the Indians, not the Spiders. Boston left town with a 9–9 record. After the final game of this series on a Saturday, Boston traveled to Chicago. Washington and Cleveland tried to play a Sunday game in Cleveland. All the players and the umpire were arrested in the first inning. Boston took two of three games in Chicago. The writer noted that Tucker had been sent home for the remainder of the trip. Before the final three stops of this trip, Soden said that Boston would make no money on any of these stops except in Cincinnati. Boston took five of six games in St. Louis and Louisville. Boston split the two games played in Cincinnati. One was rained out. Boston went 12–5 on this trip. Their record was 17–12, good for fourth place.

The home stand started on Decoration Day, May 31. In his article that day, Tim Murnane made his argument that Boston was as good or better than anyone else in the league. He quoted Selee: "I have managed three champion league teams for Boston, but the team I have this year is stronger than any I have managed before. If we don't win the championship this year it will be because the league teams are stronger than ever."[3] St. Louis was in town for a morning-afternoon doubleheader. The morning game was rained out, and Boston won the afternoon game on a very sloppy field. The postponed game was made up in a doubleheader the next day, swept by Boston. Boston did not lose on this home stand. Sweeps of (in order) Cleveland, Pittsburgh, Louisville, Cincinnati, and Chicago resulted in a record of 15–0 on this home stand. Boston moved into first place on June 21, winning one game at Brooklyn while Baltimore lost a doubleheader. Brooklyn won the next day, breaking a 17-game Boston winning streak.

Boston won the final game in Brooklyn before returning home to face Baltimore. Boston took two of three. The crowds were 15,000, 9,000, and 17,000. Boston won the second game, 10–9, on a two-out, two-run single by Tenney in the bottom of the ninth. The crowd was on the field in the first and last games of this series. That helped Baltimore win the final game, 1–0. Collins hit one into the crowd in deep center, but it was a ground-rule double and Collins did not score. In the ninth inning, Baltimore outfielder Jake Stenzel hit one into the stands in left off Nichols. South End Grounds had a short left-field porch. Collins' ball was hit farther than Stenzel's and might have been an inside-the-park homer without the crowd. But under the ground rules with the crowd in the outfield, Collins got a double and Stenzel a homer. Baltimore left town 1½ games out. This stretch of 22 of 25 games at home ended with a three-game sweep of Brooklyn. Boston won 21 of the last 22 games at home.

By this time, Selee's tweaking of the 1893 championship team into a new contending team was complete. We can see the results by comparing the two rosters:

1893		1897
Tommy Tucker	1B	Fred Tenney
Bobby Lowe	2B	Bobby Lowe
Billy Nash (Captain)	3B	Jimmy Collins
Herman Long	SS	Herman Long
Tommy McCarthy	LF	Hugh Duffy (Captain)
Hugh Duffy	CF	Billy Hamilton
Cliff Carroll	RF	Chick Stahl
Charlie Bennett	C	Marty Bergen
Charlie Ganzel	C/UT	Charlie Ganzel
Kid Nichols	P	Kid Nichols
Jack Stivetts	P	Jack Stivetts
Harry Staley	P	Fred Klobedanz
Hank Gastright	P	Ted Lewis

With the exceptions of Tucker and Nash, the players Selee let go were out of the league by 1897. Tucker and Nash were regulars in 1897, Tucker having a decent year. Both became reserves after that. Selee's pruning and replacement work was paying dividends.

Of course, injuries had to be dealt with. In the final game of the last home stand, Klobedanz suffered a split finger and sub catcher George Yeager a broken hand. Lowe was sick at the beginning of the road trip. Hence, the lineup on July 1 in New York was slightly different: Hamilton CF, Stahl RF, Long SS, Duffy 2B, Stivetts LF, Collins 3B, Tenney 1B, Ganzel C, Nichols P. Murnane said Duffy made these changes. Boston won this game, 5–4, with Long making a great play on the final ball hit, turning a 6–3 double play with runners on first and third and one out. Boston won the remainder of their games in the east, one more in New York and three in Philadelphia, before heading west to Chicago. Since their last western trip, Boston's record was 28–2.

Selee predicted Boston would win 11 of 19 in the west. Bergen was left home, injured. The trip started with a three-game sweep of Boston by Chicago. On their Sunday off after this series, Boston traveled to Cleveland.

After a court ruling, Cleveland played their first legal Sunday home game on this date against Washington. Cleveland won two of three games from Boston. During this series, negotiations were ongoing between Boston and New York regarding a trade involving Ganzel. Nothing came of these talks. Boston took two of three games in Pittsburgh. On the travel date after this series, Selee went to New Castle, Pennsylvania, to scout a pitcher. Selee, Duffy, and Soden agreed that the team needed one more pitcher. Sullivan was to be released.

Boston next took three of four games from second-place Cincinnati. This series ended on July 27, which was the first day a new name appeared in a box score for Louisville, Honus Wagner. Boston saw Wagner in the next series, playing center field. Boston took two of three. On July 22, during this series, there was a doubleheader in Pittsburgh against Baltimore. The umpire spent both games getting screamed at by the players and egged by the crowd. An article from the *Cincinnati Enquirer,* reprinted in the *Boston Globe* on July 23, praised Boston for playing clean ball and hoped they beat Baltimore for the pennant.

The Louisville series ended on a Saturday. Boston traveled to St. Louis on Sunday. There were 4 games in the west on this date. The places and attendances: Cleveland 15,000; Cincinnati 14,000; St. Louis 10,000; Louisville 6,900. Boston did not play any Sunday games this year. The final series in the west went to St. Louis, two out of three. Boston went 9–10 on the western portion of this trip. The road trip continued in the east until August 3. A make-up game in Philadelphia had the regular lineup back in place, resulting in a Boston win. The lineup did not last the entire game, Long going out with an injury. After winning the first game in Washington, Boston had a Sunday off. Selee and Hanlon gave their opinions on the race, each stating their team would win. There was a quote from NL President Nick Young and Umpire Bob Emslie on the Boston team: "They can play ball and try to win the game without browbeating the opposing player and umpires."[4] The road trip ended with two doubleheaders in Washington. The four games were split. Sullivan, who had not been released, won one of the games for Boston. Boston's record on this road trip was 18–12. Boston had 38 games remaining at home, 19 on the road. Standings on August 4: Boston 58–26, Baltimore 53–27, Cincinnati 53–28.

Ten thousand fans and Baltimore greeted Boston's return home on August 5. Baltimore won the first game, Boston the next two. In both Boston wins, the reporting stressed Baltimore abusing the single umpire and the Boston players. The assigned umpire got hurt in a dispute in the second game and had to be replaced in the finale by a minor league umpire. Umpire Tom Lynch said during this series, "A man must be a thug and stand all kinds of abuse to umpire for the Baltimores."[5] Having a good villain was

4. Boston: The Last Five Years

The Boston infield from 1897 through 1900 won two pennants, three in the Hall of Fame. From left: Lowe, Collins, Tenney (standing) and Long.

a draw just like today. The attendance for the three-game series: 10,000, 9,000, and 16,000. The next six games were against New York, three in each city. Boston won the first five before losing in New York. Two umpires worked all these games. Boston returned home on August 16 and would be home until September 18. Boston had a two-game lead at the start of this extended home stand.

Boston swept three games from Washington before the western teams came in. Sullivan, still on the team, won the middle game. Pittsburgh suffered the same fate as Washington in a three-game series. After a Sunday off, Louisville came in for four games. The series ended up as two doubleheaders due to a rainout. Boston won the first three games to get to a nine-game winning streak before losing the finale to Louisville. Cleveland won their first two games in Boston, moving Boston into second place by percentage points behind Baltimore. Boston won the final two games against Cleveland, moving back into first place. August ended with an 8–8, 11-inning tie with Chicago. Boston won the next three games from Chicago. This was the last appearance of Cap Anson in Boston. Anson had signed a 10-year contract after the 1887 season. James Hart, the Chicago owner, had announced that Anson would not be re-signed. Even though Anson was 45, he played 114 games and hit .285 in 1897. Murnane, who had known Anson as an opposing player, paid tribute to Anson in his stories about these games.

Cincinnati came in next. After the first game, a Boston win, Murnane stated, "Umpire Lynch had the satisfaction of umpiring a 9-inning game without the hint of a protest."[6] The series concluded with a morning-afternoon Labor Day doubleheader. Cincinnati won the first game with a crowd of 6,500 confined to the stands. Boston won the second game with a crowd of 12,000 spilling over into the outfield. Baltimore won a doubleheader on Labor Day, moved back into first place by percentage points. Boston swept three games from St. Louis to finish off their schedule against western teams. In the first game of that series, the pitcher Selee signed from New Castle, Pennsylvania, Charlie "Piano Legs" Hickman, made his debut, working the final two innings. Selee was out of town looking for players on September 11, the first day of a series with Philadelphia. Boston swept three games from Philadelphia. On the last day of the Philadelphia series, Selee signed Syracuse pitcher Vic Willis to pitch for Boston next year. The long home stand ended with Boston taking two of three from New York. On the date of the last Boston home game of this home stand, Cy Young pitched a no-hitter against Cincinnati. The standings on September 19: Baltimore 86–34, Boston 87–36.

On September 19, a Sunday, Boston traveled to Brooklyn and Baltimore played an exhibition game in Newark, New Jersey. After a rainout, Boston and Brooklyn split a doubleheader. Nichols was shelled in the first game, but Lewis won the second. Boston won the final game in Brooklyn with Stivetts and Sullivan combining for a shutout. On the September 23 day off, Boston traveled to Baltimore for a three-game series. This series galvanized the baseball world and was unique during the nine-year existence of the National League as the sole major league from 1892 to 1900.

The standings going into this series: Baltimore 87–36, Boston 89–37. That is how the standings were shown in the newspaper, because the team with the higher percentage was listed first. Baltimore had a higher percentage, .707 to .706. However, Boston was half a game ahead. There was no rule in place in 1897 that a team in the pennant race had to make up all postponed or tied games. Therefore, it was theoretically possible for a team to win the pennant a half-game. The odds of getting the two leading teams together near the end of the season like this were reduced by having a 12-team league. This was the only time it happened in the eight-year existence of the 12-team National League in the 1890s. Both teams had already qualified for the Temple Cup series. Neither paid any attention to that. Winning the pennant was much more important.

Selee was worried before the series that he would be without his best catcher. Marty Bergen had not made the trip to Brooklyn and was not in Baltimore when the team arrived. As we will see, Bergen was exhibiting symptoms of mental instability and had stayed home without permission. Bergen showed up before the first game of this series and played. Even though Nichols had been shelled in his last outing, Selee started his best pitcher to open the Baltimore series. Collins was hit in the eye during infield practice but played. The game ended on a Boston double play on a line drive off the bat of Wee Willie Keeler, Long to Lowe. Boston won 6–4, before a crowd of 13,000. Congressman John "Honey Fitz" Fitzgerald took time from his duties in Washington to come to the games. Honey Fitz hired a brass band to celebrate the win and to come to the next game.

Reporting the game, Tim Murnane noted that Baltimore played clean ball. Selee received congratulatory telegrams from Melrose, Louisville, and New York. Two umpires worked the game, as had been common in the second half of this season for games involving Baltimore. Klobedanz pitched the second game, a 6–3 Baltimore victory. The crowd figure was not stated in the *Boston Globe*, but other sources said it was 18,750. Baltimore left fielder Joe Kelley had the crowd on the field trained. When Baltimore was at bat, they came in about 15 feet to make it easier to get a ground-rule double. The crowd moved back when Boston was at bat. Even with that, Murnane said that Baltimore played clean ball.

That game was played on a Saturday. They had Sunday off. The final game of the series was played on Monday, September 27, starting at 3:30 p.m. In the *Globe*, Murnane stated that the paid attendance was 25,500 and that at least 5,000 more got into the game without paying. The game turned out to be a high-scoring 1890s affair. Nichols started and finished for Boston. Baltimore used four pitchers. Boston had 24 hits, Baltimore 13. Collins had five, Hamilton and Long four, and Nichols three for Boston. Keeler had four and Jennings three for Baltimore. All are Hall of Famers. Boston won,

19–10. The standings: Boston 91–38, Baltimore 88–38. Boston had one more series at Brooklyn, with Baltimore hosting Washington. Lewis won the first game in Brooklyn for Boston, Baltimore winning as well. Klobedanz won the second game, with Baltimore losing to Washington on September 30. This clinched the pennant for Boston. Selee sent his starting infield, Nichols, and Bergen home to get ready for the Temple Cup series. Boston and Baltimore both lost on the final day of the season. Final standings: Boston 93–39, Baltimore 90–40.[7]

The fans of the Beaneaters came out to support the team on October 4 for the first game of the Temple Cup series. Ten thousand saw Nichols start, and Lewis finished to get the win in a 13–12 game. That was the playing highlight of the post-season for Boston. Five more games were played against Baltimore (one an exhibition in Springfield, Massachusetts). Baltimore won them all before crowds of decreasing size. After the third game, the amount of each Boston player's share was determined at $310. That same evening, there was a banquet at Faneuil Hall attended by both the Boston and Baltimore players. The Boston team was honored for winning the pennant. Nobody mentioned the Temple Cup series. When the series moved to Baltimore, the fans showed how much they cared by not showing up. The *Boston Globe* on October 11 stated that the Boston players didn't really care about the Temple Cup. The series ended on October 11 with a game the *Globe* called a farce. Seven hundred fans attended and Baltimore won, 9–3, in an hour and 20 minutes.

Boston was a very well-balanced team in 1897. The team led the league in scoring with 1,025 runs. Baltimore had a higher team batting average and lower team ERA. Boston led the league in home runs with 45, slugging percentage with .426, and shutouts with eight. The only individual league leaders were Tenney with 566 at-bats, Hamilton with 152 runs, and Nichols with 368 innings pitched and 31 wins. But both the hitters and pitchers were strong throughout. All the regulars except Bergen had a batting average over .308. Pitchers aided the offense: Stivetts .367, Klobedanz .324, Nichols .265, and Lewis .245. The pitching staff settled into Selee's preferred three main men: Nichols, Klobedanz, and Lewis. Nichols went 31–11, Klobedanz 26–7 and Lewis 21–12. Stivetts contributed by going 11–4 in only 18 appearances and by playing 33 games at other positions. The older players (except Ganzel) were still going strong. Duffy, Hamilton, Lowe, Long, and Nichols were in their primes. The younger players contributed strongly. Tenney, Collins, Stahl, Bergen, Klobedanz, and Lewis were instrumental and should only get better. Selee had some tweaking to do, but his team was on top of the league. The fans showed their support with the largest home attendance of Selee's tenure in Boston, 334,800.

As had been shown over his career as manager, one of Selee's strengths was discovering players. Nowadays, he would be a general manager or scouting director. In those days, the manager had to perform the duties of a general manager and scout as well as running the team during the season. We have seen Selee's successes as a scout (Long, Nichols, Lowe, Collins, Tenney, Bergen, and others). Like anyone else, he had his misses. When he signed Klobedanz from the Fall River, Massachusetts, club, Selee saw the entire team. He passed on another member of that team, who signed with Philadelphia. That player was Napoleon Lajoie. Selee was alerted to a fine player from the Pittsburgh area in early 1897. Selee saw the player and passed on Honus Wagner. Selee would see plenty of those players in the future.

At the March 1, 1898, meeting of the National League owners, rule changes were passed outlawing rowdyism. Boston's pennant in 1897 was very popular outside the precincts of Cleveland and Baltimore. There was to be a three-man board to review discipline. The number of games was increased to 154 by adding two games to the season series with every other team. On the date President Soden returned from the league meeting, the list of players under contract for 1898 was released. Twelve players were under contract. Nichols and Tenney had been talking and expected to sign soon. Stivetts and Hamilton were holdouts. Selee released Ganzel. Three Baltimore players were holding out together (catcher Clarke, outfielder Keeler, shortstop Jennings).

Boston left for spring training in Greensboro, North Carolina, on March 19. Everyone signed except Nichols. Contracts took effect on April 15. Hamilton was excused for business reasons until April 28. Lewis was excused because he was still in college until May 15. Bergen had not shown up by March 26, then appeared on March 27 after not responding to letters and telegrams. At one point it rained so much in Greensboro that Selee took the team roller skating to get them some exercise. Selee distributed the new conduct rules at a meeting on April 3. In an exhibition game at Richmond on April 8, Boston lost 4–2 to Richmond pitcher Jack Chesbro. Nichols showed up, unsigned, on April 9. Nichols pitched for the first time on April 12. The team was set after the final exhibition game on April 14. Pitchers: Nichols, Klobedanz, Lewis, Sullivan, Willis, and Stivetts; catchers: Bergen and Yeager; infielders: Tenney, Lowe, Collins, Long, and Bill Keister; outfielders: Duffy, Hamilton, and Stahl. Pitcher Piano Legs Hickman had been with the team during spring training and would be farmed out. But Hickman would travel with the team until the minor league season opened. The season was to open on April 15, and Duffy said, "It is 2 weeks too early to open the season."[8]

Duffy's words were proved right in all the eastern opening games on April 15. Boston played three innings in a light rain in New York before the rain got too heavy to continue. All the eastern Opening Days were rained out (New York, Philadelphia, Baltimore). Boston scored three runs in the eighth inning to win 4–2 on April 16. The New York team kicked about umpiring decisions enough so that one player was ejected, and the crowd threw seat cushions at the umps. Both umps were given police escorts to leave the field. On this same day, the game in St. Louis ended in the first inning due to a fire in the grandstand. The New York series ended with another Boston win.

Nichols pitched and won the home opener against New York on April 18 before a crowd of 9,000. In this game, Lewis finished. Lewis had decided to report on April 15 so he could collect his entire salary. Boston went back on the road, where Baltimore took three of four. On April 22, Baltimore pitcher Jim Hughes no-hit Boston. On this same day, Cincinnati pitcher Ted Breitenstein no-hit Pittsburgh in Cincinnati. When Boston went to Philadelphia, Selee said his pitching was a bit of a mess at present. Stivetts was not in shape and not with the team. Sullivan would not pitch until the weather got warmer. Lewis had gone back to Harvard as baseball coach. Willis was too wild to count on. Only Nichols and Klobedanz were reliable. Selee had something in mind for Willis. Selee asked Jack Ryan, a retired catcher, to build a wooden target for Willis to use this for practice. After trips to Philadelphia, Washington, and one make-up game in New York, Boston returned home with a record of 8–6. Stivetts had pitched the final game of the trip in New York and lost. Willis had won two games at the end of the trip.

Boston lost the first three games at home, two to New York and one to Baltimore. This made a four-game losing streak and a record below .500. Neither of those circumstances would happen again in 1898. Sullivan had started the game on May 6, which was his last appearance for Boston. Boston won the final three games of the series with Baltimore and then swept three from Brooklyn. Lewis pitched a one-hit shutout in the sixth straight win. That game ended the home stand on May 17. The first western trip was next.

The first stop was Cincinnati. Throughout the 1890s, Cincinnati got off to good starts but could not finish off with a pennant. Cincinnati won their first game with Boston on May 19, solidifying their hold on first place. Boston won the next two to move from fifth place to third. The day after this series ended was a Sunday. All the teams from the east were in the west. On this Sunday, May 22, Boston, Baltimore, and Philadelphia did not play. Washington, New York, and Brooklyn did. Cincinnati had Pittsburgh come to town for a game. This era saw constant change and refinement in Sunday play. On this same May 22, the Indianapolis minor league team attempted to play a game. All the players and umpires were arrested.

4. Boston: The Last Five Years

Boston then split six games in St. Louis and Louisville. These had been the two worst teams in the league lately. St. Louis remained in the dumps, but Louisville was getting better after adding Honus Wagner. Boston lost the final game in Louisville in tough fashion. Louisville was up, 7–5, at the end of eight innings. Boston scored three runs in the top of the ninth, but after that half-inning it was 5 p.m. Boston had told the umpire they had to leave at 5 p.m. to catch their train to Boston. Hence, the game ended after 8½ innings. The rules then and now state that the score reverted to the last complete inning, so Louisville won, 7–5. This year the schedule maker had changed western and eastern trips so that all were not a tour of the six teams in the other geographical half of the league. Home stands and road trips were closer to current practice.

Boston hosted Chicago (without Cap Anson for the first time since 1875) on May 31. After a Boston win, the standings were: Cincinnati 27–7, Cleveland 24–12, Boston 23–13, Baltimore 17–13. In the June 1 Boston win, Selee saw a glimpse of his future. This was the first game he saw Frank Chance play for Chicago. Chance caught the final four innings. Cleveland came to town for three games, taking two. Cy Young shut out Boston in the final game of the series. Cincinnati came to Boston with a 4½-game lead over the Beaneaters. Boston cut two games off that lead by taking three of four.

By this point, Selee had settled on a four-man pitching staff of Nichols, Willis, Klobedanz, and Lewis. Those four pitched in this series, in this order. Lewis lost the finale. During this series, there was a story in the *Boston Globe* that low attendance in Baltimore would lead Ned Hanlon to sell off his best players. While that did not happen this year, it was a foreshadowing of what would happen in 1899. On the Sunday off during the next series, Tim Murnane wrote a long article evaluating all the teams in the National League. He ended this article with a sizable section about the Boston team, ending with this assessment of Selee:

> Manager Frank Selee is playing his quiet thinking part just the same as ever on the bench. Mr. Selee is responsible for the presence of most of the Boston men and therefore can credit himself with the fine position the club has held in the league race during the last eight years. The Boston team is in the race this year for a finish, and any team that beats it must have tons of phenomenal good luck or play the best game of ball that has been known.[9]

Boston took three of four games from Philadelphia on the days around this article. By the final game of the series, Long and Hamilton were injured, replaced by Stivetts and Yeager. Boston ended the home stand by taking two of three from Washington. Boston had moved into second place, 1½ games behind Cincinnati, before leaving on a three-week road trip. On the Sunday the Boston team traveled to Chicago, Chicago hosted Cincinnati. Chicago won, 10–1, before a crowd of 22,400.

This large crowd was the exception in 1898. For the first time in the history of organized baseball, the 1898 season took place in wartime. The Spanish-American War was declared on April 10, 1898. Attendance dropped throughout the country. This war would not last very long, and it did not require a huge effort on the part of the country compared to later wars. However, people in 1898 did not know that. As we saw above, paid attendance for the crucial three-game series between Boston and Baltimore in late September 1897 was 57,500 in Baltimore. For the entire 1898 season, paid attendance in Baltimore (which finished second with a record of 96–53) was 123,416.

Attendance problems were worse in Cleveland. The owners of the Spiders, the Robison brothers, also owned the Forest City streetcar company. When the union representing the workers called a strike against the streetcar company, the Robisons hired non-union strikebreakers. Other unions in the Cleveland area called for a boycott of the baseball team owned by the Robisons. This boycott was so effective that the Robisons put the team on the road for the entire second half of the season, playing 114 of 156 games on the road. The one team that had increased attendance in 1898 was Chicago, breaking their attendance record by drawing 424,352 in 89 home dates (of a total of 152 games). Boston's home attendance, despite a fine season, dropped to 229,275.

The road trip started with a four-game split in Chicago. Chicago won the first two games against complete games by Nichols and Klobedanz. Willis started the third game and gave up three runs while getting only one out before Lewis relieved. The game went 14 innings and Lewis won it. Willis also started the final game and went five innings before Nichols relieved and won the game. Klobedanz pitched much better in his next game but lost 3–2 in 12 innings in Pittsburgh. Boston and Pittsburgh split this four-game series. The next series was in Cleveland. During this series, where Cleveland won three of four, it was announced that Cleveland would play no more home games this year. Total attendance for the four dates was less than 6,000. The rough play and umpire baiting of the Cleveland team must have rubbed off on Boston. Long and Duffy were ejected from the first game and Long was suspended for three games. In three of these games, there were pitching changes for Boston. The *Boston Globe* stated that Duffy made these changes, not Selee.

In the story on the travel day to New York, Selee complained about the umpiring in Pittsburgh and Cleveland. Hamilton left the team, returning to Boston to get treatment on a knee injury. Selee said he was not looking for any position players, but was still looking for a pitcher. The most successful stop on this road trip was in New York. Boston swept three games from New York before winning a make-up game from Brooklyn. The Boston team was staying at a hotel at 38th and Broadway in Manhattan. To get to the Brooklyn game, the team dressed in the hotel, then took a tally-ho carriage to the Brooklyn ballpark. The trip ended with three games in Philadelphia. Boston lost the first two. In the second game, Philadelphia pitcher Red Donohue threw a no-hitter. Klobedanz won the final game, 2–1. Boston went 10–9 on this road trip. The standings after the games of July 9: Cincinnati 48–24, Boston 43–27, Cleveland 42–27, Baltimore 41–27.

Boston returned home for a favorable stretch of the schedule. Twenty of the next 24 games were against the three teams at the bottom of the standings: Louisville, St. Louis and Brooklyn. They got off to a good start by sweeping four games from Louisville. For the first game of this series, Boston had 12 men in uniform. Stivetts and Hamilton were out injured. The regular lineup was intact, except Yeager took Hamilton's place. The four games not against these three teams came next. Boston split four games with Pittsburgh. In the *Boston Globe* of July 18, the writer said that only five of the 12 National League teams would make money due to the war. Several minor leagues cut salary or would finish the season early. The short home stand ended with a 3-game sweep of St. Louis. In the first game in Brooklyn, Boston won 4–3 when Klobedanz, playing left field, knocked in the winning run in the ninth inning. Boston won two of three games in Brooklyn. In the middle game, a Boston loss, the Boston outfield was James "General" Stafford (an in-season pickup), Duffy, and Dave Pickett (another in-season pickup), and Klobedanz played first base. Tenney, Stahl, and Hamilton were injured.

The road trip continued to St. Louis and Louisville. Boston won three of four games in St. Louis. This made St. Louis' record in their last 27 games 2–25. Boston's stretch of success against the bottom feeders ended in Louisville, which took three of four games. Over the four days of the Louisville series, five games were played. The first was a 12-inning, 1–1 tie. The second was a Louisville seven-inning win due to rain, followed by a doubleheader and a single game. This was how Boston came into a series with first-place Cincinnati on August 6. Cincinnati won that Saturday, 2–1, walking off with a double and single in the bottom of the ninth inning off Willis. As Boston did not play Sunday games, Baltimore came to Cincinnati on August 7. Cincinnati won before a crowd of 12,500, going five games up on Boston. Boston won the remaining three games of the series to cut the lead to two games. The final date of the series was a doubleheader due to rain. Boston won the first game, and the second game started right after the first due to Boston having to catch a train. Boston chose to bat last. Cincinnati was up, 5–1, going into the bottom of the eighth inning. Boston scored five runs in that half-inning, the final three on Nichols' pinch-hit double. Nichols pitched the ninth inning to secure the game. Boston returned home after a 9–6 road trip.

The regular lineup, except Stahl, was back together for the first game against Cleveland. This was a good omen. Boston swept four games from Cleveland. In the first game of a Monday doubleheader, Boston hit three home runs (Long, Collins, Lowe), then walked off with a 4–3 win when Lewis scored the wnning run in the 10th. The crowd of 9,000 for the doubleheader was the biggest so far this year in Boston. Boston won two more against Chicago, making it nine straight wins, before welcoming Cincinnati. Boston was 2½ games up when this series started. This series turned into a two-game split. Willis won the first game, 2–1, with Nichols pitching the ninth. Long made a great one-handed catch in the ninth to save the game. After a day off, Nichols started and lost the first game of a Monday doubleheader. The second game was a 5–5 tie called after seven innings due to darkness. The two biggest crowds of the year in Boston attended these games. Boston headed west with a 2½-game lead.

The road trip started poorly. Boston lost three straight in Chicago. On August 26, Cleveland played its last home game against New York. The attendance was 400. Even though Cleveland was only five games out at this point, it was announced that Cleveland would only play road games the rest of the season. Boston lost the first game in Pittsburgh, then took Sunday off. Cincinnati won a doubleheader that Sunday and went into first place, one game up in the standings. Boston won the final two games in Pittsburgh. Selee's main concern was a judgment served on him from the New Castle club. This was a claim for $500 for the purchase price of Charlie Hickman. He forwarded this to the Triumvirs, who settled the claim.

The road trip was supposed to have one more stop. But since that stop was Cleveland, both the Boston and Cleveland clubs traveled to Boston. Cleveland treated the next three games as if they were at home. Cleveland won the first two, and the third game was a 6–6 tie in 10 innings. Maybe the fact that the crowds averaged about 2,400 per game made Cleveland feel at home. There was a make-up game on September 3 against New York. Boston won, 6–4. In the third inning of this game, Giants center fielder George Van Haltren made a putout at home plate, tagging out Kid Nichols, who was playing first base. The *Globe* said, "Captain Duffy has shown remarkable judgment this season in taking out pitchers at the right time to save a game."[10] Even with that, Boston had just gone through a bad patch. Their record in the last 12 games was 3–7 with two ties. Standings after the September 4 games: Cincinnati 76–43, Boston 72–42, Baltimore 69–42, Cleveland 67–47.

There was an immediate solution for Boston: games at home against Washington and New York. Boston took all seven to secure a 2½-game lead before heading on the road again. At the beginning of this streak, Hickman was playing first base along with the regulars. Tenney returned on

September 10. Nichols, Willis, Klobedanz, and Lewis all pitched great. Even though the Boston staff would finish 1898 with the third-best ERA in the league (after Chicago and Baltimore), their four-man regular rotation was the best in the league. Stivetts had not pitched since April and had been released. Hickman had been signed as a pitcher but got more use as a first baseman-outfielder. Of the 1,340 innings pitched by Boston in 1898, the four regular pitchers completed 1,283 of them.

Hamilton led the way to the ninth straight win in Philadelphia with three hits, three stolen bases, and a walk. Philadelphia won the second and concluding game of this series. Boston returned home for 19 straight games. The home stand opened with four games against St. Louis. Boston swept these games, making their season record 12–2 against St. Louis. In the first game of this series, something unusual happened to the St. Louis starting pitcher Jack Taylor. He had to leave the game in the third inning due to illness. Taylor led the NL in complete games in 1898 with 42. Selee would experience first-hand how often Taylor pitched complete games later in their careers.

Louisville came in for three games, winning the first. Boston took the final two to make the season series 8–6 in favor of Boston. Louisville had improved to ninth place with the addition of a couple of good players, Honus Wagner and Tommy Leach. Cincinnati had lost the last six games and was now out of the race. Baltimore had won 10 straight and moved into second place. Boston swept three games from Pittsburgh while Baltimore's streak went to 12. Baltimore was three games out. Boston got two days off, one due to rain and one due to Sunday, before a doubleheader on September 26 against Brooklyn. Boston swept the doubleheader. The second game started at 4 p.m. and was called for darkness after 6½ innings and one hour and 28 minutes. Remember there was no daylight savings time in 1898. Boston and Brooklyn split the final two games of the series, leaving Boston four games up on Baltimore.

Boston swept three games from Philadelphia. The first game of the series showed their never-say-die attitude. Klobedanz started and was shelled for six runs in three innings. Lewis came on and finished. Boston was down 10–5 going into the bottom of the ninth. Here's what happened in the Boston ninth: Hamilton, Tenney, and Long singled to load the bases; Lowe two-run single; Collins three-run home run to tie it; Stahl walk; Bergen sacrifice; Duffy ground out; Lewis walk-off, bloop single. This sweep was completed on a Saturday. The standings after this series: Boston 95–45, Baltimore 91–48.

Baltimore came to town for three games starting Monday, October 3. Boston won the two that were played (the final game was rained out and would not be made up). Both games went less than nine innings due to darkness. Boston won the first, 13–10, in 6½ innings. Baltimore was up 10–9 after four innings. Boston scored three runs in the fifth and one in the sixth. The time of the game was 2:30, more in line with modern baseball than 1890s ball. Boston won the second game 4–2, in eight innings. Nichols pitched. The game was tied 1–1 after seven. Baltimore scored a run in the top of the eight. After one out, Tenney singled, Long singled (Baltimore shortstop Jennings blocked Tenney to keep him at second), Lowe popped out, and Collins was safe on an error, with Tenney scoring. Long went to third as a wild pitch moved runners up, and Long scored on Stahl's RBI single. Both these games drew 8,000. This was the final home game for Boston. Boston had a 5½-game lead on Baltimore going on its final road trip.

The Temple Cup had died of inattention, so the pennant was the sole prize of the 1898 season. Both Boston and Baltimore went to New York. Boston won two from Brooklyn while Baltimore won two from New York. The final game of both series was scheduled for Saturday, October 8, and both were rained out. Boston went to 11th-place Washington for three games. Boston won the first two and clinched the pennant on October 11 when Baltimore split a doubleheader. Washington won the final game. The concluding series of the season was in Baltimore. Baltimore won the first game before a rainout. The final day of the season was October 15. Boston won the first game of a doubleheader. The second game was called by darkness after three innings. The final records of the top three teams: Boston 102–47, Baltimore 96–53, Cincinnati 92–60. As the schedule called for 154 games, we can see that all these teams had games that were not made up. Boston played an exhibition game in Weehawken, New Jersey, against Baltimore on October 16 and one in Connecticut against a minor league team on October 17. The season finally ended with a grand dinner in Boston honoring the team. All were present except Lowe and Yeager.

In one of his concluding articles about the 1898 season, Tim Murnane stated that only three teams in the National League (Boston, Chicago and Cincinnati) made money. One of the reasons Boston made money was the strictly enforced policy of the Triumvirs about salaries. No one player made more than $2,400 except Captain Duffy, who got more because he was captain. The salary list for the Boston 1898 National League champions:

Frank Selee	Manager	$3500
Hugh Duffy	Captain-Outfielder	3000
Herman Long	Infielder	2400

James Collins	Infielder	2400
Kid Nichols	Pitcher	2400
Billy Hamilton	Outfielder	2400
Bobby Lowe	Infielder	2300
Fred Tenney	Infielder	2150
Chick Stahl	Outfielder	2100
Marty Bergen	Catcher	2000
Jack Stivetts	Pitcher	2000
Fred Klobedanz	Pitcher	1800
Ted Lewis	Pitcher	1600
Bill Keister	Infielder	1500
Vic Willis	Pitcher	1400
George Yeager	Catcher	1400
Charles Hickman	Pitcher	1000
Charles Pittinger	Pitcher	1000
Kitty Bransfield	Catcher	900
William Mills	Pitcher	900
Total		38,150[11]

For this payroll, Boston again had a very balanced team. The individual league leader in the most categories was Kid Nichols. He led pitchers in games (50) and wins (31). If the modern save rule is extrapolated back to 1898, Nichols led the league with four saves. The team led the league with 53 homers and a slugging percentage of .377. Collins led the league with 15 homers. Everything else was consistent balance. The records of the four main pitchers were: Nichols 31–12, Lewis 26–8, Willis 25–13, Klobedanz 19-10. The batting averages of the regular lineup: Hamilton .369, Collins .328, Long .265, Duffy .298, Lowe .272, Tenney .328, Stahl .308, and Bergen .280. Bergen caught 117 games, which was quite high in this era where few catchers caught more than 100 games. **Two of my sources called this team the finest team of the 19th century.**[12] Baltimore had higher winning percentages in 1894 and 1896. Boston's 1892 team had a very similar record (102–48). However one ranks them, it was a fine team. Selee had built two championship teams in Boston. There were six players who played on both versions of the champions. Long, Lowe, and Nichols played on all these teams. Duffy and Stivetts played on all the pennant winning teams except 1891. Ganzel played on all except 1898. This was a great eight-year run for Selee, resulting in five championships. How long could it last?

BOSTON NATIONALS, 1898.
Top row, left to right: Charley Nichols, Bill Clarke, Frank Killen, Vic Willis, Martin Bergen, Ted Lewis, Charley Hickman. Middle row: Fred Tenney, Jimmy Collins, Jack Stafford, Manager Frank Selee, Hugh Duffy, Billy Hamilton, Herman Long. Bottom row: Bobby Lowe, Chick Stahl.

Team picture of the 1898 Boston Beaneaters, called by some the greatest major league team of the 19th century. Selee in the one in the business suit, just like he dressed for games.

Decline

If the teams as constituted could not beat Boston, maybe a new team could. These new teams formed through what was called syndicate ball. Owners having interest in more than one club had happened well before 1899. John Brush (owner of Cincinnati), Al Spalding (owner of Chicago) and Arthur Soden (one of the Triumvirs in Boston) all had a small share of ownership of the New York Giants. Chris Von Der Ahe had owned the St. Louis Browns in the American Association when St. Louis was the best club in that league. Von Der Ahe owned small pieces of several other clubs in the AA. By 1899, Von Der Ahe had ceased owning the St. Louis franchise, which was in the fourth-largest city in the country. The St. Louis franchise had been moribund for a few years, even though St. Louis had a great history of supporting winning baseball. The same was true in Brooklyn. Brooklyn was owned by Fred Abell, a gambling casino owner, in partnership with Charlie Byrne. Byrne died in 1898. Abell needed cash to keep running the Brooklyn team. He went looking for a partner among his fellow owners. Abell's first approach was to Baltimore owner Henry Von der Horst. After Von der Horst turned him down, Abell approached the Robison brothers, who had just experienced a very difficult season in Cleveland. When this news got out, the editor of a baseball magazine interviewed Von der Horst. Von der Horst stated, "Robison has a great team and a worthless franchise. Abell has a valuable plant and no team. These elements combined would develop a winner that would be of immense financial profit, as Brooklyn patrons are hungry for good base ball."[13]

Soon after this interview was published, Von der Horst acted on his opinion by agreeing to buy an interest in the Brooklyn club. After being rebuffed in Brooklyn, Robison gained a controlling interest in the St. Louis club. In each of these cases, the best players from one team (Baltimore and Cleveland) moved to the other team (Brooklyn and St. Louis). The two exceptions to this were Baltimore third baseman John McGraw and catcher Wilbert Robinson. McGraw had married a Baltimore woman, and McGraw and Robinson were partners in a successful saloon in Baltimore. McGraw convinced Von der Horst to make him manager of Baltimore and let Robinson stay as well. Several other players and both managers moved to the new teams. These men are listed below:

Baltimore to Brooklyn	Cleveland to St. Louis
Ned Hanlon, Manager	Patsy Tebeau, Player-Manager
Willie Keeler, Outfielder	Jesse Burkett, Outfielder
Joe Kelley, Outfielder	Emmett Heidrick, Outfielder
Hughie Jennings, Infielder	Harry Blake, Outfielder
Jim Hughes, Pitcher	Cupid Childs, Infielder
Doc McJames, Pitcher	Jack O'Connor, Catcher
Ossee Schreckengost, Catcher	Cy Young, Pitcher
Jack Powell, Pitcher	Nig Cuppy, Pitcher[14]

At the league meeting in the first week of March, the situation of the St. Louis club and the movement of players from Baltimore to Brooklyn were major topics of conversation. The ownership of the St. Louis club was in limbo at this moment. On the final day of the meeting, Selee bought catcher William "Boileryard" Clarke from Baltimore for $2,000. That was his major off-season move. Selee and the Triumvirs had faith in their two-time consecutive champion team. Selee knew he had overworked Bergen the year before. Many players had complained to Selee about Bergen's moodiness. Selee and the team needed Bergen during the second half of 1898 and gave him a bonus for his fine play. Selee signed Bergen for 1899 soon after the

1898 season ended for $2,400, a sizable raise by Boston standards. Unfortunately, Bergen had a difficult winter. His four-year-old son contracted diphtheria and Bergen had both physical and mental problems. His son died in early 1899. When Bergen joined the team, he thought everyone was persecuting him. We will see how this played out.

By March 22, all players had either signed or verbally agreed to terms. Contracts took effect on April 15. Nichols, Tenney, and Clarke had verbally agreed to terms. All were coaching college teams and said they would not sign the contracts until April 15. Lewis had signed, but he was not going to report until May 1 as he was coaching the Harvard team. Everyone else boarded the train to spring training in Durham, North Carolina. By the time the team arrived in Durham, the St. Louis situation had been resolved by the Robisons buying the franchise from the bank that had foreclosed. The move of players from Cleveland to St. Louis was announced on March 25.

Two new rules were the focus of early practices. The balk rule had been changed to require the pitcher to step toward the base he was throwing to. This must have been a major change, because stolen bases increased by 600 from 1898 to 1899. The other change required catchers to stand within the catcher's box on all deliveries. Remember catchers wore unpadded masks and chest protectors, but no shin guards. Many catchers had stood well behind home plate on pitches with no one on base and before two strikes. The umpires were told to watch out for catchers "tipping" bats while the batter was swinging. This was not a rule change, as this had always been catcher's interference. Boston stayed in Durham until April 5. By that time, all players had reported except Lewis. Over the winter, Selee had become involved in the Worcester, Massachusetts, minor league club. He had an agreement to use this team as a place to put players who did not make the major league club. There was no farm system in baseball during the 1890s. There were often informal arrangements like this. Before Opening Day, Selee reduced the roster to 15, sending three players to Worcester.

On Opening Day in Brooklyn, the Boston lineup was the same as last year: Hamilton CF, Tenney 1B, Long SS, Duffy LF, Collins 3B, Stahl RF, Lowe 2B, Bergen C, Nichols P. Brooklyn took two of three games in the opening series before the teams traveled to Boston for Boston's home opener on April 19. Boston won that game behind Nichols. This was Nichols' 10th straight home Opening Day start in Boston. The crowd at Opening Day in Brooklyn was over 20,000, and at Boston's home opener about 15,000. As had been normal on the schedule for the last few years, Boston went on the road after one home game. Boston took four straight in Washington, without using Nichols. Willis and Klobedanz pitched, as well as Hickman and a new man, Oscar Streit. All threw complete game victories.

4. Boston: The Last Five Years

Philadelphia took three of four games in the next series. In a 20–3 loss, Selee put in Streit to relieve Klobedanz. Streit gave up fourteen runs in 5⅔ innings and never pitched in the National League again (he returned to the big leagues for 10 games in the American League in 1902). In the first game in Baltimore, Boston had its first encounter with a pitcher discovered by John McGraw. Vic Willis pitched well but lost to Joe McGinnity, 3–1. After this game, Selee ordered new bats for the team. Boston ended up with a four-game split in Baltimore. Selee said he wanted another pitcher, as Lewis had not shown up by May 1. The road trip ended with one make-up game in Brooklyn, won by Boston. Boston had a decent road trip, 9–7.

Lewis showed no ill effects from missing spring training. He won his first start of the year in the first game of the home stand against Brooklyn, pitching a complete game. Boston took two of three games from Brooklyn. Marty Bergen had been home in Brookfield, Massachusetts, since the third game of the season. The latest report was that he would soon return. Selee and most of the players were convinced that Bergen was "unbalanced" but were willing to put up with it due to his talent. Hamilton, who was 33 years old, hurt the knee that had given him problems last year and was out. On the first day of the next series, Selee released Streit and Klobedanz. Klobedanz was 1–4 in 5 starts with a 4.86 ERA. Selee signed another left-handed pitcher, Frank Killen. The home stand ended with a three-game sweep of Baltimore. Boston walked off in the ninth inning of the final game. The 2–1 victory ended with Long's triple and Duffy's sacrifice fly. Boston headed to Washington and the west with a 14–10 record.

Boston won the first two games of the trip in Washington. At this point, Boston had played six games in Washington with a total attendance of 7,400. Four thousand of that came on Saturday, April 22. Tim Murnane said that Boston did not get enough money from the Washington trips to meet their expenses for the trips. The first two games in the west were wins in Louisville. Total attendance for these two games was 2,000, and the final game of the series on a Saturday was rained out. Boston was still not playing any Sunday games, home or road. Boston won two of three games in St. Louis. They then swept three in Cincinnati. All the regulars were in the lineup except Hamilton. Willis hurt his arm but was not expected to miss more than two turns. Boston returned home with an 8–2 record on this trip. Standings on May 28: Brooklyn 25–11, St. Louis 23–12, Boston 22–12, Philadelphia 20–13, Chicago 21–15. Syndicate baseball practiced by Brooklyn and St. Louis looked successful.

The next home stand opened with a Decoration Day doubleheader against Cleveland to kick off a four-game series. Boston won three of four, losing Nichols' start. Nichols won the first game of a three-game sweep of Cincinnati with the help of two Collins home runs. This short home stand ended with three games against Louisville. Boston won two of them. In the Louisville win, five fans crossed the outfield during Louisville's at-bat in the eighth inning. The umpire called the game at that point for interference, allowing a 7–6 Louisville lead to stand. Boston won three in a row at New York without Bergen. in the final series in the east before a 16-game trip west, Boston lost two of three games against Philadelphia. Boston lost in a game where their regular lineup was playing. Hamilton played but looked hurt. On this same day, Brooklyn won a game in New York on a forfeit. The umpire would not put up with any more complaining. Boston headed west with a 34–17 record, five games behind Brooklyn.

Boston started this trip in Chicago. Nichols lost the first game in relief and won the second game, throwing a 13-inning complete game. The *Globe* reported that it was dark when the 13-inning game finished. That game must have started very late, as the date was June 19, very near the longest day of the year, and the game only took 2:20. The entire team went out to Cap Anson's billiard parlor one of the evenings in Chicago. The teams split a four-game series. Charlie Frisbee was acquired by Selee to take the place of the injured Hamilton. On Sunday June 25, Boston was off. In St. Louis, the Browns played a doubleheader, the first game against New York, the second against Cleveland, losing both. Boston split four games in Pittsburgh.

The next series was scheduled for Cleveland. The other National League owners would not play in Cleveland, claiming that the low attendance and proceeds caused them to lose money on their Cleveland trips. Arthur Soden was a holdout. Boston went to Cleveland and played four games, winning three. Total attendance for this series was 2,000. The final date of this series was a doubleheader on July 1. Boston was up 7–0 in the ninth inning with Willis pitching in the first game. Cleveland scored seven runs in the ninth. Boston scored two runs in the 11th, but Cleveland scored three in the bottom of the 11th to win it. Both pitchers went the distance.

Boston won the second game, 14–0, in six innings. The second game ended when Boston had to catch a train. These games were supposed to be the final home games for Cleveland in 1899. On the Sunday Boston traveled to Washington, Washington played and lost a doubleheader in Cincinnati. This did not have much effect on the game the next day, which Washington won, 15–2. This was the only game in Washington. The next day was July 4, a doubleheader in Baltimore. Boston lost both games before winning the final game of the road trip on July 5. Their record on this road trip was 7–9. Brooklyn had just lost 10 straight games but remained in first place. Standings after the July 5 games: Brooklyn 45–22, Philadelphia 40–24, Chicago 39–24, Boston 41–26, Baltimore 37–27. Up to now, Boston had played 44 games on the road, 23 at home.

The regular lineup was back together in a three-game sweep of New

York. Chicago won two of three games in the next series. In the final game of this series, Boston lost, 9–4. Selee said Lewis pitched that entire game because there was no one to replace him. By this time, Hamilton was hurt again. Boston swept the next three-game series with Pittsburgh. In the

The troubled Martin Bergen, a fine catcher who suffered from serious undiagnosed mental problems.

game on July 15, Willis beat Jesse Tannehill, a pitcher Selee had wanted to sign in 1897, 1–0 in 11 innings. The game-winning, walk-off hit in the bottom of the 11th was hit over the fence by Collins. As there was a runner on third at the time, the hit was scored a single and only one run counted under the scoring rules. Bergen left the team again during this series. After the first game against St. Louis, the following article appeared in the *Boston Globe*. This shows how the team was dealing with Marty Bergen during the time of his mental deterioration.

> BERGEN LEAVES THE GROUNDS—HIS CONDUCT IS NOT MAKING HIM POPULAR WITH THE BASEBALL PUBLIC
> Martin Bergen was at the South End Grounds yesterday. He called at the box office to see Pres. Soden, who was busy, and referred him to manager Selee. Director J. B. Billings had a long talk with the catcher. Bergen said he would like to get away from Boston, as the players were all down on him. He gave no excuse for his absence from the club, and after his talk with Mr. Billings took his grip from the dressing room and left before the game.
> Manager Selee said last night that Bergen always had received the kindest treatment from every one connected with the team. He quoted the kindness shown Bergen last winter when he was ill in the hospital in Boston. The players have a high regard for Bergen, but have refrained from making free, owing to his bad temper, at times he did not hesitate to slap a player to the face.
> The management has the sympathy of the baseball public, as it has done all it could for this catcher who finds himself out with all the players.
> Pres. Soden is in favor of getting a good catcher at once and allowing Bergen to take care of his farm for a while, thinking it may do him good.
> Bergen is a temperance man and has many friends in this city who have grown disgusted at the attitude he has taken this season, when he has continually failed to do his best work for the club, most of the time acting indifferently and spiking the 'get there all together' feeling essential to a team's success.
> Bergen had trouble in Kansas City and his record here will make his future in baseball not a bed of roses, for in no city of the league is the management, the public, and the press so fair and considerate as in Boston.[15]

The home stand ended with St. Louis taking two of three games. Boston was four games out of first place on July 21, the day they headed west again. Bergen had boarded the train in Boston, but left the train and headed home to his farm in Brookfield, Massachusetts. Selee said he was tired of dealing with Bergen but took no decisive action yet.

After the first game of the trip in Cincinnati, Selee said that Bergen's release was in the works, but not finalized. On the date of the next scheduled game, a rainout, Tim Murnane interviewed Bergen for the *Boston Globe*,[16] and Bergen sent a telegram to Selee that he was on the way. Boston took two of three games in Cincinnati. The final two were a doubleheader on June 26. There was a doubleheader the next day in Louisville. Boileryard Clarke caught all four games as there was no other catcher with the team. Clarke was spiked in the first game in Louisville and played on. Louisville won two of three from Boston, with a doubleheader on Saturday July 29 rained out. As Boston would not play Sunday games, Louisville played a doubleheader on July 30 with Cleveland while Boston traveled to St. Louis. The first game in St. Louis was lost by Nichols in the bottom of the 14th inning on a walk-off home run by the opposing pitcher. Nichols threw a complete game. Boston won the remaining two games in St. Louis to end the road trip at 6–4 before returning home for 17 straight games. Boston was 4½ games behind Brooklyn.

Bergen returned to the lineup in the first game at home against Washington. Bergen hit a walk-off, two-run single in the ninth inning. Boston swept three games from Washington. Before and after the middle game of this series, meetings were held by the Boston team about Bergen. The meeting before the game was players only; the one after was run by Selee. All seemed to agree that it would be difficult, but they had to live with Bergen as their best catcher. Murnane noted in the Boston Globe that during the game the team gave Bergen much verbal encouragement. Selee asked Bergen to address the printed interviews in the meeting after the game. No result was discussed other than continuing with Bergen as the catcher.

Two games with Cleveland resulted in two more wins. The final game of the Cleveland series was rained out. Soden said that the four remaining games with Cleveland would be played in Cleveland. No other team had played in Cleveland since July 1. Cincinnati came to town on a 12-game winning streak and was greeted by a rainout. Cincinnati won the doubleheader the next day and three of four games in the series. Boston took four of six games from Louisville in the next three days. That's right, three doubleheaders in a row. Boston used six pitchers over this stretch. Boston won the first game of a series against Brooklyn on Saturday, August 19. That ended a week where Boston played nine games, winning six before taking Sunday off. Brooklyn won the next two games to end the home stand. Standings: Brooklyn 70–35, Boston 66–41.

By this point, Selee had run through several pitchers to support Nichols, Willis, and Lewis. Fred Klobedanz, Oscar Streit, and Charlie "Piano Legs" Hickman had been tried and released. On the roster now were Jouett Meekin and Harvey Bailey. Meekin won the first game of the road trip in Pittsburgh, pitching a 10-inning complete game. Pittsburgh won the other game of the series, the third being rained out. On the Sunday off, Selee said he had not yet signed to manage Boston next year and denied any interest in the Pittsburgh job. The next series was unique in the second half of the 1899 season. All scheduled Cleveland home games had been played at the opponent's ballpark since July 1. President Soden of Boston did not believe in that, so Boston played four games at Cleveland the next three days. Boston swept the series, which drew total attendance of 700 for the three dates. The Cleveland team was referred to in the papers as the "Exiles" and "Vagrants." After this series, Cleveland had a total of 19 wins on the season. After this series, Cleveland headed to Brooklyn to play its "home" games there. The trip for Boston ended with three games in Chicago. Chicago won two of three. Boston went 6–3 on this final western trip, returning home on Sunday, September 3 in second place, seven games out. The *Boston Globe* said second was the best they could do, even though most of the games remaining were at home.

Ten thousand fans turned out for the Labor Day single game on September 4. This was the only single game in the league, as all other teams played doubleheaders. Baltimore took two of three games before both teams traveled on the same train to New York. In the first game in Brooklyn, Boston won, 2–1. The final out was made at home plate when a Brooklyn player was thrown out trying to score. The crowd swarmed the field and tried to assault the umpire who made the call. The Brooklyn team surrounded the ump and got him off the field. Brooklyn won the remaining two games in the series, which were the final games between these two teams. Brooklyn was 10½ games up after this series.

Boston returned home to face three western teams, their final games against western teams. Selee signed a one-year contract for 1900 on September 11 for $3,500, his same salary since 1890. Boston won three of five games against St. Louis. Selee had brought up a young catcher, Billy Sullivan, and was trying him out. Boston won four of five games against Pittsburgh. There were three doubleheaders in these two series. The next two dates against Chicago were rained out. The final day of the home stand was a split doubleheader with Chicago. The second game ended after eight innings due to darkness. Boston went to New York for three games. Two were split, and the third was rained out. Selee told Long to stay home for this trip, and he played youngster Charlie Kuhns at shortstop. In the Sunday *Boston Globe,* Selee laid out some of his problems. Bergen had left the team again. Selee was not too upset about that, because he had a high opinion of Billy Sullivan. Selee said that the absence of Hamilton for half the season due to injury had really hurt his team due to Hamilton being the leading run scorer for Boston.

Boston returned home to play Washington. The schedule called for four single games. The second game was called after eight innings, tied 8–8. Hence, the teams played five games in four days, Boston winning four of them. Bergen had returned to the team, hurt his finger, and left the team again. Then Boston won five straight against New York. Meekin won one of these games. He had pitched in 10 straight games that the team won, securing seven of the victories himself. Boston and Philadelphia were in a close fight for second, and all the remaining games were with Philadelphia. The Philadelphia owner had offered his players $2,500 to be divided up in addition to the league amount if they finished second. No such incentive was given by the Boston owner. Brooklyn clinched the pennant on October 7, the date of the first game in Philadelphia. Philadelphia won the first two games at home, creating a tie for second. Boston won the final game at Philadelphia before 10,000 fans. Boston won the next day at home before 1,000 fans. After the season concluded, Boston was one game to the good in the race for second place. Standings: Brooklyn 101–47, Boston 95–57, Philadelphia 94–58.

There was a post-season series between Brooklyn and Philadelphia that started on October 17. This was an exhibition series. The *Boston Globe* printed a story that all the National League teams made money or broke even. This would not be possible for Cleveland but might be if you considered Cleveland and St. Louis together, as they had the same ownership. The article said Boston made $60,000 profit.[17] This was achieved with home attendance of 200,384.

As far as the team went, Boston had a very good year in 1899. Some of the veteran players declined slightly, as would be expected. Duffy, Long, and Lowe had lower batting averages and productivity. Hamilton's numbers were okay in all ways except games played. He was able to play only 84 games due to injury. In 1898, Bergen had caught 122 games; in 1899, he caught 72 games. His status was a major concern for Selee to address over the coming winter. The top three pitchers all were pretty good in 1899. Nichols' statistics were very good in all areas except winning percentage, going 21–19. Willis led the league in ERA and shutouts. That did not include a no-hitter on August 7, which he won, 7–1. Willis led the team with a 27–8 record. Lewis performed well with a 17–11 record. But Lewis had notified Selee and the owners that he was going to retire and take the job as coach at Harvard. He signed his contract with Harvard on October 17. Selee was not yet sure about Meekin and Bailey, so he had to try to secure more pitching. But the main reason that Boston did not finish first was syndicate ball. The combination of Cleveland and St. Louis had been handled, St. Louis finishing in fifth place. But the combination of Baltimore and Brooklyn had been too much. More of the same was to come.

Selee had to deal with two huge problems over the winter. One was within the team and had been coming for quite a while. The other was league-wide and had been foreshadowed. The biggest, and most tragic, problem was Marty Bergen. Everyone associated with the team knew that Bergen was troubled. Up to the end of 1899, these problems had been manifested in Bergen's leaving the team quite often and not getting along with his teammates and management. Bergen and Chick Stahl had gotten into a fight during the 1899 season, which precipitated one of Bergen's departures from the team. After the season, Mrs. Bergen told friends she was afraid of him. By the end of 1899, Mrs. Bergen had been diagnosed with tuberculosis, and the Bergens were behind on their mortgage. This was all too much for Bergen. On January 19, 1900, Marty Bergen's father came by his son's residence at 8 a.m., knocked on the door, got no response, and went away. He came back at noon, knocked again with no response, then opened the door and discovered the tragedy. Over the prior evening, Marty Bergen had killed his wife and two children with an ax, then cut his own throat. After a quick investigation, the county authorities declared Bergen insane. Selee had used the same word regarding Bergen in a conversation with pitcher Frank Killen in April 1899.[18]

Over the recent life of the National League as the sole major league (1892–1899), there had been many voices complaining about the size of the league. The *Boston Globe* over this time period quoted various owners saying that the optimum size of the league was eight teams. John Brush and Andrew Freedman were consistent in their advocacy of reducing the size of the league. After the experience of the 1899 season, three owners were convinced they would do better financially by taking a payout to eliminate their franchise. These were Washington (whose owner was happy to take the payment), Cleveland (whose owners owned St. Louis), and Louisville (whose owner owned Pittsburgh). After long negotiations, Baltimore became the fourth franchise to accept a buyout. The Washington and Cleveland players were made free agents and were available to anyone who wanted to sign them. As these teams finished 11th and 12th in 1899, their players were not in high demand.

All the good Louisville players moved to Pittsburgh. There were quite a few good players on Louisville, such as Honus Wagner, Fred Clarke, Claude Ritchey, Tommy Leach, Chief Zimmer, Deacon Phillippe, and Rube Waddell. They all moved to Pittsburgh. The agreement to buy out the Baltimore franchise was not concluded until March 9. The agreement said that the Baltimore players would be distributed between Brooklyn and New York. This happened for most of the Baltimore players, but not all. Before the dissolution was finalized, the Baltimore owners sold John McGraw and Wilbert Robinson to St. Louis. This happened on March 11, the same day the American League filed articles of incorporation in Chicago. There would be developments on both these stories in the coming month. All this activity resulted in an eight-team National League, split between East (Boston, Brooklyn, New York, Philadelphia) and West (Pittsburgh, Cincinnati, Chicago, St. Louis).

While all these events were taking place at a higher level, Selee was trying to put together a team for 1900. He already knew the competition would be tougher. Now there were three syndicate teams to compete against (Brooklyn, St. Louis, and Pittsburgh). Selee knew that the core of his team was getting old in baseball terms and wanted to sign some young players to eventually replace this core. The owners would not increase their budget. Hence, Selee had to keep his team pretty much the same from 1899 to 1900. Selee was able to acquire Buck Freeman as a free agent from Washington as outfield insurance. Selee wanted to acquire another catcher for obvious reasons. The budget restraints made him stick with Boileryard Clarke as the veteran and Billy Sullivan as the young backup. Another pickup from Washington strengthened the pitching staff. Bill Dinneen had gone 23–36 over the past two years on a bad team. Selee thought he would be much better with a good team behind him. As of March 6, seven players

Fred Tenney getting ready to hit. During his tenure in Boston, Tenney had a mustache some of the time.

from the 1899 team were coaching at colleges: Lewis and Hamilton at Harvard; Clarke and Willis at Princeton; Nichols at Yale; Tenney at Dartmouth; Stahl at Notre Dame. All were under contract for 1900 except for Lewis. The schedule length was not determined until March 10. Opening Day would be April 19. The actual schedule was announced on March 26. On March 31, Selee and 11 players left for spring training.

Over this same time frame, the American League was making noise. The American League at this point consisted of teams from the Western League of 1899. Several of these teams wanted to change home cities for 1900. The most newsworthy example of this was in Chicago. James Hart (the Chicago NL team owner) and Ban Johnson (the AL president) met during March 1900 and came to an agreement allowing the St. Paul franchise of the Western League to move to Chicago for the inaugural season of the American League. It was part of Ban Johnson's plan to move into cities that used to be National League cities. He successfully got teams to move to Detroit and Cleveland for the 1900 season. The American League respected National League contracts in 1900 and operated as a minor league. Some of the better free agents created by the reduction of the size of the National League ended up in the American League. Two were former players for Selee: Dummy Hoy and Steve Brodie. That would not fulfill Ban Johnson's ambition, but would do for now.

Spring training started in Greensboro, North Carolina, on April 1. Veteran players showed up at various times after April 1, Nichols first, then Clarke and Willis together. Duffy was trying to bat lefty, but never tried this in an actual league game. A new catcher, Jack Clements, was in camp. When the first game of Regulars against Yannigans was played, the Regulars were: Hamilton CF, Tenney 1B, Long SS, Stahl RF, Collins 3B, Duffy LF, Lowe 2B, Clarke(?) C. Selee had Clarke penciled in as catcher but had Sullivan and Clements as other possibilities. Selee had picked up a couple of pitchers from the free agents created by the reduction in size of the National League, Bill Dinneen and Nig Cuppy. Nig Cuppy was a veteran of eight years in the NL let go by St. Louis. Selee also picked up 28-year-old minor leaguer Charles Pittinger. These moves were insurance in case Ted Lewis decided to stick to his decision to retire.

On April 9, Selee called all 18 players to his room, gave out his rules for the season, and asked for their input. The result of this meeting was reported by Tim Murnane in the *Boston Globe*: "The most important rule was to be in bed by 11:30 pm. 'The members of the team were rather lax in living up to the rules last season. I was to blame for allowing it, but I will not stand for it this season. The public demand a run for their money, and the only way you can fulfill your part is by keeping in good condition at all times.'"[19] Selee told Murnane that he considered taking this year off due to his health and letting Duffy manage the team. Up to this spring, Selee had participated in all spring workouts. He was just supervising this year.

By the time Boston returned home to prepare for Opening Day, a major story in the league was the status of John McGraw and Wilbert Robinson. Before the dissolution of the Baltimore franchise, the contracts of both had been sold to St. Louis. Both had declined to report and tried to force a trade to New York. The New York owner had been amenable to acquiring Robinson but said McGraw would be toxic in New York. This standoff continued through the start of the season.

For most games in 1899, the league had assigned two umpires to work games. That changed for 1900, the league going back to one umpire per game. Long, Lowe, Nichols, and Selee started their 11th year in Boston on Opening Day against Philadelphia on April 19, 1900. Before a crowd of 10,000, a wild game was played. Boston was down by nine runs going into the bottom of the ninth and tied the game. An error by Lowe cost them two runs in the top of the 10th to cause a 19–17 loss. Philadelphia won their home opener the next day against Boston. Boston finally won in the fourth game of the season with Willis getting the win.

Boston went to New York for series against New York and Brooklyn. New York took two of three games, with the other game getting the most attention. In the third game of a four-game series, the game was tied 10–10 after nine innings. Boston scored three runs in the top of 10th. The first two New York batters made out in the bottom of the 10th, but then the New York team proceeded to stall outrageously. The umpire called the game due to darkness, which caused the score to revert to a 10–10 tie. The *Boston Globe* headline read "Base Ball Farce." During the New York series, Selee received a letter from Ted Lewis saying he would come back at the right price. Brooklyn took three of four games in a series where Long turned his ankle and would be out for a short time. Boston returned home with a last-place record of 3–8.

Selee had wanted to start the process of replacing some of his veteran position players by signing younger future replacements. The Triumvirs would not give him the money to do this. As has been shown by the 1898 salary figures, the Triumvirs had cost control. The veterans had nowhere else to go and had signed for salaries similar to 1898. Selee's salary was unchanged at $3,500. Ted Lewis, who had the option of going to academia as either a coach or professor, returned to the fold at the start of this home stand. Lewis pitched in the first two games against Philadelphia. He lost the first game, giving up six runs in a one-inning start. He won the second game, relieving Willis and pitching six innings to get the decision. Boston won the first game of the next series against New York, 18–11. Dinneen started and was shelled. A new left-handed pitcher, Rome Chambers, pitched four innings, gave up six runs, and got the win. This was Chambers' only major league appearance.

When Boston left for the west on May 10, it was without Long and Nichols. They hoped to be ready to play in a week. Boston's last-place record was 5–10. If you think that there are lots of new ideas in baseball, check out this quote from the May 13, 1900, *Boston Globe*. The person quoted was Tony Mullane, a major league pitcher from 1881 to 1894.

> I think they ought to be taking the pitchers out after five or six innings in a game and putting in another man. A pitcher loses his grip on the curve ball after a while when his hand gets tired, and then he can't bend them and they begin to hit him out. A catcher should be able to tell when a pitcher's gone in a game. I used to get over that by saving the curves toward the end of the game. Use the speed and the head in the first part and then bring on the curves when you couldn't fool them that way anymore.[20]

Maybe Mullane's arm was sore from his career. He averaged over eight innings per appearance in his career.

After losing the first game of the trip in Pittsburgh, there was a Sunday off. Boston was the only team in the National League that refused to play Sunday games anywhere. Pittsburgh won the remaining two games of this series. Pittsburgh player-manager Fred Clarke spiked Fred Tenney in the second game. Tenney went after Clarke, and the police came on the field to break up the fight. Tenney was out a couple of games. In the first game in Chicago, there was a 17-minute rain delay and the game finished on a wet field. Even with that, the *Boston Globe* writer said this was the first good weather day the Boston team had seen this year, on May 16. In punishment for that comment, the next two dates were rained out.

Chicago won both the games played in this series. On Sunday May 20, all teams played except Boston and Chicago. Boston lost the first two games in St. Louis, making eight straight, before winning the final game in the series. The game-winning hit was a two-run home run by Buck Freeman, who had taken over for Duffy in the outfield. Duffy missed the first game of the next series as he was out scouting. Boston won two of three games in Cincinnati. On Boston's Sunday off in Cincinnati, Pittsburgh came to town and played Cincinnati. Selee said after the Cincinnati series that he was impressed by Cincinnati third baseman Harry Steinfeldt. This was supposed to be a four-game series, but the Cincinnati grandstand burned down before the final game. This was the end of the road trip, and the next games were in Boston against Cincinnati. Selee assured the Cincinnati team that he would loan them all required equipment to replace what was lost in the fire. Boston remained in last place with an 8–18 record.

Cincinnati took the field in borrowed uniforms for the next games, a Decoration Day morning-afternoon doubleheader. Boston won both games before a combined crowd of 20,000. Boston swept four games from

Cincinnati. In the first game of the next series with St. Louis, four of the Boston starting pitchers were used. Dinneen started, then Lewis, Pittinger, and Willis pitched in a 10-inning, 17–16 win. Boston had 23 hits, St. Louis 18. Boston won two more before St. Louis took the final game of the series. Boston won two of three games from Chicago. In the first game against Pittsburgh, Billy Sullivan hit a two-run home run in a 3–2 Boston win. Long caught a line drive with his bare hand in the ninth inning and turned it into a double play. Boston completed a sweep of Pittsburgh by beating Rube Waddell. After this stretch of playing western teams, Boston's record was 21–20, and they had moved into third place. The home stand ended with a four-game sweep of Boston by Brooklyn. Attendance was pretty good for this series, with crowds of 4,000, 6,500, 8,000 and 2,500. Brooklyn had shown Boston who was the defending champion.

Boston swept a short three-game road trip to New York. On the day of the final game in New York, Brooklyn was playing in Philadelphia in a first-and-second-place matchup. That game was tied after 10 innings. Brooklyn scored seven runs in the top of the 11th. After that, Philadelphia would not throw a strike, hoping the game would be called by darkness. The umpire forfeited the game to Brooklyn. Boston returned home to take two of three games from Philadelphia before heading west again with a 26–25 record.

The trip started in Cincinnati. This June 28 game was the first game played in Cincinnati since the fire on May 28. The park had been repaired except for the left field grandstand, which was still a burnt ruin. Cincinnati took two of three games. After a Sunday off, Boston went to Pittsburgh for four games, concluding with a July 4 doubleheader. The crowd on July 4 overflowed into the outfield behind ropes. Any ball hit into that crowd was a triple. In the first game on July 4, Pittsburgh player-manager Clarke charged and bumped umpire Ed Swartwood, who hauled off and punched Clarke. No one was ejected. Pittsburgh swept the series. Chicago won the first two games of the next series, giving Boston an eight-game losing streak. Before the final game in Chicago, there was a rumor going around the park that a couple of the Chicago players were out the entire night before and had shown up drunk for the game. Boston won that game. During a four-game series in St. Louis, Selee sent a message to Duffy to come back to the team. Duffy had been scouting for the last month. St. Louis won three of four games. In the final game in St. Louis, Boston scored a run in the top of the ninth inning to tie the game. As it was getting dark, the St. Louis team hid the dark ball that had been in play for several innings, forcing the umpire to put a new, white ball in play. St. Louis scored the winning run in the bottom of the ninth. Boston won two of three games in Philadelphia, where Duffy rejoined the team. The final game of the road trip was a make-up game in Brooklyn, won by Brooklyn. Boston returned home on July 19 with a 31–38 record, good for seventh place.

Boston won two of three games against Chicago before a Sunday off. As all the series were in the east, there were no games on this Sunday. Boston swept three games from St. Louis in a series where none of the games went nine innings. Boston walked off the first two games in the 10th. In the final game, Boston scored nine runs in the first, and then there was a 17-minute rain delay. After play started again, St. Louis stalled as much as they could in the hope that more rain would come. More rain did come, but not until six innings were completed. This must have been a big storm, because all league games were rained out the next day. Boston split two games with Pittsburgh. On the date of the final game of this series, there was an article in the *Boston Globe* on the formation of a new Players Association. This was not a new league, but a new union for the players.

Boston took two of three games against Cincinnati to end the home stand. In the second game of this series, five home runs were hit. In the final game, Boston walked off in the 11th inning for a 3–2 win. The teams had agreed before the 11th that it was to be the final inning, as both had to leave town after the game. On the date of this game, Lewis was loaned out to the Worcester minor league club for one game for $50. Lewis thought he was entitled to this money. After this game in Boston, Cincinnati headed home. Boston went to Brooklyn, where they lost their ninth straight game to Brooklyn, before heading to Cincinnati. Boston lost a player (Freeman) when switching trains on their way to Cincinnati. Boston won the first 3 of 4 in Cincinnati. In a doubleheader on August 6, umpire Swartwood worked the first game, but was unable to work the second due to the heat. One player from each team umpired the second game.

Boston lost two of three games in Pittsburgh. Pittsburgh was the most improved team in the league this year due to the additions from Louisville. There were four games in the first two days at the next stop, Chicago. Chicago swept the first doubleheader, Boston the second. The final game scheduled for Chicago was rained out. The final western trip of the year ended in St. Louis. Boston beat Cy Young in the first game, when the temperature was over 100. Boston took two of three. On the way home from this road trip, the team stopped in Syracuse and played an exhibition game. Dinneen, Nichols, and Willis pitched. The Boston players mostly swung at first pitches and got the game over in an hour and a half. The record was 47–48, good for fifth place. If a move was to be made, the 27-game home stand was the time to do it.

Boston corrected one problem at the beginning of the home stand. Boston had not won any games from Brooklyn in 1900. After losing the first game, 16–8, Boston won the final two games of the series. On August

26, there was an article in the *Boston Globe* about a player in the Connecticut State League that Selee was interested in, Danny Murphy. The next week was a five-game series with New York, Boston winning three. Lewis was loaned out again to a minor league team in Norwich, Connecticut. The next Monday was Labor Day. Boston played doubleheaders against Pittsburgh on Labor Day and the day after, losing all four games. Pittsburgh won the final game for a five-game sweep. By now the pennant race in the NL was between two syndicate teams, Brooklyn and Pittsburgh.

Lewis pitched for Boston on September 6, getting the win against Cincinnati. Cincinnati won the remaining two games of the series. When Boston went to Hartford for an exhibition game, Selee said he wanted Danny Murphy and would discuss this with the Triumvirs. The Norwich club wanted $1,500 for Murphy, and the Boston directors countered with $1,000. Murphy stayed in Norwich. The other syndicate team, St. Louis, came to town for their final series with Boston. The result was a two-game split. St. Louis was on its way to a sixth-place finish, not nearly as good as the other syndicate teams. St. Louis had acquired the services of John McGraw and Wilbert Robinson in May, but they were not much help. McGraw, with his eye on going back to Baltimore or New York, negotiated contracts for Robinson and himself that did not include the reserve clause. Both would be free agents after this year.

The final visit to Boston by a western club was by Chicago. Boston swept four games in their final series with a team located west of the Appalachians. On an off-day for Boston, the umpire in the Brooklyn-St. Louis game forfeited the game to Brooklyn when the St. Louis catcher punched him, was ejected, and refused to leave the field. Boston split four games with Philadelphia. The home stand ended with what turned into four games with New York. The first game was a 14–14 tie called by darkness. Boston won the three games that counted. During this time, Brooklyn lost six straight and had a one-game lead on Pittsburgh. Boston had moved up to fourth place on this home stand with a record of 64–61. After the final game, both teams boarded the same boat to travel to New York.

The schedule called for four games in Brooklyn followed by three in Boston against Brooklyn. In each series, there was a tie, so the teams played nine games with seven results. Brooklyn won three of four in Brooklyn before sweeping three games in Boston. The result of the season series between the two teams was 16–4 in favor of Brooklyn. The *Boston Globe* reported that Selee was not sure of his status for next year as of October 1. In all the years prior to this, he knew by September 1. This story had some effect, because Selee signed his contract for 1901 on October 2. The series with Brooklyn ended the home season for Boston with a record of 42–29. Home attendance held steady with a total of 202,000.

Willis had been sent home after pitching on September 27 for some rest. He returned to the team on October 5 and was shelled in New York by the last-place team. Boston lost two games in New York and two were rained out, not to be made up. Brooklyn had been cured by the games with Boston and clinched the pennant on October 6. Selee wrote a letter to the directors during the New York series, stating that the team needed to spend more money to get back in contention. Boston finished the season in Philadelphia. Philadelphia won three of four games to make Boston's record in their last 15 games 2–13. Boston ended with a road record of 24–43. Their final record was 66–72 and a fourth-place finish. Brooklyn and Pittsburgh agreed to play a best-three-of-five series for a cup donated by the *Pittsburgh Chronicle-Telegraph*. Brooklyn won the series, 3–1.

The *Boston Globe* printed a list of reserved players for the Boston Beaneaters for 1901 on October 9. The list: Kid Nichols, Vic Willis, Ted Lewis, Bill Dinneen, Charles Pittinger, Harvey Bailey (pitchers); Shad Barry, Chick Stahl, Buck Freeman, Hugh Duffy, Billy Hamilton (outfielders); Boileryard Clarke, Billy Sullivan (catchers); Fred Tenney, Bobby Lowe, Herman Long and Jimmy Collins (infielders). Both the Triumvirs and Selee thought they would be able to keep these players for 1901.[21] However, a change was brewing.

The first shot was fired in the next baseball war on October 24, 1900. The American League announced its member teams for 1901. The teams would be in Philadelphia, Washington, Baltimore, Brooklyn, Chicago, Detroit, and one other city in the west, which turned out to be Milwaukee. The Players Association, the organization that wanted to represent the players, welcomed this development. The Players Association said players would sign with the American League if it was to their financial advantage. John McGraw and Wilbert Robinson had already agreed to go to Baltimore and start up the franchise there. By the end of October 1900, it appeared there would be a new major league.

In *The New Bill James Historical Baseball Abstract*, published in 2001, James lists 10 baseball wars. The first was in 1876, and the last in 1994. The first five wars were as follows: Founding Revolution of National League, 1876; First American Association Skirmish, 1882–1883; Union League Incident, 1884; Players Association War, 1890; Second American Association Skirmish, 1891.[22] Arthur Soden, the lead Triumvir of the Boston owners, had been involved in all these conflicts. He was a leader of the National League in all except the first, where he followed William Hulbert. The only conflict the National League lost was the First American Association Skirmish, which led to a two-league system from 1882 through 1891, with the interruptions of the Union League in 1884 and the Players' League in 1890. The result of the First American Association Skirmish was reversed after the

4. Boston: The Last Five Years

1891 season, with the merger of the AA and NL. That result was refined in 1900 when the NL reduced from the 12 teams agreed to in the merger to eight teams.

Soden had invented the reserve clause. Soden was known to be stingy with his payroll in most situations. He would spend money when he had to, like when he bought Mike Kelly and John Clarkson for $10,000 each. But Soden felt that baseball was a business where the goal was to make a profit. The Boston NL team was profitable during his ownership through 1900. Unfortunately for the position Soden had taken by 1900, the rules were changing over the 1900–1901 off-season. Ban Johnson and the American League declared themselves a second Major League. The American League teams said that the reserve clause was not binding, and they would try to sign anyone not under contract from the National League. Where players from the National League in 1900 would play in 1901 would depend on money in most cases.

Selee's position in this new war was dependent on Soden. Selee had recommended that the budget be increased for 1901. Soden did not think the American League was a major threat and did not increase his budget. Soden wanted to sit out this war. After being a militant in five conflicts since 1876, he was a pacifist in this one. The results of this stance became clear by March 1901. Duffy had signed with Milwaukee of the AL as player-manager. Collins was negotiating with Soden and fellow Triumvir Billings at the beginning of March. Starting catcher Clarke signed with Washington of the AL on March 1. There was a report in the March 4 *Boston Globe* that Collins, Stahl, and Dinneen had signed with the Boston AL team. The next day's story said these three plus Buck Freeman had signed with Boston AL. Selee said Willis had signed with Philadelphia AL team. Ban Johnson said Billy Sullivan had signed with Chicago AL on this same date. On March 7, Tenney and Long signed with Boston NL.

The Boston AL team started work on their ballpark this same day. On March 8, Boston NL had eight signed players. Brooklyn had eight signed players. Pittsburgh had 15 signed players. Soden said the reserve clause would hold. Willis acknowledged he had signed with Philadelphia. Jimmy Sheckard, last of Brooklyn in 1900, had signed with Brooklyn of the NL and Baltimore of the AL. Selee was able to sign Nichols and Hamilton by March 15. Lowe was holding out. Lewis was going to retire. A new catcher, Mal Kittridge, was signed along with infielder Shad Berry. Lowe signed on March 21.

Dinneen consulted a lawyer in his hometown of Syracuse. The lawyer said the reserve clause would hold, so Dinneen signed a two-year deal with Boston NL, voiding his deal with Boston AL. Jimmy Slagle did the same thing to Washington AL, voiding his signed contract and returning to Philadelphia NL. The Philadelphia NL team sued the Philadelphia AL team in state court regarding Nap Lajoie. Ban Johnson made the decision that this would be the test case regarding the reserve clause. He advised the AL owners not to dispute any other voided contracts, like Dinneen's and Slagle's. Connie Mack of the Philadelphia AL team had signed Vic Willis and Christy Mathewson. Both Willis and Mathewson had second thoughts and went back to Boston NL and New York NL respectively. Mack honored Johnson's decision and did not dispute these moves.

By the start of spring training on April 1, Selee had lost much of his offense from 1900. On April 7, Selee gave the *Boston Globe* his assessment of his team for the upcoming year. He said his pitching was first-rate, the defense would be good, but he was not sure of his hitting. Selee learned that Yale had played the Boston AL team, so he cancelled an upcoming game with Yale. Boston did not go south for spring training this year, playing games and practicing in New England. The pitching was done by Nichols, Willis, Dinneen, Pittinger, and Faulkner. Faulkner did not make the team, which started the season with Nichols, Willis, Dinneen, and Pittinger as the pitchers. By the final exhibition game on April 16, the rest of the roster read: Shad Barry, Fred Crolius, Hamilton, outfielders; Gene DeMontreville, Long (captain), Lowe, Tenney, infielders; Kittridge, Pat Moran, Fred Brown catchers; Nichols, Willis, Dinneen, Pittinger, pitchers. On the day before Opening Day, Ted Lewis decided to sign with Boston AL when his coaching at Harvard was concluded.

After all the permutations that took place before the start of the seasons of both leagues, it was clear that Selee was left with a reduced team. This was the result of the budgetary decision of the Triumvirs. Soden had lost his taste for combat and was willing to see his team decimated. Half of the eight regular position players from 1900 were in the

Vic Willis in 1898, the rookie year of a Hall of Fame career that finished up with Pittsburgh.

American League (Collins, Stahl, Clarke, Freeman). Boston was going into this season with an unbalanced team.

There was one new rule in the National League for 1901, the "foul-strike" rule. Before this, a foul ball did not count as a strike. This rule became the rule we are familiar with today. Boston got its Opening Day game in on April 19, beating New York, 7–0, in Boston. The next two games in New York were rained out. On April 22, Pittsburgh had a game scheduled at home, but the field was under water from a flood. There was another experimental rule in place this year. The team coming to bat could end the pitcher's warmup by being ready to hit. This was noted in the story about the April 23 game in Philadelphia. "It is amusing to see the players rush to the plate as soon as an inning was over to prevent the pitcher from warming up."[23] Boston split two games in Philadelphia, with one rainout. Through April 25, Boston had played three games and had three rainouts. The road trip ended with a scheduled four-game series in Brooklyn. Brooklyn won two of three and there was one rainout.

The home stand started with another rainout, which made the count six games played and five rainouts. The first game of the home stand featured a great pitching matchup. Nichols, close to the end of his career, faced Christy Mathewson, at the beginning of his. New York won, 2–1, in a game that lasted 93 minutes. The two-game series was a split. On May 5, the game in St. Louis was called as a 4–4 tie in the 10th inning due to a fire in the grandstand. The next series, with Brooklyn, was the first of the year with no rainout.

Boston took three of four games, but that was not the big baseball news in Boston. The Boston AL team played its first home game on May 7, receiving more space in the *Boston Globe* and outdrawing the NL team, 11,500 to 5,500. On the day of the next rainout, Selee proposed hot and cold shower baths for the home clubhouse. He tried to acquire Johnny Dobbs, an outfielder from Cincinnati, but was unsuccessful. Philadelphia swept two games from Boston in a series umpired by Billy Nash, who had played 10 years for Boston NL. A new pitcher, Bob Lawson, pitched the game against Philadelphia on May 13. St. Louis came in next for four games. This series was split, without a rainout. That was corrected at the beginning of the Cincinnati series, which started with a rainout, a Sunday off, and a rainout. Cincinnati won the two games that were played. In the finale, Boston struck out 16 times in a nine-inning game. That was quite unusual for anyone in 1901.

A four-game series with Pittsburgh was next. Pittsburgh won two of three, both Pittsburgh wins shortened by rain before the inevitable rainout. The *Boston Globe* commented that Selee did not have the tools to do the job. Their figures said Boston NL had 14 players with total salary of $30,000, and Boston AL had 16 players with total salary of more than $40,000. This long home stand, which was against every other team in the NL, ended with four games scheduled against Chicago. The first two were rained out. All contests on Decoration Day in the NL were morning-afternoon doubleheaders. The Boston-Chicago doubleheader was split. That was not the big news from that day. Total attendance for the Decoration Day doubleheaders in the National League (separate admissions): New York 32,000, Philadelphia 18,700, Brooklyn 13,500, Boston 4,500. This was in line with the figures for Boston on this long home stand. The average attendance for the 18 games played on this home stand was 2,050. The Boston AL team had been at home from May 7 through May 30 and averaged over 5,000. Weather had been a problem. After Decoration Day, Boston NL had played 25 games and had 12 rainouts.

The next trip was a stop in New York for a couple of make-up games and the first venture west. The first game in New York was rained out. New York won the one game played, another 2–1 win for Mathewson over Nichols. Boston went west to play the four western teams. The first stop was Chicago for three games. The teams split the first two before the inevitable rainout. During this series, the *Boston Globe* commented, "It's nearly time that Selee and Hanlon gave some other managers a chance."[24] This after Selee and Hanlon had won all the NL pennants from 1891 to 1900. The same pattern held in St. Louis. St. Louis won the first two games of the series before a rainout. The three games in Cincinnati changed the pattern somewhat. Boston won the first two, and the third ended in a tie called by darkness after 12 innings. The Cincinnati left field grandstand had burned down the year before. During this series, there was a big pile of lumber where the grandstand should have been, with no fence in front of it. One of the Boston runs in the final game came when a Boston player hit a ball into this pile of lumber and the Cincinnati outfielder could not find the ball. The final stop in Pittsburgh was the only stop on this trip where the series was completed as scheduled. Pittsburgh took two of three games without a rainout, even though the final game was played through a constant, light rain. Boston ended the trip 4–6–1, coming home with a 15–20 record in seventh place. They came home on June 16, having played only 35 games in the first two months of the season.

This home stand would start with another test of the relative popularity of the AL and NL teams. Both were scheduled to be in Boston for the week of June 17. The home stand started with a sweep of two games against Philadelphia. On June 18, it was announced that the lowest ticket price at the NL ballpark would be dropped from $.50 to $.25, same as the AL ballpark. This was announced one day after a paid attendance of 300. The next two series were with the bookends of the National League: Chicago (last) and Pittsburgh (first). Boston swept five games from Chicago over three days, making up a couple of rainouts. The pitchers for Boston in this series were Willis (consecutive day complete games), Dinneen (complete game win against Rube Waddell), and Lawson (two complete games with one day of rest). Selee saved Nichols and Pittinger for the doubleheader against Pittsburgh on Saturday. Those five men (Nichols, Willis, Dinneen, Pittinger, and Lawson) did all the pitching for Boston NL in 1901.

The Saturday doubleheader with Pittsburgh was split. In the six days from June 17 through June 22, the two Boston teams played 16 games in Boston, winning 15 of them. Total attendance: Boston AL, 38,000; Boston NL 12,000. The Pittsburgh series was completed with a split of Monday and Tuesday games. In the final game, Willis pitched and Nichols played left field and got two hits. Nichols was not much affected, pitching a complete game the next day in a 3–2 loss to St. Louis. St. Louis took two of three. In the first game against Cincinnati, Selee used three pitchers in an 11–3 loss. Dinneen started, went three innings, and lost. Pittinger pitched three innings and Lawson finished up. This was the last game Lawson pitched for Boston in 1901. Boston swept a doubleheader the next day, both Willis and Dinneen pitching complete games. Cincinnati ended the home stand by winning the final game. All teams in the league spent the next day traveling from east to west. Boston ended the home stand with a record of 27–26, in sixth place.

The road trip started with a morning-afternoon July 4 doubleheader in Cincinnati, which was split. The remaining two games of the series were split as well, even though Boston only had four regular position players playing. The regulars playing these final two games in Cincinnati were Long, DeMontreville, Hamilton, and Lowe. Nichols played first base when not pitching. On July 6, Nichols had four hits, including an inside-the-park home run while playing first base. That same day, Philadelphia released Jimmy Slagle, an outfielder Selee was interested in. The next series was four games at first-place Pittsburgh. Pittsburgh swept the series, including a 1–0 win in 12 innings. Both Dinneen and Jack Chesbro pitched complete games. Slagle joined Boston for the final game in Pittsburgh, immediately moved into center field. That game was the first game this year for Boston that had two umpires. Boston's batting average after this series was .250, last in NL.

The next stop was in Chicago. The four games there were split. On the date of the third game, July 15, Christy Mathewson threw a no-hitter in St. Louis. On July 16, the *Boston Globe* reported that Mathewson was in Chicago (New York's next stop on their road trip). The *Globe* said, "Mathewson spent an hour pitching batting practice to Boston, sat on Boston bench for the game. He said he stiffened up in St. Louis and needed the workout."[25] Boston took New York's place in St. Louis for the next series. Chicago was in last place, and St. Louis was second. Hence the attendance in Chicago averaged about 1,000 per game and in St. Louis about 4,700 per date. Boston won four of five games from St. Louis. In the July 19, Boston 8–1 victory, the umpire did not show up. Nichols and a St. Louis player umpired the game. The trip continued in Philadelphia. Philadelphia swept four games while Boston scored just seven runs. The road trip ended with four games in New York, swept by Boston. The final game featured another Nichols-Mathewson matchup, won by Nichols in 10 innings, 5–4. Boston returned from this six-stop road trip with a record of 38–40, in fifth place.

Both teams went to Boston for the next series. They each won one game before Brooklyn came to town. Boston took two of three games in a series where Boston scored six runs. During this series, a manager said something exaggerated about a player that turned out true. Manager Fred Clarke of Pittsburgh had moved Honus Wagner to shortstop about a month earlier. On August 3, Clarke said Wagner was the finest shortstop ever.[26] If Clarke was off, it was not by much. Boston concluded this short home stand with three games against Philadelphia. Boston won the first before a rainout. The doubleheader forced by the rainout was swept by Philadelphia. At the end of this home stand, Boston NL home attendance was 75,000, lowest in both leagues.

The next road trip was against these same eastern teams. Brooklyn won the first game in Brooklyn with the style of play that was emerging in the 1900s. They scored two runs in the bottom of the ninth inning to win this way: walk, bunt single, sacrifice, two-run single. In the doubleheader split the next day, Dinneen won the first game with a complete game. The second game went to the eighth inning with Pittinger pitching. Pittinger was hit on the right hand with a line drive in the eighth and had to leave. The *Boston Globe* said, "Dineen and Nichols volunteered to finish, and Long selected Dinneen." Brooklyn took two of three games before a rainout. Boston went across town to play New York. This was to be a five-game series in three days. Boston won three of the first four before the final game ended in a 5–5 tie. The first and last games of this series were matchups between Nichols and Mathewson. The road trip finished with a three-game sweep in Philadelphia by the Phillies. Boston headed home with a 46–50 record, in fifth place.

The home stand started with a two-game sweep of New York. The first game was another Nichols/Mathewson matchup. On August 22, the *Boston Globe* reported, "Manager Selee says he has lines out for a few young players." Boston took two of three games from Philadelphia. On the last day of this series, there was an article in the *Boston Globe* written by Ban Johnson, President of the American League. Johnson explained his rationale for cracking down on dirty play and continual "kicking" (arguing) against the umpires. Johnson claimed that troublesome managers and players wanted more than their fair share, and were covering for themselves when either the team or individual were having a bad time.[27] In the week of August 26, Boston played Brooklyn seven games in six days in Boston. Boston won three games in this series. The average attendance for the six dates was 3,700, which was very good non-holiday attendance for Boston NL this year. First-place Pittsburgh came to town next and showed why they were in first. Pittsburgh swept the three games in two days, the first two coming on Labor Day. As had been the case all year, the Boston pitchers pitched well and got little support. The scores in this series were 5–3, 3–0, and 5–2. The attendance for this series was the best of the year for Boston NL, averaging over 4,800. The Boston crowd saw Honus Wagner at shortstop in these games. St. Louis was the next western team to visit on this final home stand. Boston won the first two games in different, walk-off fashions. Boston won 3–2 in the bottom of the ninth inning of the first game with a walk, sacrifice, passed ball, and Lowe's walk-off single. They were behind 5–0 after 6½ innings in the second game. In the bottom of the ninth, Demontreville hit a two-out, walk-off, three-run home run. St. Louis won the final game.

During this series, Pittsburgh won six games in three days from New York, moving into a 4½-game lead. Cincinnati came in next for four games, which Boston. The four regular pitchers went in this order: Dinneen, Pittinger, Nichols, and Willis. They allowed one, one, three, and two runs. In this series, that was good enough. The average time of game in this series was one hour 26 minutes. The foul-strike rule was shortening games as the rule makers intended. Chicago was the final western team to visit this year. Boston swept three games. The final two games were a doubleheader won by Boston, 2–1 and 1–0. Hamilton scored all the runs for Boston on this date. The home schedule ended with a make-up game against New York. Boston won this to finish the home stand with a 10–1 stretch. Boston left for its final road trip with a record of 62–61, in fifth place. The *Boston Globe* said that Boston NL players were not signing their contracts for next year, waiting for offers from American League teams.

The final road trip would see the Beaneaters visit every city in the league except Brooklyn. The first stop was to finish the schedule with New York. A make-up doubleheader was split on September 17. On this date, the Boston AL team was eliminated in their pennant race. They would end up in second place. Boston NL headed west for final visits to the western teams. Two doubleheaders were scheduled in Chicago for the two days of this series. Boston swept the first doubleheader. There was a story in the Chicago paper after this doubleheader that Selee would be hired by New York next year. Selee would not confirm or deny it. The final doubleheader was scheduled for Saturday, September 21. Chicago walked off with a 1–0 win in 17 innings. Both pitchers threw complete games. By the time this game was finished, it was too late to start the second game. The final game scheduled between Chicago and Boston was not played. It could have been played the next day, but Boston did not play any Sunday games.

While Boston traveled to St. Louis, Pittsburgh came to Chicago and won, 15–9, on Sunday. During the first game of the St. Louis series, the news broke that Boston NL had engaged Al Buckenberger to manage the team next year. Selee would finish out the season. The story said that Director Billings wanted the change, convinced the other Triumvirs to make the change, and then negotiated the deal with Buckenberger. St. Louis won two of three games in this series. The lineup in the middle game featured Tenney at catcher, Cooley at first base, and Dinneen in center field. That was the only game Boston won in this series. Nichols played center field in the final game. After this series, the *Boston Globe* paid tribute to Selee: "Goodbye Frank Selee, you gave Boston 5 pennants in 12 years."[28] The year finished out with two games in Cincinnati and the final rainout in a year filled with them, two games in Pittsburgh, and one in Philadelphia. Boston ended up with a 69–69 record, in fifth place. The Boston fans showed which team was preferred. Total home attendance for Boston NL was 146,502, Boston AL 289,448.

One judgment made much later showed what Selee was up against in his last year in Boston. In his 2001 publication of *The New Bill James Historical Baseball Abstract,* James selected the best pitching staff of every decade from the 1880s thru the 1990s. James ranked pitching staffs by his Win Share method, which is too complicated to explain here. Per this method, the best starting pitching staff of the 1900s decade, and the 20th century, was the 1901 Boston Beaneaters.[29] James ranks the top four starters who started 136 of the 140 games. The fifth pitcher, Bob Lawson, pitched in six games and none after June 26. The four main starters on this staff were all good, even though their won-lost records in 1901 would not confirm this. Nichols was 19–16, 3.22 ERA. Willis was 20–17, 2.36. Dinneen was 15–18, 2.94. Pittinger was 13–16, 3.01. The staff ERA was 2.90, which put them third in the league. The main reasons James rates this staff so high are (1) all four had ERAs better than the league average; (2) their home park was the best hitters' park in the league; (3) their average innings were 304 per pitcher; and (4) the offense of the Boston team was genuinely pathetic. Boston was last in the league in batting average, slugging percentage, runs scored, and several other offensive categories. Selee was able to retain his pitching staff from the fine years in the 1890s, but not his hitters. The pitchers held up their end, but the hitters he secured were not up to snuff, as the best went to the American League.

Frank Selee had a truly outstanding run as manager in Boston. He started and ended his run in Boston during two difficult years due to the Players' League and American League. Both those years were unsuccessful due to factors beyond Selee's control. In the other ten years of his employment, Boston finished first five times, second twice, and below that three times. He was able to blend the players returning from the Players' League with the new players he had secured in 1891 to the tune of three straight pennants. After that team aged, he rebuilt it over the next three years into another two-time pennant winner. Selee seemed quite happy in Boston. During his employment there, he lived in Melrose, either with his parents or brother. Selee made no fuss about his contract, resulting in the same salary over his 12-year tenure. On October 13, 1901, Hugh Duffy said, "Selee should have left long ago and taken one of several good offers, instead of remaining at a very small [$3500] salary."

Selee showed throughout his tenure his eye for talent. Coming to town with Nichols, Long, and Lowe was a very good start. Securing outstanding veteran players like Duffy, McCarthy, and Hamilton for minimal cost helped greatly. Discovering youngsters like Tenney, Willis, Collins, Stahl, and Dinneen showed he still had this ability late into his tenure.

Selee maintained his reputation as a nice guy with his behavior on not being rehired. There were no statements to newspapers burning his bridges to Boston. When he wrote an article for *Baseball Magazine* after his retirement, he only had good things to say about the players and owners in Boston.

> Collins in my opinion is the greatest third basemen I ever saw... During my connection with the Boston Club I had a good lieutenant in Hughey Duffy, Captain of the Club; our associations were very pleasant... Mr. Soden, President of the Club, was one of the truest gentlemen I ever met. During my twelve years' stay in Boston, I never heard him use an impatient word.[30]

It seems true that Selee was taught and practiced the old saying, "If you don't have anything good to say about somebody, don't say anything."[31] How would this help in the next step of his career?

5

Chicago

A New Start

As Hugh Duffy said, Frank Selee was in demand. There had been a story that New York NL, which finished seventh in 1901, wanted Selee for 1902. As it turned out, there was a turnover of three of the eight managers in the National League from the end of 1901 season to the beginning of 1902 season. The new manager in Boston was Al Buckenberger. New York replaced George Davis (an unwilling player-manager) with Horace Fogel. And Selee was hired by an old friend.

As was discussed in the Oshkosh and Omaha chapters of this book, Frank Selee managed against James Hart in 1887 and 1888. After the 1888 season, Hart was hired as manager of the Boston NL team. After the 1889 season, Hart resigned for a step up the front office ladder. Hart recommended Selee for the manager's job in Boston. Hence, we know Hart had a high opinion of Selee.

After the 1889 season, James Hart went to England at the behest of A. G. Spalding, the owner of the Chicago NL team and his eponymous sporting goods firm. Hart's assignment was to start an English baseball league and try to sell some sporting goods. Hart did this job until the end of 1890, when Spalding called him back to Chicago. Hart had been named Secretary of the Chicago NL team before heading to England. At the annual meeting of the corporation that owned the Chicago club in April 1891, Hart was elected President. By spring 1891, Spalding was a hands-off owner of the Chicago NL team, spending most of his time building up his sporting goods business. Hart was given control of the day-to-day operations of the team. Hart controlled the budget and was the boss of Cap Anson, the player-manager. Hart and Anson did not get along, but Anson was under contract until 1897.

In 1895, Spalding announced his intention to sell his majority share of the team. Spalding offered his share in the team to Anson for $150,000. Anson was given 60 days to raise the money. He was not able to raise the money, so Spalding sold his share to Hart. The amount Hart paid was never made public. Anson suspected a backroom deal to let Hart buy this interest for much less than $150,000, and this belief further poisoned the relationship between Anson and Hart.[1] Anson was let go when his contract expired after the 1897 season. Hart hired Tom Burns to manage in 1898–1899. Burns had two years over .500 and was fired after the 1899 season. Tom Loftus was hired to manage in 1900–1901. Loftus' record over these two years was 118–161. Loftus was let go as soon as the 1901 season ended. Selee was hired by Hart before the end of October 1901 for the 1902 season. No salary was disclosed, but it was a safe bet Selee earned more than $3,500.

Before we get to the baseball action in the 1902 season, a short diversion to Selee's personal life. There is almost nothing in the record about Selee's personal behavior during his tenure as a Major League manager. It was known that he lived in Melrose, Massachusetts. His family was still there. It was thought he lived with either his brother, a real estate broker, or his parents. Selee and Sid Farrar opened a haberdashery shop in Melrose after the 1891 season, but I could not find anything about how long this shop remained open or whether it was successful. One change that happened after the 1901 season was noted. Selee got married to a woman from St. Louis named Mary. The only reference to this event that I could find was in the *Chicago Tribune* on August 31, 1902. The story said that Mrs. Selee was a native of Ireland. It stated that the marriage was such a secret that even their closest friends did not know the date. The new couple lived during the season in the apartment of Jimmy Ryan, a player for Chicago from 1890 to 1900 who was now with Washington in the AL. Mrs. Selee made clear that they lived in the Boston area, and that they would return there after the season.

Selee got to work in December 1901. Kid Nichols, who left the Boston NL team to become part-owner and manager of his hometown Kansas City minor league team, contacted a couple of players in that league on behalf of Selee, as reported by the *Boston Globe* on December 5, 1901. Selee met with Jack Doyle, the 1901 captain of the Chicago NL team, in Boston, on December 6. Selee stated that he was going to try and acquire Lowe for Chicago for 1902. On December 17, Lowe was released by Boston and signed by Selee for Chicago. Selee also acquired Jimmy Slagle from his old employer. Selee went to Chicago to confer with James Hart on February 2, 1902, then proceeded to Hot Springs, Arkansas, with Herman Long. On February 8, the *Chicago Tribune* listed the 31 players under contract to the Chicago NL team for 1902. In the final week of February, Selee released Jack Doyle, who signed with New York NL, and signed pitcher Pop Williams from Toronto.

In the month before the team left for spring training on March 29, there was turmoil surrounding the leadership of the National League. There was an attempt to remove President Nick Young and replace him with A. G. Spalding. That move was blocked by Arthur Soden. After various court challenges, Spalding gave up the battle and Young was reinstated in his office. The war with the American League was ongoing. Chicago NL had lost some players to the AL after the 1901 season, notably outfielders Topsy Hartsel and Davy Jones. During March, pitcher Rube Waddell was threatening to jump, and catcher Frank Chance asked to be allowed to work out in Oakland, California, and report late (Chance lived in Los Angeles). A result of all these maneuvers was that when spring training officially started on March 29, only nine players were there. The schedule for the NL had not yet been made, due to the dispute over who the president would be.

One of the facts about Selee's building of the Chicago NL team had puzzled me when I was researching my prior book (*The Cubs and A's of 1910*). Several of the young players acquired in the next three years were scouted for the Chicago NL team by George Huff, then signed by Selee on Huff's recommendation. As I know from living in Champaign, Illinois, George Huff was a prominent name in the athletic history of the University of Illinois. However, nothing in Huff's papers at the University library explained why he had a relationship with Selee. The research for this book revealed the answer. When the Chicago Colts (or Remnants or Orphans) left for spring training on March 29, 1902, their destination was Champaign. The team would be working out with the University of Illinois baseball team, coached by George Huff. From March 30 through April 15, all exhibition games except two would be played against the U of I, and practices would be joint. The connection made between Selee and Huff paid serious dividends for the Chicago NL team.

The dispute about the presidency of the NL continued. Both factions agreed to offer the presidency to William Temple of Temple Cup fame, but he turned it down. The two factions agreed on Arthur Soden of Boston, John Brush of New York, and James Hart of Chicago as a committee to run the league. Ex-president Nick Young was named Secretary-Treasurer. Young submitted his schedule to the committee on April 4. The schedule for 140 games was issued the next day. The schedule called for 20 games against every other team in the league.

Players reported in such a way that by April 11 there were 24 in camp. Frank Chance, Jimmy Slagle, and John Kling were late arrivals. Several of these players were young infielders. Selee had acquired Bobby Lowe to play second base. The rest of the infield was in flux. In spring training and during the season, Selee experimented with different players at first and third base. But he made up his mind on his new shortstop in spring training. Per the testimony of the winner, in spring training of 1902,

5. *Chicago*

There were ten infielders trying for the Cubs that spring and when I learned that I was prepared to return to Portland [his prior team] at any moment. I never dreamed that I had a chance and my hopes were blasted into nothingness when Seeley [sic] asked me what position I liked most, and after learning that I considered myself nothing but a third baseman announced that he wanted me to play shortstop. I told him then that I might just as well return to Portland, as I had anticipated would be the upshot of my trial with the Cubs. He looked me over and said, "I know that you are going to make a good shortstop, and furthermore you won't be returned to Portland."[2]

This was how Joe Tinker became the shortstop of the Chicago NL team. Another player who impressed Selee during spring training was pitching for the University of Illinois. Carl Lundgren, a senior at the U of I, pitched four times against Chicago in the spring. His final appearance was a complete game victory in the final exhibition game on April 15. That would not be the last time Selee saw Lundgren pitch in 1902.

The season started the next day. Selee set his roster. The starting lineup was: Joe Tinker SS, Frank Chance C, Bunk Congalton RF, Jimmy Slagle CF, Dakin "Dusty" Miller LF, Hal O'Hagen 1B, Bobby Lowe 2B, Charlie Dexter 3B. Substitutes were: John Kling and Mike Kahoe, C; Mike Lynch OF, Germany Schaefer IF. Pitchers were Jack Taylor, Jocko Menafee, Jimmy St. Vrain. Jim Gardner, Bob Rhoads, and Pop Williams. This roster was not the only thing about the Chicago NL team that was set in pencil at the beginning of the 1902 season. The *Chicago Tribune* published an article on April 16 that debated what the Chicago NL team should be called. The popular choices for them were Remnants and Colts. The first of these names came from what was left over when Cap Anson left the team. The Colts name was due to the low average age of the team. The *Chicago Tribune* decided to use the name Colts. As we will see, the low average age of the team would lead to the lasting nickname.

Joe Tinker much later in his career with Chicago. Tinker thought he had no chance to make the team in 1902, but Selee selected him and stuck with him.

Selee's strength as a manager was looking at his players and determining how they would fit in. That was his main concern at the beginning of the 1902 season. The only player he was confident in had been named Captain by Selee. That was Bobby Lowe. Not much surprise there, as Selee and Lowe had been together for 12 years in Boston. Selee thought enough of Jimmy Slagle to acquire him twice. The rest of the team had to prove themselves to their manager. This process started on Opening Day in Cincinnati on April 17. The Colts won three of four games in this series. Selee managed his first Sunday game in the National League on April 20 before a crowd of 13,000. Selee used five pitchers and two catchers in this series. He made the only public comment I could find that denigrated an opposing player: "Those college pitchers up at Champaign showed us more than Swormstedt [the Cincinnati pitcher on Opening Day] had today."[3] The team returned to Chicago for the home opener with St. Louis. This was to be a two-game series, but only the opener was played. Chicago won, 4–3, on a sacrifice fly by Tinker. The Colts went on the road for a series against the champion Pirates. Chicago won two of three. During this series, a Louisville paper published an article headlined "Quiet Management Best." The two managers cited in this article were Selee and Ned Hanlon.[4] Now Chicago did something Selee had not experienced before. They had a long home stand early in the season. His Boston teams had always opened with long road trips after an Opening Day or short home series. Chicago would be home from April 27 to May 25.

The home stand started with one game against Pittsburgh, won by the champions before a crowd of 17,000, which spilled over to the outfield. The next game showed several things that were different about baseball in 1902 as compared to 2020. The game between Cincinnati and Chicago was called for darkness after 12 innings as a 0–0 tie. This game started at 4 p.m. and lasted two hours. As there was no daylight savings time, it was dark enough to call at 6 p.m. Both pitchers (Jack Taylor and Noodles Hahn) went the distance. The records for this game went into the yearly statistics, but the game had to be completely replayed, not suspended.

This created one problem for Selee, who had been evaluating his two main catchers, Chance and Kling. Selee had already decided that Kling was the better defensive player and that Chance's bat needed to be in the lineup. One factor keeping Chance at catcher was that Taylor liked to pitch to Chance. Jack Taylor was the Colts' best pitcher. Chance had caught all 12 innings of this game and was on the way to catching 29 games this year. Soon Selee would have to make his choice about the catching position. Chicago won two of three games from Cincinnati. St. Louis won the first game of a series before the next two were rained out. Five games against St. Louis had been scheduled so far in Chicago, and three had been rained out. This was followed by a four-game series with New York. Chicago won three, and the final game was rained out. Selee released pitcher Mal Eason and tried to sell catcher Mike Kahoe to New York. The sale did not go through. The next series was five games with Brooklyn. The first three were shutouts, Brooklyn winning two and Chicago the third. After Chicago was shut out for 26 of 27 innings by Brooklyn in these three games, "Selee celebrated victory with a cigarette, his 1st in several years. 'Have to do something unusual after a game like that.'"[5] He had another unusual thing to experience before this series was over.

The war between the NL and AL was ongoing. Near the end of the 1901 season, James Hart had purchased a 21-year-old outfielder from the Rockford, Illinois, minor league team. That outfielder, Davy Jones, got an offer at the same time from the Milwaukee team in the AL. Jones went with the Milwaukee offer, playing 14 games for Milwaukee in 1901. The Milwaukee franchise moved to St. Louis for the 1902 season. Davy Jones told the story of what came next in *The Glory of Their Times*:

"I'd been with the St. Louis club about two or three weeks in the 1902 season when we went to Chicago to play the White Sox. [Jones played 15 games with St. Louis in 1902.]

After the game that day [May 13] I got a phone call from James A. Hart, the owner of the Chicago Cubs. He'd been pretty sore ever since I'd jumped from the Cubs to the American League the previous August. Mr. Hart said he'd like me to come over and talk with him at his office the next morning. Well, why not?

'I see you're going pretty good,' he said to me after I got there.

'Yes, that's right,' I said. 'We've got a good club.'

'You know,' he said, 'I've lost a lot of good ballplayers to the American League, men like Clark Griffith and Jimmy Callahan, not to mention yourself. I'd like to try to get some of you fellows to move the other way. What would you think about jumping back to the Chicago Cubs?'

'Well, what have you got to offer?'

So he thought a minute, got up, walked into the next room, and sent the clerk for some cash. I guess he thought I'd find green cash more tempting than a check. He was right.

Finally he came back. 'How about a two-year contract for $3,600 a year, the highest salary on the club, plus a $500 bonus that you can have right now. Here's the $500.'

Well, what could I do? I was playing for $2,400, and here was a 50% raise plus $500 in cold cash, stacked up right in front of me. And, after all, I wasn't even twenty-two years old yet. Besides, everybody was jumping all over the lot in those days: Sam Crawford, Larry Lajoie, Clark Griffith, Willie Keeler, Jack Chesbro, Ed Delahanty. You name him, he was jumping from one league to the other.

So I signed.

Mr. Hart immediately called up the ball park and got the manager of the Cubs, Frank Selee, on the phone. 'I've just signed a new outfielder,' he said. 'I won't tell you who he is, but take it from me he's OK. Put him in center field this afternoon.'

So Selee went out on the field and one of the players told me later he looked sort of bewildered.

'Mr. Hart just called me,' he said. He says we've got a new outfielder and I should play him today, but he won't tell me who he is. Things are getting funnier and funnier around this place.'"[6]

Jones showed up at West Side Park for the May 14 game against Brooklyn. He played center field the rest of the home stand, which concluded against Boston, Philadelphia, and New York. Chicago won enough games to end the home stand with a record of 20–10, second to Pittsburgh's 27–5. As of their travel day, May 26, Chicago had played 26 games at home, four on the road. President Hart was impressed enough that on May 24 he purchased the stock of his two minority stockholders and now owned the franchise 100 percent. On May 27, the *Chicago Daily News* coined a new name for Selee's team. It reported, "Frank Selee will devote his strongest efforts on the team work of the new Cubs, this year."[7] This was the origin of the nickname the Chicago NL team still carries. However, the *Tribune* continued to call the team the Colts until after the end of Selee's tenure.

The road trip started with three games in St. Louis, Chicago winning two. The next games were on Decoration Day in Pittsburgh. In the first game of this doubleheader, another incident occurred that was recorded by Davy Jones in *The Glory of Their Times*. This incident was not reported in the *Chicago Tribune* story, but this game is the only game on record that fits the circumstances. In Jones' words:

> We had a young pitcher on that club named Jimmy St. Vrain. He was a left-handed pitcher and a right-handed batter. But an absolutely terrible hitter—never got a loud foul off anybody.
>
> Well, one day we were playing the Pittsburgh Pirates and Jimmy was pitching for us. The first two times he went up to bat that day he looked simply awful. So when he came back after striking out the second time Frank Selee, our manager, said, "Jimmy, you're a left-handed pitcher, why don't you turn around and bat from the left side, too? Why not try it?"
>
> Actually, Frank was half kidding, but Jimmy took him seriously. So the next time he went up he batted left-handed. Turned around and stood on the opposite side of the plate from where he was used to, you know. And darned if he didn't actually hit the ball. He tapped a slow roller down to Honus Wagner at shortstop and took off as fast as he could go ... but instead of running to first base, he headed for third.
>
> Oh, my God! What bedlam! Everybody yelling and screaming at poor Jimmy as he raced to third base, head down, spikes flying, determined to get there ahead of the throw. Later on, Honus told us that as a matter of fact he almost did throw the ball to third.
>
> "I'm standing there with the ball in my hand," Honus said, "looking at this guy running from home to third and for an instant there I swear I didn't know where to throw the damn ball. And when I finally did throw to first, I wasn't at all sure it was the right thing to do!"[8]

The two teams split this doubleheader before a total crowd of 18,500. Chicago then had two rainouts in two days in two different cities. The final game in Pittsburgh was scheduled for Saturday, May 31. It was rained out after three innings. there was no Sunday ball in Pittsburgh. Both teams traveled to Chicago to play on Sunday, June 1. That game was rained out before it started. Then Chicago headed to New York. Lots of train time. The *Chicago Tribune* story about the trip to New York noted, "Before the train started Mr. Selee pulled off the customary drawing for upper and lower berths, he and Captain Lowe taking the same chance as the others. Schaefer, who makes his first trip with the team, drew an upper and could not understand how Chance, Kling and some of the old-timers were lucky and secured lowers. Selee holds the slips face downward in his hand and the players take turns at drawing. Chance told Schaefer he could see through the backs, but the latter was suspicious."[9]

Taylor pitched the first game in New York with Chance at catcher and Schaefer at first base. Taylor did what he commonly did. He finished the game. Taylor finished every game he started in 1902, 1903, 1904, and 1905. New York won two of three games in this series, which featured more important moves off the field. New York had protested two Chicago victories on May 7 and 8 in Chicago because the pitching distance was too short. To everyone's surprise, the protest was upheld and the teams were told to replay the games when next in Chicago. On June 4, Selee signed two players from the University of Illinois, Carl Lundgren and Jake Stahl. Selee asked George Huff, the University of Illinois coach, to scout Harvard players for him. This was the start of an important relationship for the Chicago NL team.

When the team moved on to Brooklyn, Selee moved Schaefer to third base. Brooklyn took three of four games. Their first game in Boston featured a ceremony before the game. Selee was presented a gold watch from "Boston Friends" before the game was rained out. Boston swept the two games played. The Colts then lost two of three games in Philadelphia. The road trip ended with two games in Cincinnati. Carl Lundgren made his major league debut on June 19, winning 7–5, with Chance as his catcher. Chicago won the final game for a two-game sweep of Cincinnati. They returned home with a record of 27–21, in second place.

The next series started with a classic game. Both Jack Taylor and Deacon Phillippe pitched 19 innings in a 3–2 Chicago win over Pittsburgh. Chicago walked off on Kling's single with one out, a stolen base, and Lowe's RBI single, his fourth hit of the game. Selee spent this entire year adjusting his roster. On the next day, June 23, he secured Jimmy St. Vrain's signature on a contract for 1903 and sent St. Vrain to the minors in Memphis for the rest of the year. That was understandable, as St. Vrain was 19 years old. St. Vrain's contract situation was complicated by claims from other teams he had played for in the minors, and St. Vrain never returned to the Chicago team or to the majors.

Pittsburgh won the remaining three games of the series. Tinker got into a fight with Wid Conroy of Pittsburgh, and both were suspended for

10 games. Tinker left the team to return to his home in Kansas City and was gone when his suspension was reduced to two games. Selee telegraphed Tinker to come back to the team. Tinker was present for the next series in St. Louis. The first date was a doubleheader. Kling caught both games, including one with Taylor as pitcher. Selee had seen enough of his catchers to decide that Kling was going to be his main catcher. There was another doubleheader the next day. Chance caught the first game, Kling the second. This was followed by a rainout, then another doubleheader. The catching was split again. This six-game series was split.

The next day was July 4, a doubleheader in Chicago against Boston. Boston won both, plus the next game for a sweep. Pittsburgh came to town for one game on July 6, a Sunday, as Boston still did not play Sunday games. Chicago beat the first-place Pirates. Kling caught all these games, and Chance played right field. Selee had acquired a first baseman named Fred Clark who had been playing the last few games. Clark hurt his hand but refused to come out. New York came to town, and big news was announced the day of a doubleheader. John McGraw, who had been in the American League since the beginning of 1901, had signed as manager of the New York Giants. McGraw's preferred rough style of play and umpire baiting had led to many conflicts with AL President Ban Johnson. This was McGraw's solution. The doubleheader turned out to be the only games of this series. The first date was rained out, then the doubleheader (second game shortened by rain), then another rainout.

In the doubleheader, the style of baseball that was coming into prominence in the 1900s was on display. In the 1890s, particularly after the change in pitching distance, baseball was an offensive game featuring high scoring. By 1902, pitchers had adjusted to the pitching distance and were beginning to dominate the game. In the July 8 doubleheader, three runs were scored. New York won the first game, 1–0, behind Christy Mathewson. Chicago won the rain-shortened second game in seven innings, 2–0, behind Carl Lundgren. Philadelphia came to town, and Chicago won two of three games. In the middle game, Chance started as catcher. Chance was hit in the head on the follow-through swing of a batter but remained in the game. Later he tried to stop a wild pitch with his bare hand and had to come out. This was the last game Chance caught this year.

July 13 was supposed to be an off-day for both Chicago and New York. But because of the rainouts earlier this home stand, New York came to Chicago for a doubleheader. John McGraw was present as manager of New York. Carl Lundgren and Bob Rhoades gave up one total run for a Chicago sweep. Brooklyn came in next and took two of three. Lundgren played shortstop in the first two games due to an injury. This home stand was broken up by a short trip to Pittsburgh. The first-place Pirates won two of three games. Chicago returned home for one more series against Cincinnati. Cincinnati won three of five games in another series marred by a rainout. Selee had been trying to find the best spot to play Frank Chance now that he had decided on Kling as his catcher. Chance had been playing the outfield. On July 23 against Cincinnati Chance played first base for the first time this year. He would play first base 39 times in 1902, all after July 23.

The next road trip started in Boston, where Chicago won three of five. In the second game, Jack Taylor beat Vic Willis, 1–0. The Colts run scored when Chance walked, stole second, and scored on Tinker's RBI single. The next game was won, 3–1, in 13 innings. In the 13th, the Colts scored two runs on a walk, Tinker's RBI double, and Lowe's RBI single. Before Chicago left Boston, the *Chicago Tribune* commented, "Selee made a good move in putting Chance at first base."[10] Chicago went to Philadelphia and swept three games. They won the second game, 7–2, in 12 innings. In the 12th, Chance hit an inside-the-park grand slam.

During this series, there was a small item in the *Chicago Tribune*: "Terre Haute's best pitcher has been sold to the St. Louis Nationals, but will not leave until their race is over."[11] No name was given, but one famous pitcher fits this description, Mordecai Brown. We will hear more of him later. After much shuffling of players due to lack of performance and injuries, Selee settled on a lineup for the Philadelphia series: Davy Jones RF, Jimmy Slagle LF, Frank Chance 1B, Johnny Dobbs CF, Joe Tinker SS, Bobby Lowe 2B, John Kling C, Germany Schaefer 3B. The road trip would finish in New York against both New York and Brooklyn. The first game against New York led to adding another game. It was a 3–3 tie in 13 innings. This caused a doubleheader on Saturday, August 9, which was split before 12,000 fans. There was no Sunday ball in New York. Another doubleheader was to be played on Monday. The first game was started late due to wet grounds. It ended up a 3–3 tie after 11 innings before being called for darkness. The Colts and Giants had two more games to make up. Brooklyn won the first two games before Chicago won the final game of the road trip. Bobby Lowe was ejected for arguing in the second game of the series, and Taylor finished the game playing second base. Taylor threw a complete game victory in the final game. Chicago returned home with a record of 51–44.

Chicago started the next home stand with a roster of 13 players. In the first game against New York, pitcher Jocko Menafee played right field and batted leadoff. Menafee played first base in the finale against New York, who won both games. By the start of the next series against Philadelphia, Chance and Jones were out. Jones had typhoid fever and would be out the rest of the year. Pitchers Menafee and Pop Williams played in the field. Philadelphia swept the three games. In the final game, local Chicago semi-pro player Chick Pedro played right field. His entire career was two games, and he went 0-for-6. Boston came to town for two games. Chicago lost the first for an eight-game losing streak, putting them one game below .500. Chicago broke out offensively in the second game against Boston, scoring 14 runs in a win. Brooklyn finished the home stand with three games in two days. Chicago swept the doubleheader on August 24 to end the home stand. The final inning of the second game was the bottom of the 12th. Chicago walked off on a two-out walk and an RBI double by Dobbs. Chicago ended the home stand with a record of 54–53.

The next road trip started in Pittsburgh. Pittsburgh ran away with the pennant in the National League, ending up with a 103–36 record and a 27½-game margin. Pittsburgh took two of three games in this series. At the end of the prior home stand, Selee had contacted an unnamed scout in the east and asked the scout to send him an infielder. The scout sent a 5'9", 125-pound, left-handed hitter from Troy, New York. Johnny Evers made his first appearance with Chicago on Labor Day, September 1, in Philadelphia. The infield that day was Chance 1B, Lowe 2B, Evers SS, Tinker 3B (all are in the Hall of Fame). Chance played on September 1, but not on September 2, suffering another minor injury.

In his first game, Evers had eight chances and made four errors. After the game, Evers thought he would be sent back to Troy. After dinner, Selee told Evers to get some sleep (Evers had not slept or eaten on his train ride from Troy to Philadelphia) and what time to report for tomorrow's game. Evers said, "Then you are not going to can me, after the fizzle I made?" Selee replied, "We don't do things that way in the big leagues. I heard of you riding down from Troy in the smoker car, without eating anything for 12 hours. No wonder you had a bad afternoon. I'll bet a hat that you will have a better one tomorrow."[12]

Philadelphia took three of four games over these two days. A pitcher picked up from the minors, Frank "Deacon" Morrissey, pitched the first game of the next series in Brooklyn. He lost, but the next game was won 1–0 by another new pitcher, Alex Hardy. In the game on September 4, Tinker played shortstop, Evers second base. Brooklyn won the series, two games to one. Kling had caught every game for two months. Selee acquired a backup catcher to give Kling an occasional break. Selee did not want to put Chance back behind the plate. A trip to Boston resulted in another series loss, two of three. The final stop on this trip was New York. The teams split four games in two days. Morrissey and Hardy pitched in this series. Chicago's record on returning home was 60–64.

The home stand started with a make-up game against St. Louis. The starting infield for this game was Chance 1B, Evers 2B, Tinker SS, Schaefer 3B. Lowe was injured and out for the rest of the year. Chance played four innings in this game before suffering another minor injury. Later in

Johnny Evers soon after he started with Chicago. He got off to a bad start, but Selee stuck with him just like Tinker.

the game, there was a double play listed as Tinker to Evers to Menafee. Cincinnati came to town for four games. In the second game, there was a double play listed as Tinker to Evers to Chance, the first time this appeared in a box score. That happened during the second game of a doubleheader on Sunday, September 14, before a crowd of 8,500. The single game on the following Monday drew a crowd of 260. Cincinnati won three of four games before both teams headed to Cincinnati for two games. After a rainout, Chicago swept a doubleheader, then headed back to Chicago. Pittsburgh swept a doubleheader, ending their season series. The home season ended with a doubleheader sweep of St. Louis after two rainouts. The season ended with a doubleheader in St. Louis, which Chicago swept. The *Chicago Tribune* stated that the Chicago team broke even financially this season. After several exhibition games in the Midwest, Selee returned to Chicago on October 11. He went to the doctor and was confined to his hotel room with pleurisy.

The 1902 season was mostly an open tryout run by Selee to see what he had and what he needed for the Chicago NL team. Twenty-eight position players and 11 pitchers were used in 1902. Remember that the normal roster size on any date during 1902 was 15–16. A lot of this movement was due to the AL-NL war. There were hopes of a peace settlement between the leagues in the upcoming off-season. However, Selee had signed pitcher Jake Weimer for the 1903 season. Chicago AL owner Charles Comiskey claimed in the October 18 *Chicago Tribune* that he had Weimer under contract as well for 1903. Peace had not yet been secured. Home attendance for Chicago NL increased from 205,071 in 1901 to 263,700 in 1902. This was still behind the total for Chicago AL, which had won the pennant in 1901 (total home attendance 354,350) and lost after a close race in 1902 (337,898).

The best performers for the Colts would be coming back in 1903. Jack Taylor was the steadiest pitcher with 36 appearances, 33 starts, 33 complete games and a record of 23–11. Jocko Menafee did well enough for a

Frank Chance later in his career with Chicago. Note the bat, not much thinner at the handle than the hitting end.

34-year-old with a 12–10 record. Of the several young pitchers tried out, Selee kept Carl Lundgren, who had a 9–9 record with a 1.97 ERA in 18 starts. In the outfield, Selee would keep Jimmy Slagle and Davy Jones. Slagle had a fine year, hitting .315 with 40 stolen bases. Jones did well in limited action, hitting .305 in 64 games. And he had a contract for 1903. Selee was convinced he had found his first baseman in Frank Chance. Chance was not sure yet, still thinking he might be a catcher. Selee was sure. Selee saw that the competitiveness in Chance would cause fewer problems at first base than at catcher. Chance's attitude was summarized best by Christy Mathewson in his 1912 book *Pitching in A Pinch*: "Chance is the sort of athlete who is likely to get injured…. If he has to choose between accepting a pair of spikes in a vital part of his anatomy and getting a put-out, or dodging the spikes and losing the put-out, he always takes the put-out."[13]

Bobby Lowe had been adequate at second base before getting injured, but Selee knew how much Lowe had played the last 13 years. Johnny Evers had played well in his 24-game trial. Lowe was 33, Evers 20. Joe Tinker had made it through the entire season, mostly playing shortstop. Tinker's fielding was iffy. He committed 74 errors, 72 at shortstop. His offense was quite good for a shortstop, batting .273 with 28 stolen bases. Selee was satisfied with Tinker and willing to give Evers a long look next spring. Germany Schaefer had been poor at third base, hitting .196. John Kling had been excellent at catcher, hitting .286 and fielding very well in 112 games. The normal workload for a catcher in the National League in 1902 (other than Kling) was 80 games. Selee's work over the winter would be to find an outfielder, a third baseman, a backup catcher, and some pitchers.

Building Another Championship Team

After much negotiation, peace was achieved between the American and National Leagues over the winter of 1902–1903. The contracts that were in place were all to be honored, and a three-man commission would settle any disputes. This commission consisted of AL President Ban Johnson, NL President (vacant), and Cincinnati owner Garry Herrmann. Herrmann had been a major force behind the peace settlement, and the AL owners trusted him to give them a fair shake. On March 3, 1903, Harry Pulliam was named NL President. The *Chicago Tribune* said that Pulliam was a straw man for the three owners in the NL that had the most power: Chicago owner James Hart, Pittsburgh owner Barney Dreyfuss, and Cincinnati owner Garry Herrmann. However this played out, the war was over. Selee could build his team without worrying about players jumping from the AL to NL and vice versa.

One of the consequences of the peace settlement was that the Chicago NL team was awarded Jake Weimer instead of the Chicago AL team. Selee secured another new pitcher from St. Louis NL over the winter. He traded Bob Rhoads, a 22-year-old right-hander, for Bob Wicker, a 24-year-old right-hander. These pitchers were comparable in 1902, but Selee saw something in Wicker that led him to make this deal. Before the peace settlement took effect, Selee and Hart persuaded a veteran player from the Detroit AL team to jump. This player would fill the perceived gap at third base. Doc Casey (a dentist in the off season) was 32 years old and had been in the big leagues as a third baseman since 1898. They had a line out on another player to replace Johnny Dobbs in the outfield. Dick Harley was 30 years old and had been in the big leagues since 1897. By the time the team left for spring training, Dobbs was still on the team and Harley was a free agent. Casey and Dobbs were among the group that left Chicago on March 6. Their destination was Los Angeles, where spring training would be held. Selee was already in LA, having spent some of the winter there for his health. While the team was in transit, the news broke that wherever the team finished in the pennant race, they would have a post-season series. Hart and Charles Comiskey signed a contract for a 15-game series to take place between the Chicago NL and AL teams from October 1 through 15, 1903.

The first exhibition game showed that this spring training was a bit different from last year in Champaign. The Colts beat the LA minor league team, 7–6, in 10 innings, before a crowd of 7,000. The team remained in LA until March 24, playing five exhibitions and having three rained out. Selee signed a contract for the team to return for spring training in 1904. Captain Bobby Lowe praised the team on March 18, saying they would have a say in who won the pennant. From March 25 through April 12, the team barnstormed through a tour that ended in Chicago. The stops were: Deming, New Mexico; Albuquerque; Pueblo, Colorado; Denver; Omaha; Davenport, Iowa. The team either played the resident minor league team or an intrasquad game. The *Chicago Tribune* weighed in on the pros and cons of a trip like this, which were conducted by both Chicago teams before the 1903 season. The *Tribune* came out against these trips, and Ban Johnson agreed with this opinion.[14] The weather did not improve on their arrival in Chicago. An intrasquad game scheduled for April 12 was hailed out after three innings. The season was to open in St. Louis on April 14. The team traveled to St. Louis on the 12th so they could practice on the 13th. That was rained out.

One piece of business Selee had not yet accomplished was convincing Frank Chance that he was a first baseman. When the lineup for the first game was turned in, it read: Jones RF, Slagle LF, Kling C, Dobbs CF, Tinker 3B, Evers SS, Lowe 2B, Bob Hanlon 1B. This lineup held for the first series, which was a four-game split. In the final game of the series, St. Louis won a five-inning, rain-shortened game. The St. Louis pitcher, making his major league debut, was Mordecai Brown. On the way to Chicago after this series, the Colts played an exhibition game against the University of Illinois team. Carl Lundgren pitched for the Colts, and Selee said after the game that he had a verbal contract with Jake Stahl to join the Colts after he graduated in June. Frank Chance was the catcher in this game. While there is no record of this, I suspect that Selee made an agreement with U of I coach George Huff to scout for the Colts after the U of I season was over. We will see the results of that agreement later.

Opening Day in Chicago was rained out. The scheduled four-game series with Cincinnati turned into three, with Chicago winning two. The final game of this short home stand was on Sunday, April 26 against Pittsburgh. The overflow crowd surrounded the field to the point that the Colts had to call more police to control the crowd. The paid attendance was 24,255. The *Chicago Tribune* said that at least 30,000 fans saw the game, including those on rooftops. The Colts won, 9–6.

The team went on the road until May 30, with one exception that will be noted, visiting all the other cities in the league. The first game at Cincinnati saw Chance at first base for the first time this year. The lineup on April 28 was: Jones RF, Slagle LF, Chance 1B, Dobbs CF, Tinker SS, Casey 3B, Lowe 2B, Kling C. The series was a four-game split. The next series started in Pittsburgh with a Saturday game won by Chicago. No Sunday ball was played in Pittsburgh. The teams traveled to Chicago for a game on Sunday. Pittsburgh won, 3–2, in 11 innings before another overflow crowd of 15,000. Kling was given the day off. Tommy Raub, the third catcher, started and had to leave with a split finger. Per the *Chicago Tribune*, Captain Lowe made these changes: Chance from 1B to C, Lowe from 2B to 1B, Evers to 2B. The teams returned to Pittsburgh after the game. Evers was back on the bench for the next game but played the day after. The *Chicago Tribune* reported: "Captain Lowe sent Evers in his place and the youngster put up a good game. Lowe has a bad knee, but could have played. He wanted to give the youngster a chance."[15] Pittsburgh won three of five games in this series played in both home parks.

During the next series in St. Louis, Dobbs was released and Harley signed to replace him. Pitcher Alex Hardy was released after pitching in his third game. Chicago swept four games in St. Louis. Both teams got on the same train after the final game to travel to New York. Lowe started the series in Brooklyn in the lineup at second base. He had three stolen bases in a Chicago win and returned to the bench the next day. Evers returned to the lineup the next day for Chicago's eighth straight win. Chicago took three of four games from Brooklyn. Lowe played first base in the third game after Chance was ejected for arguing with the umpire.

The next stop was Boston. The first game there was on Saturday, May 16. The largest crowd of the year so far in Boston, 4,904, turned out to greet Selee. Chicago swept the three games. Selee's mother attended the game on May 19, which was rained out after two innings. This was the first time it was noted that Selee's mother attended a game he managed in his career. During the next stop of the road trip in Philadelphia, Selee took the entire team to a hat store and bought them all Panama hats, courtesy of James Hart. During the series, Dick Harley had the team over to his new home in Philadelphia. The team responded by sweeping the four-game series. The final stop of the trip was in New York. Chicago lost the first two games by one run. Taylor won the final game, 7–1. The crowds in New York averaged over 10,000 per game. Chicago went 17–5 on this road trip, returning home one game behind New York in second place.

The home stand started with three games against St. Louis. Chicago swept this series and the next two-game series with Brooklyn. This six-game win streak moved the Colts into first place, 3½ games ahead of New York. New York took care of that lead in the next series, sweeping four games in Chicago. A good example of Chicago's problems took place in the sixth inning on June 6. The score was 4–3 in favor of New York. Chicago's half of the sixth went: Slagle 1B, Chance ground-rule 2B, Jones 1B, Slagle scored and Chance out at plate, Tinker 1B, Jones to second, Jones caught stealing third, Kling walk, Wicker out. Chicago had three singles, a double and a walk and scored one run to tie the game. New York scored three runs in the ninth to win. James Hart could take solace at the attendance figures for the series: 9,000; 5,500; 15,000; 20,000.

In the first game of the next series against Boston, Selee elected to bat first to change their luck. It worked in the first game. Chicago swept the three games against Boston. The home stand concluded with four games scheduled against Philadelphia. The first game on June 11 was "colded out"[16] per the *Chicago Tribune*. Philadelphia won two of the three games played. The *Tribune* complained that the June 12 game was too slow, lasting 2:30 for a nine-inning game. The June 13 game was lost due to two errors committed by the infield in the ninth inning. The score was 2–2 when a Philadelphia batter hit a grounder to Evers at shortstop. Evers made a bad throw and the batter went to third base. Chance threw to third to try to get the runner, made a bad throw, and the batter scored. Nowadays we call that a Little League home run. Chicago went on the road with a 34–17 record, tied with Pittsburgh for second place behind New York.

Tinker had been gone for about a week due to a sick mother. He returned to the team in Pittsburgh when the road trip started. Lowe had been playing second base and Evers shortstop. By this point, it was clear that Lowe was going to be the utility man in the infield, which would consist of Casey, Tinker, Evers, and Chance. None of those players hit in the first game, won by Pittsburgh, 3–0. Pitcher Jocko Menefee got the only hit for Chicago. Pittsburgh swept the two-game series. In the next series, two umpires were assigned to the games in New York. As had happened in the late 1890s, the National League would assign two umpires to games with the team they considered the rowdiest. In the late 1890s, that was Baltimore with John McGraw. Now, it was New York, managed by John McGraw.

The series in New York was supposed to be four games. After two rainouts and a Sunday off, three games were played. Chicago won two of three. Pittsburgh was on a 14-game winning streak and took over first place from New York on June 20. The rain continued during the next series in Brooklyn. A doubleheader on June 25 were the only games played. The doubleheader was split. Pittsburgh lost a game on the 25th after an 18-game winning streak. Next came four games in Boston with a Sunday off. Boston won the first three games. For Sunday, Selee had scheduled an exhibition game in Troy, New York, Evers' hometown. The team returned to Boston for another game, which ended in a 0–0 tie after nine innings when rain came. Selee had signed a young left-handed pitcher named Jake Doscher. Doscher got the one decision of his career with Chicago in Philadelphia, a loss. The winning pitcher in this game was Pop Williams, whom Selee had released three weeks ago. Philadelphia won two of three games. The final game started a half-hour early so Chicago could catch a train back to Chicago. The road trip ended with the standings: Pittsburgh 43–20, New York 38–21, Chicago 38–26.

The home stand started with a July 4 doubleheader against New York. Chicago won the first game, and the second was rained out. In the next game, the New York catcher was hit by a foul ball, resulting in a split finger on his throwing hand. McGraw called Roger Bresnahan, a regular player for New York who had been given the day off and was sitting in the stands, out of the stands to replace the injured catcher. Selee protested due to the rules saying a player must be in uniform starting the game to play. This protest would be denied. New York won the final two of the three-game series.

By the start of the next series against Philadelphia, Chicago had some serious injuries. Lowe was out for the year with a broken kneecap. Chance and Casey were out with minor injuries. Casey came back for the second game in the four-game series. Before the third game, Selee had a clubhouse meeting to select a new captain. Lowe had been the captain and would not play the rest of the year. Instead of announcing his selection, which was how Selee had picked a captain in the past, Selee allowed the active players to elect one. Per Johnny Evers' account, Selee made it known he preferred Doc Casey to be elected. The players voted Chance 11, Casey 4, Kling 2. Selee named Frank Chance captain before the July 9 game.[17]

Chicago won three of four games against Philadelphia. Before the first game against Brooklyn, Lowe was given a watch by the Chicago players, Selee making the presentation. The four-game series with Brooklyn was split. Selee had picked up utility infielder Otto Williams from St. Louis. Selee thought Tinker was worn out, so he sent him home for a couple of days. Williams would be the fifth infielder the rest of the year. Four games against Boston were split. The final game was the second game of a doubleheader on July 18. Boston won, 5–4, after 8½ innings due to an agreed-on end time so Boston could catch a train.

First-place Pittsburgh came to town for three games. Chicago swept this series. Tinker returned in the second game after a five-day rest. Cincinnati came for a four-game series, which was split. The final two games were a doubleheader that started at 2 p.m. There was no problem finishing the games before darkness, with both games lasting less than two hours. The final series of this home stand, which had featured every National League team, was against St. Louis. In the first game, the regular lineup made its appearance for the first time in a month. This lineup was: Slagle LF, Casey 3B, Chance 1B, Evers 2B, Jones CF, Harley RF, Kling C, Tinker SS. Chicago won three of four games. Mordecai Brown pitched in the game on July 28 in relief for St. Louis.

During this series, first-place Pittsburgh issued a challenge to first-place Boston of the AL to meet in a post-season series if both won the pennant. Bobby Lowe agreed to be the manager of Denver in the minor leagues for the rest of the year. Standings after the Colts' longest home stand of the year: Pittsburgh 57–28, Chicago 54–36, New York 48–34.

Four games in Cincinnati were split. Both the Chicago wins were shutouts, pitched by Weimer and Wicker. While the prior home stand had been against all the other teams in the NL, there was one more home series before a long road trip. Pittsburgh came to town for four games. Menefee pitched another shutout in the first game. The only run was scored in the first inning when Slagle singled, Casey sacrificed, and Chance drove in the run with a single. Taylor won the next game before both teams were off on August 6. On August 7, the Colts played an exhibition game in Woodstock, Illinois. All the regulars played except Kling. The final two games against Pittsburgh were played on Saturday and Sunday. Total attendance for these two dates was 25,500. After this series, the standings were: Pittsburgh 61–32, New York 55–36, Chicago 58–40.

On the way east, the Colts stopped in Manchester, New Hampshire, for an exhibition game on August 11. A member of the Manchester team, James Murray, had secured a judgment against the Chicago team after his tryout with Chicago in 1902. All the Colts' proceeds were seized. The game was played to its completion before the Colts headed to Boston. Chicago won two of three games in Boston. While in Boston, Selee was told that the Philadelphia series was off due to the collapse of the grandstand at the Philadelphia ballpark. Selee was able to arrange three exhibition games for this stretch. Regular play resumed in Brooklyn on August 19. This four-game series was split. Chicago moved into second place, ½-game ahead of its next opponent, New York. Three of the four games scheduled with New York were played, but the final game was a rainout. Chicago won two of three. The rainout would not be made up, as this was Chicago's last trip to New York this year. Cincinnati swept two games in Cincinnati before both teams got on the same train to Chicago.

The first two dates in Chicago were rained out. Chicago won the first game on August 31. On this date, Joe McGinnity pitched and won both games of a doubleheader for New York. Cincinnati won the final game between the two teams on September 1. Selee saw something he would see several more times in the next game. On September 2, St. Louis beat Chicago. The winning pitcher was Mordecai Brown. Chicago swept a doubleheader the next day to take the series. Selee had soured on Dick Harley in the outfield, so he signed free agent Jack McCarthy for the final month. Pittsburgh came to town for a make-up game before both teams headed to Pittsburgh. The league office must have been confused, because no umpire showed up for this game. Players Menefee (Chicago) and Harry Smith (Pittsburgh) umpired a Pittsburgh win that started 15 minutes early so both teams could make their 5:30 train. The Colts had publicized this Sunday game, which drew 12,000. These two teams finished their season series in Pittsburgh with a five-game series. Nineteen thousand fans came to the first date, a Labor Day doubleheader. Chicago won four of five. Chicago was the first team since 1900 to win a season series from Pittsburgh. The standings after this series: Pittsburgh 83–40, New York 74–49, Chicago 73–50.

Before the next series, Selee purchased outfielder Archie Marshall from the Troy, New York, minor league club. He was still experimenting with the third spot in the outfield. Slagle and Jones both played over 130 games this year, but the other outfield spot was up for grabs. In the first game against Brooklyn, Selee started Clarence Currie, a 22-year-old, on a tryout. Brooklyn and Chicago split the four-game series. Philadelphia came to town for four games. A doubleheader was scheduled for September 15 and rained out. A doubleheader was scheduled for September 16 and rained out. Doubleheaders were played on September 17 and 18. Chicago won the first three games. In the final game, Chick Fraser of Philadelphia no-hit the Colts in a 10–0 game. This was the first no-hitter in the NL this year. Pittsburgh clinched the pennant on September 18. Chicago was 1½ games behind New York for second place, with New York coming to town for four games. After the Philadelphia series, Selee made an argument in the *Chicago Tribune* for abolishing doubleheaders. "From the standpoint of the players and public, it is too much of a strain on the players, who cannot maintain top speed for three of four hours as well as for half the time."[18] No one was listening. The town was still interested in the race for second place. The attendance on Saturday and Sunday was 10,000 and 24,000. The series was split, so New York remained in 2nd by 1½ games with three games to play. Chicago won two of three games from Boston in the final series. Final standings: Pittsburgh 91–49, New York 84–55, Chicago 82–56.

After the 1903 season, there was the 15-game series to be played against the Chicago AL team. James Hart had offered a "substantial prize" to his players if they won the series, per an article in the *Chicago Tribune* on September 27. John Kling had been sent home for a five-day rest. When the series started on October 1, the regulars for both teams played. Jack Taylor pitched a shutout. We may think that all the attention of baseball fans would be on the World Series at this time. That would be incorrect. There was a World Series this year, best of nine between the pennant winners Pittsburgh and Boston. But at the same time, the Chicago teams played a series, Cincinnati played St. Louis AL, and Cleveland played St. Louis NL.

The 15-game Chicago series ended in a 7–7 tie with one rainout, as the teams could not agree to play another game. Charles Comiskey, the Chicago AL owner, awarded his team $2,500 (total) to split. One statement made after the series showed potential problems. Jack Taylor had pitched a shutout in the first game and was shelled in his three other starts. Taylor was allegedly quoted as saying, "Why should I have won? I got $100 from Hart for winning and $500 for losing." The record of the two leagues in the interleague games, including the World Series, was 29–20 in favor of the American League. The attendance figures for 1903 reflected the performance of each club in Chicago this year. Chicago NL attendance was 386,205 with a third-place finish. Chicago AL attendance was 286,183 with a seventh-place finish.

Selee had done a fine job of building up the Colts. Going from 53–86 in 1901 to 68–69 in 1902 to 82–56 showed considerable improvement. The team had three 20-game winners in 1903: Jack Taylor 21–14, Jake Weimer 20–8, and Bob Wicker 20–9. Carl Lundgren was 11–9 and Jocko Menefee 8–10. Menefee was 35 years old and would not return. It appeared Selee had settled on four pitchers and was looking for one more. He was happy with his infield. Chance was the best first baseman in the league with an average of .327 and 67 stolen bases. Evers and Tinker were developing young players. Doc Casey was steady at third base. These three all hit over .290. Kling had caught 132 games and hit .293. No problem there. Jones and Slagle both hit over .290 in the outfield. Selee was still looking for another outfielder. Chance had proven himself a good leader as captain. This year showed that

5. Chicago

the National League could become a two-level league. Pittsburgh, New York and Chicago were much better than the other five teams. Pittsburgh was three-time champion, but now had two serious teams to contend with.

After spring training in 1902, Selee had hired George Huff, the athletic director and baseball coach of the University of Illinois, as a scout. The first fruit of that relationship had been Carl Lundgren, now established on the Chicago pitching staff. Selee had a verbal agreement with Jake Stahl from the U of I to join the Colts after his 1903 graduation. Boston AL came in with a better offer, and Stahl signed with Boston. During the 1903 college season, the U of I had played Notre Dame. Huff was impressed with a pitcher for Notre Dame, Ed Reulbach. After the college season, Huff heard of a good pitcher in Sedalia, Missouri, named Lawson. By the time Huff got to Sedalia, Lawson had disappeared. Huff then heard of a good pitcher in Vermont named Sheldon. After visiting Vermont, Huff realized that Lawson and Sheldon were really Ed Reulbach, a common practice among college players at the time to earn some money during the summer. Huff signed Reulbach to a contract to play in the minors in 1904 while under the control of the Colts. Huff was just getting started in his contributions to the Colts.

There were rumors about Jack Taylor throwing three of his games during the series with the Chicago AL team after the 1903 season. Taylor had been a workhorse for the Colts since 1898. He was working on a string of 80 straight complete games. His records for the Colts in the last three years were 13–19, 23–11, and 21–14. Taylor was 29 years old and in his prime. But Hart and Selee believed the rumors about Taylor and made him available for trade. They consulted Chance, who recommended Mordecai Brown as a target. This resulted in a trade with St. Louis: Jack Taylor and catcher Larry McLean to St. Louis for Mordecai Brown and catcher Jack O'Neil. O'Neil had been the main catcher for St. Louis in 1903, but the Colts did not need a catcher. Brown was the main component in the trade for Chicago. Brown had gone 9–13 for a last-place team in St. Louis and had impressed the Colts hitters and Selee. This turned out to be a key move in building the Chicago team.

On February 28, NL and AL owners met in New York to try to set up non-competing schedules, a major factor in leagues that shared five cities (St. Louis, Chicago, Boston, New York, and Philadelphia). Selee arrived in Los Angeles for spring training on March 2. Four Chicago players were already there: Chance, Tinker, Kling, and McCarthy. The remaining players were to leave Chicago on March 3. The 13 players on the train were: O'Neil, Weimer, Wicker, Lundgren, Brown, Briggs, Corridon, Casey, Evers, Moriarity, Slagle, Jones, and Holmes. The schedule was issued on March 4. The length of the season was increased from 140 to 154 games (two more games against each team). The two Chicago teams had 12 conflicting dates.

On March 6, Selee told the *Chicago Tribune*, "Pittsburgh should not be considered the favorite for the NL pennant. Cincinnati and New York should be favorites along with Chicago, if I can get two more hard-hitting outfielders."[19] Practice started on March 9. Hitting practice stressed bunting and hit-and-run plays. Selee gave his starting lineup: Slagle CF, Casey 3B, Chance 1B, McCarthy LF, Tinker SS, Kling C, Jones RF, Evers 2B. The pitchers would be Weimer, Wicker, and Lundgren as carryovers, joined by Mordecai Brown and Herbert "Buttons" Briggs. Briggs had been in the majors from 1896 to 1898 with the Colts and in the minors since. Selee remembered him and got him back for 1904. Frank Corridon had been in spring training with the Colts in 1903. He had made the team, then suffered a season-ending illness in May. The utilitymen would be determined during the residence in Los Angeles and the tour heading back to Chicago.

Chicago played games in Los Angeles from March 12 to March 15, then hit the road. From March 16 to March 23, games were played in various California town, from Bakersfield to Fresno to San Francisco to Sacramento. The next stops, Reno and Granger, Wyoming, were snowed out. After watching a traveling actor threaten a waiter on the train for slow service and get thrown off the train, the team arrived in Denver. The team stayed in Colorado from March 26 to April 10, playing in Denver, Colorado Springs, and Pueblo. On April 9, Jones yawned and dislocated his jaw. Doc Casey was called and popped the jaw back into place. Jones was able to eat that evening. Two more games, in Grand Island and Omaha, ended the exhibition season. The team returned to Chicago on April 13, dropped belongings at their rooms, and boarded a late train to Cincinnati. The roster was set at 16 players: Kling and Jack O'Neill C; Chance, Evers, Tinker, Casey IF; Slagle, Jones, McCarthy OF, Otto Williams utility; Brown, Briggs, Corridon, Lundgren, Weimer, and Wicker P.

The season opened on April 14 in Cincinnati. A crowd of 13,000 turned out, requiring special ground rules as the overflow stood in the outfield behind ropes. Weimer was the pitcher for the Colts in a 3–2 loss. The next day was a 5–5 tie called by darkness. The final two games of the series were split. The final game was on Sunday, April 17. Mordecai Brown made his first start for the Colts before a crowd of 16,000 (in the outfield again) and was shelled. The Colts lost, 12–3. As Mordecai "Three Finger" Brown would end up in the Hall of Fame, games like this were rare. Before the first game in St. Louis, Kling split a finger in practice. Chance caught this game, which would be his last appearance as a catcher in the major leagues. Jack O'Neill had been left behind in Chicago. Selee telegraphed O'Neill to get on the next train to St. Louis. Chicago won the game with Chance catching. O'Neill had not yet arrived for the next game. Selee used Tom Stanton, a local catcher recommended by the St. Louis team. Jack Taylor beat the Colts this day. The Cardinals had several stolen bases. During this and the next season, Selee matched wits with Cardinals manager Kid Nichols.

The Colts' home season opened with St. Louis on April 21. O'Neill had gotten injured in practice as well, so Casey was the catcher in the home

Mordecai Brown later in his career with Chicago. He has his right hand curled up, so we cannot see where he got his nickname "Three Finger."

opener. The Colts won the first game. The next game, with Kid Nichols pitching, was a 2–1 loss to the Cardinals. St. Louis bunted several times with Casey at catcher and rookie George Moriarty at third. On this date, Selee's wife left for Boston to attend the funeral of her brother. Brown pitched the finale against his old teammates on Sunday, losing before a crowd of 11,000. This was the date of the first Sunday game in Brooklyn, which drew a crowd of 14,000. After the first pitch, three players were arrested. The rest of the players stayed and played the game. Kling returned by the game on April 27. Moriarty was sent to the minors. Chicago won the only game played against Cincinnati on this date after two rainouts. The next series in Pittsburgh was expected to be postponed. The Pittsburgh ballpark was near the confluence of the Allegheny and Monongahela Rivers, and it was under water on April 18. One game was played in Pittsburgh, won by Chicago, before the two teams went to Chicago for the next series. In the month of April, the Colts won five games, lost five, and had five rainouts.

The Colts would be at home for a month, playing every NL team except Cincinnati. The first game was Sunday, May 1, against the defending champion Pirates. A crowd of 18,000 saw Pittsburgh win. Chicago won the three remaining games against Pittsburgh. The Pirates turned a triple play in one of these losses. Boston came to town for four games, which were split. In one game, Slagle was spiked while running the bases. Wicker played the outfield in his place. In the first game of the next series against Philadelphia, the deadball style of baseball was demonstrated in a 1–0 Phillies win. Each team had one chance to score. Lundgren was on first base and tried to score on a double by Casey. He was out at the plate. The *Tribune* story about the game did not say who was coaching third. Remember there were no coaches on any team. Players would fill the coaching boxes when they felt it was necessary. The lone run scored by Philadelphia was on a sacrifice fly to Wicker, playing center field in place of Slagle. Wicker made a strong but inaccurate throw. In the Colts' ninth, Jones failed to sacrifice with runners at first and second and no one out. The *Tribune* blamed Jones, saying Selee must have either told him to sacrifice or trusted him to do it on his own. This was one of several examples of the writer covering the Colts running down Jones as a player.

Chicago won the three remaining games in the series. In the third game, each team used 12 players in a two-hour game. Both these facts were unusual enough to be noted in the story reporting the game. By the start of the next series against Brooklyn, the outfield was Kling LF (O'Neill was healthy), Wicker CF, and Jones RF. Chicago swept four games from Brooklyn. Kling hit an inside-the-park home run in one game, and Chance cleared the fence for a home run in another. Wicker returned to pitching in one of these games after playing center field for a week straight.

When New York came to town on May 20, Chicago was in second place, ½-game behind New York. Chicago won two of the first three games, beating Christy Mathewson in the first. The third game of the series was on Sunday and drew a crowd estimated at 20–25,000. The fourth and final game was played on Monday, May 23. The game ended in a 5–5 tie after 11 innings. It was called so New York could catch a train. After the fourth inning of the next game against St. Louis on May 25, three pitchers were playing. Lundgren pitched a complete game. By the fourth inning, McCarthy was injured and Chance ejected. Wicker went to center field and Corridon to first base. Chicago won anyway. Chicago swept three of what should have been a five-game series, thanks to two more rainouts. This long home stand ended with a win against Pittsburgh. The Colts' record was 23–10, putting them in a tie for first place with New York.

The road trip started with a Decoration Day doubleheader, and the Colts would be on the road until June 26. The doubleheader was split in Cincinnati. Chance was hit by a pitch five times in these two games. The third one in the first game left him unconscious for a few minutes. A doctor was called out of the stands. When he regained consciousness, Chance stayed in the game and also played the second game. The Decoration Day date were the only games in Cincinnati this stop. Both Colts catchers were hurt in these games, so Selee signed another. After two rainouts, the next series started in Philadelphia. A new signee, Aleck Smith, was playing center field due to an injury to Slagle. Chicago swept the two games that were played. Chance was hurt again on a slide.

Chicago arrived in Brooklyn in first place by half a game. Brooklyn took two of three games with another rainout. The next series with New York started with New York half a game in the lead. Christy Mathewson shut out the Colts on one hit in the first game. Manager McGraw and two players from New York were ejected. Chicago beat Joe McGinnity in 12 innings in the second game, 1–0. Wicker pitched a shutout. Chicago scored in the 12th on Chance's single and a two-out, RBI single by Evers. Two umpires worked the game before a crowd estimated at 38,500. This was McGinnity's first loss of the season, on June 11. Six balls were lost to fans during this game, a fact unusual enough to be reported. Selee was still looking for another outfielder. June 12 was a Sunday, which meant no game.

June 13 saw the first matchup between Chicago pitcher Three Finger Brown and New York pitcher Christy Mathewson. Chance and Evers had the only hits for Chicago in a 3–2 win. Brown and Mathewson would match up many times for these two teams over the next nine years. Chicago left for Boston with a ½-game lead. Chicago won one of three games in Boston, going 6–5 on its trip east. The next stop was for six days in Cincinnati. In the first game on June 18, Chicago fielded its regular lineup for the first time since early May. The six-game series was split. On June 22, there was a note in the *Tribune* that Herman Long quit baseball. He had been playing for the Toledo minor league club. On the way to Pittsburgh, Chicago stopped in Sharon, Pennsylvania, for an exhibition game. One game was played in Pittsburgh, won by Chicago, before both teams headed for Chicago. Chicago came home in second place with a 34–19 record.

Pittsburgh came to town for four games, which were split. New York was in the process of winning 18 in a row, giving them breathing space in first place. Chicago went to St. Louis for five games. The start of the July 2 game was delayed due to the running of the St. Louis Derby horse race across the street from the ballpark. St. Louis won three of five. The Colts went to Pittsburgh for a July 4 doubleheader. The Pirates swept before a crowd of over 24,000. Jones was hurt in a collision at the plate and was sent home to Chicago on crutches the next day. Chicago won the one game played between two rainouts. Now the Colts returned home for three weeks. New York had opened a large lead: New York 49–17, Chicago 38–26.

Chicago won the first game against Brooklyn, 1-0, on a pitcher's hit. In the bottom of the eighth, Otto Williams led off with a single, and when Button Briggs singled him to third, Williams was hit by the throw and scored. This was the first victory of a four-game sweep. The games in this series averaged one hour 40 minutes in duration. During the series, Selee tried to trade a pitcher to Brooklyn for an outfielder. Brooklyn turned him down. Chicago won the first three games against Boston, for an eight-game winning streak, before losing the last game. There was an innovation at West Side park in the final game on July 15. The pitcher's name for both teams was posted on the scoreboard. Remember no one wore numbers before the late 1920s.

The first game against Philadelphia was a classic deadball game. Chicago scored in the sixth after Slagle singled and was sacrificed to second. On Chance's short fly to right, Slagle tagged and went to third, where the Phillies third baseman (a pitcher playing there due to injury) misplayed the throw, scoring Slagle. The Phillies had the bases loaded with one out in the ninth inning when the final play of the game was a Tinker to Evers to Chance double play.

Selee had suspended Weimer for the prior three games for "indifferent work." Weimer was reinstated on July 17. John McGraw said that if New York won the NL pennant, they would not play the AL winner in a series after the season.[20] Chicago won three of four games from Philadelphia before New York came to town. New York was seven games up at the start of this series. New York won three of four games. President Hart announced that the attendance was the greatest in the history of the club for a four-game series. Hart did not cite any specific figures. Review of the articles about the New York series did not show specific figures for any game, just that the crowds were large. Prior rainouts against Cincinnati would be made up in the next series. Hart denied a rumor that Selee was going to the AL club in New York next year. Selee stated he had a contract for "a couple of more years." The game on July 30 featured free admission for children, a once-a-year opportunity at West Side Park. The size of the crowd was not listed but was described as sizable. Chicago won three of the five games played, and one was rained out. St. Louis came to town for one make-up game on July 31. Lundgren pitched a complete game and hit a three-run triple in a 9–5 win. Chicago went 15–7 on this home stand. New York was in the lead by nine games. As Chicago had 23 home and 47 road games remaining, New York was in good shape.

On this last home stand, another product of George Huff's scouting came to the Colts. Selee had told Huff that he was looking for outfielders. Huff went to Des Moines to scout an outfielder and was not impressed. He saw a player at shortstop named Artie Hofman who impressed him. Huff talked to Hofman and his manager and learned that Hofman had played all over the field for Des Moines. Huff recommended Hofman to Selee. Selee bought Hofman from Des Moines about the same time he traded Corridon to Philadelphia for outfielder Shad Barry. Barry would see more playing time than Hofman the remainder of the year, but Hofman would be the more important acquisition. Later in the year, Huff made a trip to Syracuse to scout two outfielders there. Huff recommended both Mike Mitchell and Frank Schulte. Later at year, Selee acquired both.

The trip started with one make-up game in Pittsburgh, won by the Pirates. Four games were scheduled in New York for the next four days. The series ended up as three games in two days, with two rainouts. New York won two of three. The only extra infielder on the Colts, Otto Williams, was sent back to Chicago with an injury. The two dates in New York drew more than 24,000 fans. There was an off-day during the next series in Brooklyn. Selee went to Newark to scout minor leaguers. This was the day he acquired Mitchell and Schulte. They were to finish their minor league season before reporting to Chicago. The four-game series in Brooklyn turned into three games, swept by Chicago. Selee missed the last date, which was rained out, because he went to New England to scout. Selee returned to the team in Philadelphia.

Chicago won the first three games in Philadelphia, lost one, and won the final game. Jones played in his first game since getting injured in mid–July. He was able to play one game, then had to sit again. Tinker was notified of his mother's death and left the team for the funeral. Outfielder Barry played shortstop while Tinker was gone. This road trip ended in Boston. The first date was to be a doubleheader. Chicago won the first game and the second was rained out. That made the next day a doubleheader, which was split. Chicago won the final game. By August 18, the last day of the road trip, Chicago had signed four more outfielders than had been on the roster when the road trip started (Mitchell, Schulte, Harry McChesney, and Bill Carney). None were with the team on this trip. The trip had been successful, resulting in a 10–5 record. The standings on August 18: New York 72–29, Chicago 63–39, Pittsburgh 59–41, Cincinnati 61–45.

The home stand started with three games against Boston. Chicago won two of three even though the left side of the infield was out. Barry played shortstop, Aleck Smith third base. Tinker and Casey were back by the start of the next series with New York. Chicago had a day off on August 23 while New York played a doubleheader in Pittsburgh. New York split that doubleheader and got to Chicago to play another doubleheader on the 24th. New York won the first game as Christy Mathewson pitched a shutout, not allowing a runner past first base. The second game was a 2–2 tie in 10 innings, called by darkness. The attendance was not listed, but the *Tribune* reporter complained about the crowd's rowdiness. Play had to be stopped several times due to glass bottles being thrown at the New York players. As had been common this year in games involving New York or Brooklyn, there were two umpires. In game involving other teams, there was usually one umpire.

The tie called for another doubleheader on the 25th. New York swept that. In the first game, it was tied 1–1 in the top of the 10th. Jake Weimer, who had started, put the first two men on and was then ejected for arguing balls and strikes. Bob Wicker came in, with no warmup, and gave up three runs. Wicker pitched the second game, getting shelled. Brown won the final game of the series for the Colts. Philadelphia came to town for three games. Chicago won two of them. Selee made news during this series by (1) signing Carl Lundgren for 1905; (2) announcing that Frank Schulte would join the team on September 10; and (3) signing Ed Reulbach for 1905.

Brooklyn won two of three in the next series in Chicago. A couple of occurrences during this series showed some differences between baseball then and now. During one game, the lone umpire missed a fair/foul call while umpiring behind the pitcher. In the final game on September 1, Brooklyn was out of available pitchers. They signed a local Chicago pitcher, Koukalik, for this game only, paying him $10. The home stand ended with a three-game sweep of St. Louis. During this series, Selee signed pitcher Jeff Pfeffer for next year. He had played for George Huff at the University of Illinois. Even after this good home stand, Chicago lost ground to New York. New York was at 85–32, Chicago 72–46.

The second game of the prior series with St. Louis took place on September 3, which was the last day of the Olympics in St. Louis. The World's

Fair was still going on in St. Louis, which was where both teams played their next series, starting with a Labor Day doubleheader. There were no bases on the field for the first game, just "a few old sticks for bases."[21] This was a morning/afternoon doubleheader with separate admissions. The Colts went across the street to the World's Fair clubhouse for lunch between games of a victorious sweep. Chicago won two more before St. Louis won the final game of the series. Chance split a finger in the final game and was sent home to Chicago. The next stop in Pittsburgh was not so successful. Pittsburgh swept four games. On the final day of this series, Kid Nichols of St. Louis pitched both games of a doubleheader. It was also the first day of the Colored World Series in Chicago, being played at the Chicago AL ballpark. Both teams got on the same train to Chicago after the final game.

The final scheduled home stand started on September 12 with one make-up game against Pittsburgh. Pittsburgh won, making it five straight against Chicago and moving into second place. By this time, Jones' leg injury had put him out for the year. Selee was trying all the new outfielders he had acquired, thinking that the Jones injury would not heal in time for next year. It turned out that Jones was not re-signed and played the 1905 season in the minors. Cincinnati came to town for five games. Chicago won the first four. The final game played was to be doubleheader, starting at 1:30 p.m., and had to end before both teams caught a train. This first game went 17 innings. Both pitchers went the distance. Chicago walked off in the 17th on McCarthy's two-out RBI single. There was one more possible home game on October 9, but it would only be played if it meant anything in the standings. As the records on September 18 were New York 99–35 and Chicago 80–52, that was unlikely.

Chicago had to catch the train to Syracuse. They played an exhibition game there. Frank Schulte played for Syracuse in this game, then joined Chicago. Schulte played his first game for Chicago in Philadelphia, getting three hits. Philadelphia won three of four games. Artie Hofman made his Chicago debut in the final game of the series at shortstop. The next five-game series in Brooklyn featured a couple of notable performances. Wicker pitched the first game. The writer covering the Colts thought Wicker threw a no-hitter. Only one Brooklyn player reached base. Chance made a bad throw to Wicker covering first, and it was scored a hit. The Chicago writer thought it was an error. Schulte hit his first major league homer in this game. In another game, Brooklyn pitcher Doc Reisling featured a new pitch called a "spit" ball.

Chicago won four of five games in Brooklyn. New York had clinched the pennant by now. New York was disinterested in the three-game series with Chicago and it showed. Chicago won all three. Chicago and New York split their season series. The final game took one hour 15 minutes to play. Chicago won three of four games in Boston. The outfield for the final game in Boston was Schulte LF, McChesney CF, and Hofman RF. During this series, Hart announced there would be no post-season series with Chicago AL. John McGraw confirmed that New York NL would not play pennant-winning Boston AL in a World Series. The season ended with three games in Pittsburgh. Pittsburgh won two of three, but that was not enough to improve their position. The final standing for the first four teams in the National League were: New York 106–47, Chicago 93–60, Cincinnati 88–65, Pittsburgh 87–66. Selee's prediction before the season that New York, Chicago and Cincinnati would be better than Pittsburgh was borne out. Home attendance continued to grow. The total was 439,100 for 1904.

There was plenty of news around the Colts in October, even without a series with the White Sox. Jack Taylor threatened to sue James Hart about the insinuations that Taylor threw games in the prior year's series against the White Sox. Taylor had told Hart after that series, when the claims of throwing games reached the papers, that he would not play for Hart again. Taylor said Selee tried to talk him out of that, but Taylor held firm. The Colts made out fine as a result of this mess, getting Three Finger Brown. John Brush, owner of the New York Giants, admitted on October 17 that he and John McGraw had made a mistake in not playing the AL champion in a post-season series.[22] The post-season series between the pennant winners of separate leagues had been played many times before. All had been arranged between the teams and had not been required. Brush submitted a set of rules to the National Commission requiring the champions of the National and American Leagues to meet in a World Series at the conclusion of their seasons. This was the start of the official World Series as we know it, to start in after the 1905 season. John Kling of the Colts said he might buy the Kansas City minor league club in partnership with Kid Nichols (both Kansas City natives). If he did, he would quit the Colts.

The 1904 season had been a success for Frank Selee. The team continued to improve, from 82–56 to 93–60. Selee had gone through many players in search of aiding the roster. The pitching staff was now stable. The five main starters started all but 15 games. Their records were all good: Weimer 20–14, Briggs 19–11, Lundgren 17–10, Wicker 17–8, and Brown 15–10 with a 1.87 ERA.[23] The infield of Chance, Evers, Tinker and Casey were solid. The only question was Casey at third, due to his age of 33. Kling was established at catcher. The outfield had been the main place of experiment during the 1904 season. Slagle was set in center. Jones had been released after a serious injury. The corner outfielders were not set. McCarthy, Barry, McChesney, Schulte, Hofman and several others had been used in left and right. Selee would bring some of these to spring training in 1905 to determine the best.

That is, if Selee went to spring training in 1905. Selee and his wife went to Los Angeles on October 20 to spend the winter there. Spring training was to be in Santa Monica in 1905. But the reason the Selees went to Los Angeles was not related to baseball. Selee's lung condition had worsened during the 1904 season. Selee followed the normal medical advice of the time regarding a condition like his and moved to a warm, dry climate. Selee intended to manage the Colts in 1905 but was realistic enough to know that his health would be the ultimate determining condition.

The Colts arrived in Santa Monica on March 1, 1905, for spring training. Chance and Weimer, who lived in southern California, joined Selee in greeting the others. The first three days of practice were run by Chance, due to Selee's weakened condition. Selee was present and told the team to work on hit-and-run plays. The Colts played exhibition games in the Los Angeles area from March 3 through 12. After games in Bakersfield and Fresno, the team stayed in San Francisco from March 18 through 26. Selee missed a couple of workouts due to illness. On March 26, James Hart talked to the press and said Selee was in poor health and had lost 15 pounds. Selee wrote in *Baseball Magazine*:

> In the Spring of 1905 the Club trained at Santa Monica, Ca. I was not feeling at all well. I met Mr. Hart at the St. Francis Hotel in San Francisco, and told him I wanted to throw up the management as I did not feel that I was able to take charge again that season. Mr. Hart was sick himself at the time, and asked me to go on with the Club, which I finally agreed to do. During our conversation at the St. Francis he remarked that he would like to sell out. I did not think he really meant it, but when I got back to Chicago and he had returned also I said to him "Were you in earnest about selling out?" He replied, "Yes, you bet I was, and you can have the first chance at the Club for a less price than any one else." While in Los Angeles I had met Mr. Auten, formerly half owner of the Pittsburg Club. He told me if I saw a good chance in baseball he would like to go in with me. After my conversation with Mr. Hart relative to the purchase of the Club, I started downtown to telegraph Mr. Auten the situation, when I was taken sick on the street and had to return home and finally gave up everything.[24]

After leaving San Francisco, the team had games scheduled in both Salt Lake City and Denver snowed out. One game was played in each city before the team headed further east. Games were played against colleges in Kansas. The exhibition season ended in Kansas City and Omaha with split squad games played over four days. Chance had not yet played in the spring due to an injury. Selee said he had not yet decided on his outfielders except for Slagle. The last day before the season was spent traveling to St. Louis. Selee told the press, "We are out for the pennant."[25] Selee released McChesney and Otto Williams. Selee listed his lineup for the first game as: Casey 3B, Billy Maloney RF, Barry 1B, McCarthy CF, Slagle LF, Tinker SS, Evers 2B, Kling C, Lundgren P. The other players on the team were: Chance (injured); Schulte and Hofman OF; O'Neill C; Brown, Weimer, Wicker, Briggs, and Pfeffer P.

In its article on April 14 regarding Opening Day in St. Louis, the *Chicago Tribune* used the name "Cubs" for the first time. Chicago and St. Louis split the four-game series. Cincinnati came to Chicago for Chicago's home opener. Cincinnati took two of three. The Chicago team got its first look at Orval Overall, who pitched for Cincinnati in the final game. Overall won with a 10-inning complete game before 10,000 fans on a Saturday. Pittsburgh came to town next. Chicago won the first game on a Sunday before 20,000 fans. Brown pitched a shutout and scored the only run in a 1–0 game. On this same date (April 23) the Chicago AL team played and drew 20,000 fans at home. Chicago won another game from Pittsburgh before both teams headed to Pittsburgh.

In the first game at Pittsburgh, McCarthy threw out three runners at home from center field. Pfeffer won 2–1 and drove in the winning run. Chance took his first exercise since he was injured in Santa Monica. Pittsburgh won the remaining two games at their home. Schulte was inserted into the lineup in right field in the final game in Pittsburgh. Chicago (called the Zephyrs in an article on May 1) split a four-game series in Cincinnati before returning home. Evers had gotten hurt in Pittsburgh and Chance was still out. Hofman was playing second base and Barry first. This midwestern portion of the schedule ended with a four-game sweep of St. Louis in Chicago. During that series, Kling was called home to Kansas City because his mother was sick. The Chicago team approved of its new clubhouse at West Side Park, which had six "shower baths." There was a case of smallpox found in the boarding house where Bob Wicker lived. Wicker was quarantined for two weeks. Before heading east, the standings were: New York 14–4, Pittsburgh 12–7, Chicago 12–8.

There was an exhibition game scheduled on the way to Boston, in Lynn, Massachusetts Somehow the Lynn team forgot about it, and the game was canceled. A four-game series in Boston was split. Slagle had an unassisted double play, from left field, at second base in one of the games. Chance made his first appearance, as a pinch-hitter, on May 11. Selee saw two pitchers he had acquired face each other on May 12. Brown beat Willis in a 10-inning game. The team went on to New York. New York showed their stuff as defending champions by sweeping four games from Chicago. Ed Reulbach joined the team in New York and lost one of the games. New York shut out Chicago for the first 28 innings of the series, Chicago scored two runs total in this series.

Chicago got back on track, winning three of four games in Brooklyn. What was supposed to be Chicago's regular lineup made its first appearance in Brooklyn on May 18: Casey 3B, Schulte LF, Maloney RF, Slagle CF, Chance 1B, Tinker SS, Evers 2B, Kling C. After this series, Barry was sold to Cincinnati. The eastern trip ended in Philadelphia. Per the *Tribune*, Selee remained in New York to "finish the Barry trade. Chance ran the team in Philadelphia."[26] It is likely that Selee had a medical problem. This would be the pattern the rest of the time Selee remained as manager. Selee would not travel with the team, and Chance would run all the road games. In Chance's first stab as manager, Chicago won one of three games in Philadelphia. The team returned home in fourth place: New York 25–8, Pittsburgh 19–15, Philadelphia 16–15, Chicago 18–17.

At the start of the short home stand, Selee complained that New York got to spend most of May at home. Two games with St. Louis were split. In the second game, Pfeffer started, threw 10 straight balls, and was replaced by Brown. Pfeffer took the loss. Cincinnati came to town for four games and won three. The only Chicago win was Ed Reulbach's first career win by a 1–0 score. The only run was scored by Chicago on Slagle's single, a walk, and Tinker's RBI single. The last out was a man thrown out at home by Schulte. Overall beat the Cubs again in the final game of the series. Chicago went to Pittsburgh for two games, which were split. Both teams traveled to Chicago after this series. Chicago would be home from June 4 through June 27 except for a short trip to St. Louis.

The home stand started with a doubleheader loss to Pittsburgh. The fans still believed, as the attendance at this doubleheader was 12,000. Chicago won the two remaining games in the series to move their record to 23–24. Chicago swept four games from Boston. During this series, George Huff and the University of Illinois baseball team attended one of the games. At the start of the series, Boston was down to its third catcher. In the third game, a Chance foul tip dislocated a finger on the throwing hand of the Boston catcher. Chance pulled the finger back in place, and the Boston catcher had to continue playing as there was no sub available. Chicago stole six bases against this catcher in both the third and fourth games of the series.

Chicago won the first game of the next series against New York. The teams then split 1–0 decisions. In the first, Mathewson faced 28 men, beating Brown with a no-hitter. In the second, Wicker beat McGinnity. The Cubs run scored on Chance's walk, a Tinker sacrifice, and Casey's RBI triple. After Casey reached third, he was physically stopped by O'Neill, who was coaching third. Casey was called out, but as that was the second out, the run counted. For this series only on the home stand, two umpires were assigned.

Chicago swept three games from Brooklyn. Before the first game of the next series with Philadelphia, a groundkeeper working in left field when he was hit by a piece of coal thrown from the bleachers. The groundkeeper pulled out a pistol and fired it into the air, getting the attention of everyone in the park. That was the end of the incident. Chicago and Philadelphia split four games. Selee purchased the contract of Hans Lobert from

Des Moines. The break in the home stand came next, with one game in St. Louis. It was a heck of a game, won 2–1 by Chicago in 18 innings. Ed Reulbach and Jack Taylor both went the distance. Chicago scored in the 18th on a Schulte triple followed by Maloney's sacrifice fly. This home stretch ended with three games against Cincinnati. Chicago won two of them. There were two exhibition games in the Chicago area before the start of the next road trip. Selee tried to attend a game in Fowler, Indiana. He was sent back to Chicago with "acute attack of intestinal indigestion."[27] Chance would continue handling the team on the road.

Chicago won one game in Cincinnati and two in St. Louis on July 1 and 2. Chicago and St. Louis traveled to Chicago on the same train for a Fourth of July doubleheader. Chicago swept this doubleheader. Pittsburgh came to town for five games to end this mostly home stretch. Pittsburgh won three, Chicago one, and one game was tied. Selee was moved from his home to a hospital during this series for a complete exam. The final game was a 2–2 tie that ended at 5:30 so both teams could catch a train east. Chicago would play in the east until July 29. It was hoped that Selee could join the team at some point, but that would depend on the medical verdict. As this developed into the end of Selee's career as Chicago manager, we will not review the games played and instead will tell what happened next at the level of ownership and the manager's job.

James Hart had told Selee the truth at before the 1905 season. Hart wanted to sell the team. After giving Selee the chance to buy the team, Hart spread the word around the National League that the team was for sale. Hart owned and ran the Chicago Gravel Company as his main business and thought his health would not allow him to run both. The person who acted on this knowledge lived in Cincinnati. Charles Murphy was an ex-newspaper man who had transitioned to public relations. Murphy's clients included John Brush, the owner of the New York Giants. Murphy heard about this opportunity from Brush. Murphy had $15,000 saved. Murphy contacted Hart and made a bid of $100,000 for the team, adding $5,000 to pay Hart as a finder's fee. Hart and Murphy agreed to an option for Murphy to buy the Colts at this price.

Now Murphy had to find the remaining $90,000 to close the deal. From his newspaper days, Murphy knew Charles Taft, the owner and publisher of the *Cincinnati Enquirer* (and older half-brother of the Secretary of War, William Howard Taft). Murphy persuaded Taft to loan him the $90,000, to be repaid out of the operating profits of the Chicago NL team. The option was exercised on July 15, 1905, with the payment to take place in November. Murphy was named the executive vice-president of the team on July 15, and Hart left on a long vacation.

This was announced in the *Chicago Tribune* on July 16, along with an

5. Chicago

inaccurate story about who was backing Murphy. The *Tribune* said New York money was financing Murphy, with no mention of Taft. On July 26 a story in the *Tribune* stated that Charles Taft was backing Murphy. On July 28, 1905, the announcement was made that "Selee is forced to quit the game." Hart granted Selee a leave of absence for sickness. Hart stated that he expected Selee to return at the beginning of 1906 as manager and that Chance would remain the manager for the rest of 1905. The article said Selee had been operated on for appendicitis and had not recovered, taking this action on the advice of his physician. The article added that Hart would relinquish control on October 15, 1905.[28]

The record of the Colts on July 27 was 52–38. Chance led the team for the rest of the year. The Colts' record under Chance's official management was 40–23. The official reason this change was made has been detailed above. There was another version, which was that Murphy wanted to make the change to Chance and saw the opportunity due to Selee's illness. My presumption is that both are partially true. There had been no announcement of the real nature of Selee's illness. Appendicitis, indigestion, and pleurisy had been mentioned. The correct diagnosis was tuberculosis. There was no cure for tuberculosis in 1905. Selee had not been able to give his full attention to his job for a while due to his health. Murphy had not hired Selee. Most new owners or executives want to have their man in charge. Murphy used this opportunity to make the change, nominally on a temporary basis.

Selee stated that he would go to Colorado and New Mexico for his health. Someone else needed to do the job during that time. Selee issued this statement on the date of his leaving: "It is with sincere regret, as it is hard for me to sever myself from the pleasant associations I have enjoyed under you [Hart]. The Chicago League Ball Club is today not only a grand ball club as far as playing ability goes but is composed of manly young men of whom I am proud. I wish you and the boys success, and I hope to be with the club again in the spring."[29] A benefit game was scheduled by Chicago for September 28, 1905, with the proceeds to go to Selee for his medical expenses. This game was announced on August 26, and the first mention was made that he was critically ill and the illness was of long standing. A crowd of 5,000 attended the regularly scheduled game on September 28 against St. Louis. $4,000 was raised and contributed to Selee. The final mention of Selee as being involved with the Chicago club came on September 28. A trade to be executed after the season with Cincinnati was announced. Chicago would trade Jake Weimer to Cincinnati for third baseman Harry Steinfeldt and another player. Selee gave his endorsement to this trade.

Selee had effected a large transformation in the fortunes of the Chicago NL team (which with the endorsement of Frank Chance would henceforth be known as the Cubs). The record of the Cubs in 1901, their final season before Selee's arrival, was 53–86. Under Selee, the records for 1902–1905 were 68–69, 82–56, 93–60, and 92–61. Home attendance continued to rise, reaching 509,900 in 1905. The base had been built up for the Cubs to have the best regular season decade in baseball history. In 1906, the Cubs set the record for most wins in one season (116, tied by the Seattle Mariners in 2001 in a longer season). From 1904 through 1913, they also set records for regular season wins in consecutive seasons for every number between two and 10.[30] Their managers during this time were Selee, Chance (mid-1905 thru 1912), and Evers (1913). But the core of this team was built by Selee.

In a prior book about the 1910 Cubs, I listed the 12 members of the Cubs who had been on the team from 1906 thru 1910, when the Cubs won four pennants and won 104 games the season they did not win the pennant. These 12 players—Chance, Evers, Tinker, Steinfeldt, Hofman, Schulte, Kling, Brown, Reulbach, Overall, Pfiester. Chance, and Kling—were on the team when Selee took over. Selee made the major decision that Kling was the catcher and that Chance should be the first baseman. Selee acquired and played Tinker, Evers, Hofman, Schulte, Brown, and Reulbach. That was one hell of a base for Chance and Murphy to build on. Chance and Murphy did build on it, as the results indicated.

The best modern tribute to Selee's effectiveness as a manager was stated by Bill James. James said that the best teams in the majors before the 1927 Yankees were the 1898 Boston Beaneaters and the 1906 Chicago Cubs. Those two teams had Frank Selee in common.[31]

6

Endgame

Pueblo and Denver

Mr. and Mrs. Selee moved to Colorado for Frank's health after the 1905 baseball season. Selee stated in in *Baseball Magazine,* "To make a success a baseball manager must enter into his work with every bit of energy he can command, and I believe what little success I have attained is probably due to my earnestness and strict attention to business and having the confidence and respect of the players."[1] Selee also said, "Well, it looks as though I were done with baseball, as it is too strenuous work for me as a manager. I may be connected with the Pueblo Club in a business capacity the coming season."

As has been shown many times before and since, someone who has had success at the highest level in sports finds it hard to walk away. Selee had an excellent reason (tuberculosis) to stay away from baseball and had left as a great success in the major leagues. But the siren song of the game pulled him back. The Pueblo (Colorado) Indians of the Western League offered him the job of manager, and he accepted in early March 1906. The president of the Western League heard the news on March 8 and commented that the addition of Frank Selee to the Western League would add prestige to the League.[2]

Selee spent most of March and April gathering players for the upcoming season. The Pueblo team had gone through its initial season in 1905, finishing sixth in a six-team league. Eleven players who had been reserved from the year before came to spring training in Pueblo, three weeks before the start of the season. During these three weeks, Selee added several other players. By the first game, he had made several changes and had 15 players to start the season.

The community was excited about this touch of the big time in small-town Colorado. Spring training took place on the county fairgrounds while a new ballpark was built. This park was named Selee Park and was ready for the first game on May 2. The opponent was defending champion

Des Moines, managed by Joe Cantillon, who would be in the major leagues as a manager in 1907. The rest of the league consisted of Denver, Lincoln, Omaha, and Sioux City. President O'Neil had stated that he wanted to take advantage of Selee's presence as much as possible. He helped Pueblo out by having them at home for their first 12 games. Des Moines won three games, followed by Sioux City and Omaha each sweeping three. Lincoln won the first game of their series in Pueblo, making 10 straight losses to start the season. Pueblo won the final two games at home before their first road trip. After an Opening Day crowd of 2,700, attendance averaged about 500, which was better than the year before.

Selee showed his inveterate optimism by stating that a couple of new players would make the difference, in a statement to the *Pueblo Chieftain* when the team left for its first road trip under his leadership. The owners of the team (which included Selee as a minority shareholder) were confident as well. They started work on a 2,000-seat grandstand at Selee Park. By the time the Indians returned to Pueblo, they were securely in last place. The road trip covered all the other teams in the league, and Pueblo won four games on the trip. As two of the wins were against Denver, the hometown paper was pleased with their performance. There had been an instance of rowdy play and rowdy fan behavior in a game between Omaha and Sioux City during this time. A league meeting was called to address this. It was discussed in the press that President O'Neil was in trouble and that Selee could replace him. Nothing came of this.

Pueblo improved during their next home stand. The bloom was still on the rose as far as attendance went. Several games during this home stand had attendance of more than 2,000. At a doubleheader on June 11 against Des Moines, the crowd was more than 3,000. The newspaper report on this date complained of the rowdyism of the Des Moines players. There was a fight in the first game, where each player (one from each team) was fined $10. The crowd felt that the Des Moines player initiated the fracas and raised $60 to pay the Pueblo player's fine. The story said that the excess went to the Pueblo player. The story also said both games were long, drawn-out affairs. The time of game was 2:10 for the first game and two hours for the second. By the end of the home stand, Pueblo was still in last place but had closed the gap to two games behind the fifth-place team.

During the first series of the next road trip, Pueblo faced Lincoln pitcher "Spit Ball" Jones twice. These games were split, the Pueblo paper commenting on Jones' unorthodox pitch. Pueblo remained in last place during this road trip. The team finished with a couple of wins against Denver, which pleased the home fans. By the time the next home stand started, the division in the league was clear. Des Moines, Omaha and Denver had winning records, with Des Moines easily in the lead. Sioux City, Lincoln

6. Endgame

and Pueblo had losing records, with Pueblo remaining in last place. Pueblo had steadily improved from its 0–10 start. By July 8, they were in last place by 2½ games.

On July 10, Pueblo beat Denver at home. On this same date, Manager Holmes of Lincoln protested a call from the umpire in a unique way. That evening, Holmes saw the umpire on the street, went up to him, and punched him in the jaw. Holmes was suspended by the league president. On July 14, Pueblo hosted a doubleheader with Omaha. A short notice in the *Pueblo Chieftain* explained that it would be a split morning-afternoon doubleheader because "one game following another is rather tiresome, [so] the management had decided to try the morning and afternoon arrangement."[3] By the end of this home stand, Pueblo had improved to ½-game out of fifth place.

The following road trip was a regression. By the final series, the headline in the *Pueblo Chieftain* after another loss was "Indians Continue to Lose with Painful Regularity." Selee was still doing his best. The stories mention that he was travelling with the team on all the road trips so far. Before the first game of the upcoming home stand, Selee signed two new players. One showed what could happen to a player due to events out of his control. Clarence Henley pitched 45 games for San Francisco of the Pacific Coast League in 1905, winning 24. He had not pitched so far in 1906. The reason was the San Francisco earthquake of 1906, which cancelled the season of the San Francisco team. No one had signed Henley so far. Selee picked him up.

After losing 14 straight games on the road, Pueblo returned home on August 4. The streak was broken with a win against Sioux City. The losing streak had moved Pueblo deeper into the cellar. A series win against Sioux City made some dent in their eight-game deficit. Des Moines came to town and put an end to any hope of quick improvement. After a Des Moines win on August 10, Des Moines had an 11-game lead over second-place Omaha at one end of the standings. Pueblo was 7½ games behind Lincoln at the other end. A headline right next to the story about the Des Moines-Pueblo game told Selee what he was missing: "Cubs Romping Pennantward."[4] Des Moines completed a sweep of Pueblo on August 12. Pueblo returned to the road still in sixth place.

The road trip started with five straight losses to Des Moines and Lincoln. Pueblo won the final game in Lincoln to close the gap between fifth (Lincoln) and sixth (Pueblo) to nine games. On August 29, the small story about Pueblo's victory at Omaha was overshadowed by a neighboring story that Selee would promote a wrestling match at Selee Park before a scheduled boxing match on September 3. It was clear that Selee was not devoting all his energies to the ballclub. Pueblo continued its good performance against Denver by winning three of four games in Denver before returning home to face Denver. Pueblo won again on September 4.

The bigger story in the *Pueblo Chieftain* was about the fact that September 5 would be "Bargain Day at Selee's Ball Yard." There would be two games and wild bull riding. This had been scheduled for Labor Day but had been rained out. Since the middle of June, Fridays had been Ladies Day in Pueblo. Selee was trying everything to make the experience of going to a ballgame in Pueblo enjoyable. It wasn't working. Attendance for the Omaha-Pueblo game at Selee Park on September 11 was 100. The State Fair started that day in Pueblo. The team announced they would move the rest of the games on this home stand to their old park on the grounds of the State Fair. This certainly worked on September 12. A win over Omaha drew a crowd of 3,000. Fifteen hundred came for a doubleheader on September 16. Pueblo won the first game against Sioux City on a forfeit when Sioux City would not stop complaining to the umpire, then won the second game in normal fashion.

The next series was against the defending and soon-to-be repeat champions of the Western League, Des Moines. Pueblo won their final home game against Des Moines on September 23 to move their record to 56–81. That was seven games behind Denver in last place. Des Moines' record was 95–45, good for a 24-game lead over Lincoln, the only other team in the league with a record over .500. The final home series against Denver resulted in two more wins for Pueblo. The season ended on September 30 in Denver. Final standings for the Western League in 1906: Des Moines 98–50, Lincoln 75–73, Omaha 72–72, Sioux City 68–80, Denver 67–81 and Pueblo 61–85.

Selee's old team in Chicago won the National League by 20 games in 1906. On October 2, Selee announced an exhibition game against Denver for the next day. Selee stated that he would live in Pueblo over the winter. In another story, the triumvirate that had owned the Boston National League Club for 30 years announced that they had sold the franchise.

Selee had tried to improve the Pueblo club during the 1906 season. He had used over 25 players during the year. Nothing worked. His first baseman, Bill McGilvray, led the league in batting average, with Henry Melchior and Jim Cook not far behind. No one else stood out as a successful player. Selee made all the road trips during the year and seemed to be doing well with his health. He promised to keep trying to improve the club.

By the beginning of the 1907 season, the manager of the champion Des Moines team had gotten his reward. Just like Selee in 1889, Joe Cantillon was able to move to the major leagues off a fine season in the Western League. Cantilion became the manager of the Washington team of the American League, lasting from 1907 to 1909. Selee was still in Pueblo. He made some more moves over the winter to try and improve the team. These did not make much difference at the beginning of the year. Pueblo opened the season on the road for three weeks. By the date of their first game at home on May 7, the Indians were in sixth place. There was a picture in the *Pueblo Chieftain* of Selee on May 7 where he was called "Col. Frank Selee" and looked like a prosperous undertaker.

Selee had made the first road trip with the team and was still trying to improve the team. By the end of May, Pueblo's record was 11–24, which was good for last place, five games behind the fifth-place team. On June 1, the team announced they had signed Lew Drill as a playing manager. Drill had been in the American League from 1902 to 1904, playing for three different teams. Most of his experience was as a catcher. The article reporting this announcement said that Selee had been part of the decision and was fine with it.[5] By the time Pueblo came home from a long road trip on June 17, the newspaper featured Drill as the manager who wanted to make changes. While the ballpark was still called Selee Park, there was no mention of Frank Selee in the article. However, there was a mention that a new infielder, Vandegraft, had been signed on the recommendation of "baseball expert George Huff." Selee was still involved, but not running the team on a day-to-day basis. The team was still in last place with a 15–36 record.

By June 30 the team had improved to 25–40 and was in last place by two games. By July 25 the team had moved into fifth place. None of the stories about games mentioned Selee as involved as manager of the team. The only mention of his name was Selee Park. Pueblo kept improving, getting to 51–65 by August 22, which was two games out of fourth place. By September the *Pueblo Chieftain* was calling the team the Drillers after their playing manager. The season ended on September 15. Pueblo's record was 67–73, in fourth place. A bit of quick math shows that their record under Selee was 11–24, and under Drill 56–49. No wonder the story in the *Pueblo Chieftain* on September 16 said, "Drill has been an unqualified success as catcher-manager, and no doubt the directors will insist on his return." The article went on to say that the team lost money at the gate but made enough on selling players to the majors to break even. The only mention of Selee was that he would attend an amateur tournament in Albuquerque and try to sign replacements for the players sold to the majors.

These predictions did not work out for the Pueblo club. Manager Drill went elsewhere. Selee did not come up with better players at the amateur tournament. The manager at the start of the 1908 season was Ham Patterson, a first baseman. Pueblo had a new pitcher, described as a "little white-haired boy" named Kid Nichols. It was not clear if Selee found this avatar for his outstanding pitcher in Boston. This Nichols was not related to the major league pitcher. By May 6, Pueblo had taken up residence in the

Western League cellar. They were still in last on June 12. A good stretch at home moved Pueblo into fifth place by July 2.

A story on July 3 stated that the club had been sold. Three directors sold their shares, and the new investors took their places on the board of directors. Selee was on both the old and new boards of directors. Patterson was listed as the manager. The story stated the club would make money in 1908. New officers of the corporation were elected on July 14. Selee was not among them. In an interesting side note, a game in Omaha was called due to cold on July 6, 1908. On August 10, Pueblo beat Des Moines at home to stay in fifth place. There was a story in the *Pueblo Chieftain* that day regarding a game in New York between Chicago and New York (NL) that drew over 30,000 fans. The attendance in Pueblo that day was 700. On August 19, Lincoln did not show on time for a scheduled game in Pueblo due to train trouble. The game was rained out anyway.

At their next-to-last home date, Pueblo drew a "vast crowd" of 2,400 to a doubleheader win against Omaha on August 24. After a win in Omaha on September 3, Pueblo's record was 60–67, good for fifth place. On that same date, there was a smaller story about the outstanding pennant race in the National League. On September 14, player-manager Ducky Holmes of Sioux City hit a home run to win the pennant on the final day of the Western League season. Pueblo finished fifth with a 64–77 record.

Selee had not been able to work his magic in Pueblo. The team improved, but only after Selee stopped being an active manager. There was no mention of him running the team after Drill was named manager in 1907. There was no mention of any health problems in any of the newspaper articles about Selee and the Pueblo team. But, knowing what we know, Selee must have been deteriorating fast and physically unable to do more with Pueblo. He sold his stake in the Pueblo team after the 1908 season and returned to Denver to live. The Pueblo team was eventually sold to ex-big leaguer Frank Isbell, who sold the franchise to a group from Wichita after the 1911 season. Minor league baseball never returned to Pueblo.

Death and Legacy

Frank Selee died in Denver on July 5, 1909. He had moved into a sanitarium, the Rev. Frederick W. Oakes Home for Consumptives, in early 1909. Selee and his wife had been trying to make a go of life since they heard he had tuberculosis back in 1905, but it had become too much. They had been living in Denver since after the 1905 baseball season, for Frank's health. The experiment of working in Pueblo had not worked out, and moving to the sanitarium was the final stop. Frank Selee was 49 years old.

6. Endgame

Frank Selee was buried in Melrose, Massachusetts, on July 17, 1909. The cost of transporting his body from Denver to Melrose was borne by the Elks of Denver. Selee had been a member of the Elks since moving to Denver. The service took place at the Methodist Episcopal Church of Melrose, where Selee's father Nathan had been employed during Frank's youth. The pallbearers were drawn from three parts of Selee's life. Billy Hamilton and John Morrill (manager of Boston NL from 1882 to 1888) represented baseball. Two friends from Melrose and two members of the Elks rounded out the six.

The two most prominent tributes to Selee soon after his death were by Tim Murnane and Ted Lewis. Murnane stressed that Selee was a follower of Harry Wright as a manager. As was pointed out many times during Selee's career, his teams played clean baseball, particularly in comparison to the Baltimore Orioles and Cleveland Spiders of the 1890s. Murnane summed it up this way: "For no one ever accused clubs working under Wright and Selee of anything but cleancut methods. Neither would stand for umpire baiting. Neither would stand for dissipation among the men and both ever gathered around them boys who could appreciate the fact that the public wanted nothing but open, clean methods. And for this Messrs. Wright and Selee stood as personal examples."[6]

The most complete tribute from one of his former players came from Ted Lewis. Lewis, who by this time was a professor at Williams College in Massachusetts, wrote this letter to the weekly *Sporting Life* about his former manager that was published on July 24, 1909.

> As one who knew Manager Frank Selee intimately, having worked under him for over four years, I should like to add a word to the many tributes to his memory that will be written and printed. When I was about to break into the game Mr. Selee was generally considered to be among the three or four great leaders of the day. It was with a good deal of interest, therefore, that I looked forward to meeting him. Such a manager, I imagined, must be a keen, shrewd, aggressive, hustling and almost boisterous sort of individual. Imagine my surprise then when I met the quite little man, with the calm, placid countenance, the unobtrusive manner and the forehead—high and broad—which lent a strongly intellectual cast to the expression! He seemed, as such men always do seem, quite ordinary; and I was almost willing to agree with one of the players that the team might profitably get along just as well without him.
>
> But as the weeks and months passed by I gradually began to realize that I had been mistaken; that here, after all, was a powerful hand and a dominating personality—a man thoroughly indispensable to the success of the team. Finally he impressed me as one in a thousand. And now, after the years have gone, when we who read the papers and see how managers come and go, and when we consider his wonderful record of 12 years in Boston, we are inclined to think that it is not too much to say of him that he was one of the greatest managers that the game has known.
>
> His remarkable success was due in part, probably, to a large acquaintance with the men of his profession and the help that came thereby. But certainly it was not wholly

due to that. For Frank Selee possessed a thorough knowledge of men, and especially of the ball player; he possessed the rare ability to weld men into a harmonious working body, and the distinctive gift of drawing out all that was in the young fellows. For the latter he had, in fact, a veritable genius. By wise counsel, by splendid tact, by kindly encouragement, and by a real sympathy with his every earnest effort, he inspired the youngster to do his best. Moreover, his power was not limited to "breaking in" the colts; he also knew how to get the most out of his well-trained thoroughbreds and how to drive the balky. His hands were always on the reins and could always be felt; when necessary they were strongly firm, but only in one case do I recall that he was sternly severe. He controlled his men not by inducing fear, but by inspiring loyalty.

His conduct both on and off the field was always most exemplary, and in consequence the moral respect of his team came to him unsolicited. He strenuously objected to unfair and ungentlemanly methods, whether indulged in by friend or foe. I have heard him frankly, but quietly, reprove a player whom he personally greatly respected. Everywhere, as I knew him, his influence was sound and wholesome. To know this man—Quiet, simple, lovable, modest, even to shyness—was indeed a rare pleasure; to work under him and with him as I did was the privilege of a lifetime. I venture to predict that when the final history of base ball will be written it will record few, if any, worthier of more beneficent lives than that of Frank Selee. Sincerely yours, Edward M. Lewis.[7]

Ted Lewis was an English professor and sounds like it. His points are well taken. Frank Selee never indulged in behavior we came to associate with a tough baseball manager. He never wore a uniform in the major leagues. He never came out on the field to argue with an umpire. Players on his team argued with umpires, but to a much lesser degree than players and managers on opposing teams. The Selee player who argued most with umpires was Frank Chance, who succeeded Selee in Chicago as manager. Chance was captain under Selee for about two years before Selee's retirement. Even though Chance took over a team built by Selee and had great success with it, Chance did not like Selee or his style. That's understandable, because Chance was extremely combative as a player and manager. Chance found his own style and stuck with it.

As I stated at the beginning of this book, there are several basic types of manager. Selee was a great example of a players' manager. There have been other managers like Selee since, but they are few and far between. Bill James, in his book *The Bill James Guide to Baseball Managers from 1870 to Today*, published in 1997, said there were three schools of managers: the Connie Mack family, the Branch Rickey family, and the Ned Hanlon family. The Ned Hanlon family was the biggest. Ned Hanlon managers included John McGraw, Wilbert Robinson, Miller Huggins, Leo Durocher, Casey Stengel, and many others. They tended to be noisy and combative. Connie Mack's descendants were fewer in number and pretty much died out by the 1970s. Even though Mack's manner had more in common with Selee than Hanlon, Mack played for Hanlon and respected him as a manager.

6. Endgame 183

Mack was offered a job by Selee at the beginning of both their careers but declined the offer. The Branch Rickey family was started by Rickey during his tenure with the Dodgers. I would call this the predecessor of the analytic school of managing in vogue today. Rickey was the first front office figure to hire a statistician while he was with the Dodgers. Rickey's managers stressed fundamentals and tried to impose a philosophy throughout the organization.

There was no Frank Selee school of manager. Several of his players went on to become managers, but only one had measurable success. That was Pat Moran, who had been with Selee in Chicago. Moran became a successful manager in the National League but drank himself to death before developing any successors as a manager. Frank Chance was successful but managed in his own style. Jimmy Collins was successful but did not develop any other managers. All the other men who had played for Selee were not successful managers. These included Bobby Lowe, Kid Nichols, Charlie Ganzel, Hugh Duffy, Chick Stahl, Fred Tenney, Johnny Evers, and Joe Tinker.[8]

It is unlikely that someone like Selee could become a manager today. First, the job is different. The main part of the job when Selee held it was talent selection and development. The selection part is now done by the front office. Many people (scouts, general managers, presidents of baseball operations, etc.) take part in this process. The development of players is also managed by the front office until a player gets to the major leagues. All that was done by the manager until about 1930, and longer than that for teams that did not have minor league systems. All discussions of Selee that I reviewed stressed how good he was at spotting talent. Like anyone else who did the same job for a substantial time, he had his misses. The biggest miss was Napoleon Lajoie. Selee signed Fred Klobedanz from the same minor league team but passed on Lajoie. He did not have many other misses.

The list of players brought to the majors by Selee who went on to great success is long. Herman Long, Bobby Lowe, Kid Nichols, Jimmy Collins, Fred Tenney, Chick Stahl, Vic Willis, Bill Dinneen, Joe Tinker, Johnny Evers, Frank Schulte, and Ed Reulbach are just some of them. He was a judicious trader, which was part of the job. He acquired Billy Hamilton for a player about the same age (Billy Nash). Hamilton went on to have six more good years, while Nash had one more before becoming a backup. The trade of his best pitcher with Chicago (Jack Taylor) for a second-year Mordecai Brown was a foundation for the Chicago team in the 1900s.

Another difference between today's style of play and Selee's era is the control exercised by the manager during a game. Selee had some control, but not much direct control. None of the newspaper articles I reviewed cite

Selee as making a call for a bunt, hit-and-run, or other offensive actions. There are many instances where the captain of Selee's team was credited with making a change in pitchers or other players during the game. All the references to his style of management state that he let the players play and call their own plays. He set the philosophy. Selee favored the bunt. He was instrumental in developing the hit-and-run play, per many witnesses. He discussed with the players the best time to use these plays. But there is no testimony that he signaled the play from the bench. I tend to believe that he did not. There were many instances cited in newspaper articles crediting the captain on the field with a pitching change. There are also many instances crediting Selee with the pitching change. We know Selee did not go to the mound in his business suit for a conference. In this case, I expect both parties had something to do with it. There is no testimony of signals from Selee to the captain for a change during an inning. It is not clear who made the decision for a change. Selee would make the change if it happened between innings.

Selee had no coaches at any time during his tenure as a manager. Base coaches were players who were not up at bat or on base. There are stories of a player in the lineup coaching at first or third, when they were not the on-deck hitter. These folks in the coach's box did not give signals. Bunt, hit-and-run and double steal signals were given by the participants in the play. Selee was doing this like everyone else. Even someone like John McGraw did not give many signals at this stage of his career, per the testimony of some of his players in *The Glory of Their Times*.

Frank Selee found good players, trained them in the style of ball he wanted them to play, then let them play. The style of ball played by Selee's teams varied during his career. Early in Boston, the team was in flux in 1890. In 1891–1893, he had championship teams. These teams could win any kind of game. In 1891–1892, pitchers dominated the game, to the extent that the owners changed the pitching distance for the 1893 season. After 1892, hitters dominated. Selee's teams led the league in runs scored in 1891 and 1894. They led the league in complete games by pitchers in 1890–1891. After rebuilding this team to win pennants in 1897–1898, the team played the kind of ball dictated by high-scoring games. The team led the NL in runs scored in 1897, and in home runs and slugging percentage in 1897–1898.

The pitching improved. By the time the syndicate teams overtook Boston in 1899, Boston had the finest pitching staff in the NL. This staff remained intact through the 1901 season. The staff could not lift the team to a record over .500 because most of the hitters left for the American League. By the early 1900s, baseball had changed from a high-scoring to a low-scoring game. Selee built a team in Chicago that could win low-scoring games. It is a bit amazing to realize that the Chicago NL team from 1904 thru 1913 holds the record for most regular season victories over a ten-year span. Surprisingly, only four players from that team are in the Hall of Fame. These are Frank Chance (mostly as a manager), Mordecai Brown, Johnny Evers and Joe Tinker. I have not seen anyone claim that Chance and Brown should not be in the Hall of Fame. I have seen folks say that Evers and Tinker should not be there due to their relatively weak batting statistics. However, since the team they were on had the best winning percentage of any team in modern (post-1900) baseball history, isn't this team underrepresented? This was the team Frank Selee built and Frank Chance perfected.

Frank Selee was successful as a manager everywhere he went after he served his apprenticeship in the New England minor leagues. He won pennants in 1887, 1889, 1891, 1892, 1893, 1897, and 1898. He built the team that would win pennants in 1906, 1907, 1908, and 1910 and World Series in 1907 and 1908. His health would not allow him to complete the job in Chicago. He attempted to regain his powers in Pueblo, but his health would not allow that either. Frank Selee showed that when healthy, a gentleman who preached clean play could win in the most rough-and-tumble era of baseball's history. He fully deserved his place in the Baseball Hall of Fame, and on the list of great managers.

Showing that Selee was not alone in his condition at the end of his life, one of his best players suffered the same fate in the same place. On September 17, 1909, Herman Long died penniless in Denver of tuberculosis.

Frank Selee's Record as a Manager			
Minor Leagues			
Year	Team/League	Won-Loss	Place
1884	Waltham Massachusetts State	11–5	3rd
1884	Lawrence Massachusetts State	27–2	2nd
1885	Haverhill Eastern New England	29–15	3rd
1886	Haverhill Eastern New England	27–23	3rd
1887	Oshkosh Northwestern	76–41	1st
1888	Omaha Western Assn.	55–48	5th
1889	Omaha Western Assn.	83–36	1st
1906	Pueblo Western	61–85	6th
1907	Pueblo Western	11–24	6th through May 31
Total		380–279	

Major Leagues			
Year	Team/League	Won-Loss	Place
1890	Boston National	75–57	5th
1891	Boston National	87–51	1st
1892	Boston National	102–48	1st
1893	Boston National	86–43	1st
1894	Boston National	83–49	3rd
1895	Boston National	72–60	5th
1896	Boston National	74–57	4th
1897	Boston National	93–39	1st
1898	Boston National	102–47	1st
1899	Boston National	95–57	2nd
1900	Boston National	66–72	4th
1901	Boston National	69–69	5th
1902	Chicago National	70–69	5th
1903	Chicago National	82–56	3rd
1904	Chicago National	93–60	2nd
1905	Chicago National	37–28	4th
Total		1,286–862	

Sources for standings listed above:
1884-Waltham Daily Tribune, Lawrence Daily American
1885,6-Haverhill Evening Bulletin
1887-Oshkosh Daily Northwestern
1888,9-Omaha Daily Herald
1890 thru 1900-Nemec
1901 thru 1905-Neft, Cohen and Neft
1906,7-Pueblo Chieftain

Baseball Hall of Fame Players Managed by Frank Selee

Kid Nichols	Boston	1890–1901
John Clarkson	Boston	1890–1892
Mike "King" Kelly	Boston	1891–1892
Hugh Duffy	Boston	1892–1900
Tommy McCarthy	Boston	1892–1895
Jimmy Collins	Boston	1895–1900
Billy Hamilton	Boston	1896–1901

6. Endgame

Vic Willis	Boston	1898–1901
Frank Chance	Chicago	1902–1905
Joe Tinker	Chicago	1902–1905
Johnny Evers	Chicago	1902–1905
Mordecai Brown	Chicago	1904–1905

In the *Bill James Guide to Baseball Managers from 1870 to Today* (published in 1997), Frank Selee is listed as the 12th most successful manager.

Chapter Notes

Chapter 1

1. Frank Selee Hall of Fame file.
2. Norman Macht, *Connie Mack and the Early Years of Baseball* (Lincoln: University of Nebraska Press, 2007), 7.
3. *Melrose Record*; October 6, 1875.
4. Frank Selee Hall of Fame file.
5. *Ibid.*
6. *Waltham Daily Tribune*, April 10, 1884.
7. Frank Selee Hall of Fame file.
8. Macht, *Connie Mack and the Early Years of Baseball,*10.
9. *Waltham Daily Tribune*, April 17, 1884.
10. *Waltham Daily Tribune*, April 22, 1884.
11. *Waltham Daily Tribune*, April 21, 1884.
12. Macht, *Connie Mack and the Early Years of Baseball*, 9.
13. *Waltham Daily Tribune*, May 4–15, 1884.
14. *Waltham Daily Tribune*, May 28–June 5, 1884.
15. *Waltham Daily Tribune*, June 6, 1884.
16. *Waltham Daily Tribune*, June 9, 1884.
17. *Waltham Daily Tribune*, June 15–30, 1884.
18. *Waltham Daily Tribune*, July 22, 1884.
19. *Lawrence Daily American*, July 26, 1884.
20. *Lawrence Daily American*, August 9–10, 1884.
21. *Lawrence Daily American*, August 16, 1884.
22. *Ibid.*
23. *Lawrence Daily American*, August 18, 1884.
24. *Lawrence Daily American*, August 19–31, 1884.
25. *Lawrence Daily American*, September 1–30, 1884.
26. *Lawrence Daily American*, October 1–7, 1884.
27. Frank Selee Hall of Fame file.
28. *Ibid.*
29. *Haverhill Evening Bulletin*, May 6, 1885.
30. *Haverhill Evening Bulletin*, May 12, 1885.
31. *Haverhill Evening Bulletin*, May 17, 1885.
32. *Haverhill Evening Bulletin*, May 19, 1885.
33. *Haverhill Evening Bulletin*, May 20, 1885.
34. *Haverhill Evening Bulletin*, June 9, 1885.
35. *Haverhill Evening Bulletin*, June 16, 1885.
36. *Haverhill Evening Bulletin*, July 7, 1885.
37. Frank Selee Hall of Fame file.
38. *Haverhill Evening Bulletin*. July 10, 1885. The quotes are from the papers listed but were printed in the *Haverhill Evening Bulletin* on this date.
39. *Haverhill Evening Bulletin*, July 1, 1885. All remaining newspaper citations in this section are from this paper unless noted.
40. *Boston Globe*, April 1, 1886.
41. *Boston Herald*, June 10, 1886.
42. Frank Selee Hall of Fame file.

Chapter 2

1. Frank Selee, "Twenty-One Years in Baseball," *Baseball Magazine*, December 1911: 55.

2. *Ibid.*
3. Buck Ewing Hall of Fame file.
4. *Oshkosh Daily Northwestern*. All references to articles in this chapter are from this paper unless noted otherwise.
5. William (Dummy) Hoy Hall of Fame file.
6. Frank Selee Hall of Fame file.
7. *Ibid.*
8. *Ibid.*
9. *Ibid.*
10. James Hart Hall of Fame file.
11. *Oshkosh Daily Northwestern*, August 29, 1887. *Sporting Life* is quoted in the newspaper article cited.
12. Frank Selee Hall of Fame file.
13. *Ibid.*
14. *Ibid.*
15. *Ibid.*
16. *Ibid.*
17. *Ibid.*

Chapter 3

1. Arthur Soden Hall of Fame file.
2. Bill James, *The New Bill James Historical Baseball Abstract* (New York: Free Press, 2001), 21–34.
3. *Ibid.*, 18.
4. David Nemec, *The Great Encyclopedia of 19th Century Major League Baseball* (New York: Donald I. Fine, 1997). All statistics cited in this book for major league baseball up to 1900 are from this source.
5. Arthur Soden Hall of Fame file.
6. John Montgomery Ward Hall of Fame file.
7. Robert Ross, *The Great Baseball Revolt: The Rise and Fall of the 1890 Players League* (Lincoln: University of Nebraska Press, 2016).
8. Macht, *Connie Mack and the Early Years*, 74.
9. John Montgomery Ward Hall of Fame file.
10. *Boston Herald*, April 14, 1890. All newspaper citations for 1890 are from the *Boston Herald* unless otherwise noted.
11. *Boston Globe*, April 21, 1890.
12. Nemec, *Great Encyclopedia*, 378.
13. *Ibid.*, 381.
14. *Boston Herald*, June 12, 1890.
15. Paul Hines Hall of Fame file.
16. *Boston Globe*, July 18, 1890.
17. *Boston Globe*, July 27, 1890.
18. *Boston Herald*, August 31, 1890.
19. Macht, *Connie Mack and the Early Years*, 360.
20. Billy Nash Hall of Fame file.
21. *Boston Globe*, May 12, 1891.
22. Cap Anson Hall of Fame file.
23. Frank Selee Hall of Fame file.
24. James, *New Bill James Historical Baseball Abstract*, 60.
25. Nemec, *Great Encyclopedia*, 458.
26. *Boston Globe*, May 2, 1892.
27. *Boston Globe*, June 9, 1892.
28. *Boston Globe*, July 15, 1892.
29. *Boston Globe*, July 23, 1892.
30. James, *New Bill James Historical Baseball Abstract*, 59.
31. Frank Selee Hall of Fame file.
32. Hermann Long Hall of Fame file.
33. Bobby Lowe Hall of Fame file.
34. *Ibid.*
35. *Boston Globe*, March 27, 1893.
36. Macht, *Connie Mack and the Early Years*, 101.
37. *Boston Globe*, August 8, 1893.
38. *Boston Globe*, August 15, 1893.
39. *Boston Globe*, September 8, 1893.
40. *Boston Globe*, September 22, 1893.
41. *Boston Globe*, September 23, 1893.
42. James, *New Bill James Historical Baseball Abstract*, 65.
43. James, *New Bill James Historical Baseball Abstract*, 60. Lowe's comment on p. 52 of this book.
44. Hugh Duffy Hall of Fame file.
45. Tommy McCarthy Hall of Fame file.
46. Charlie Bennett Hall of Fame file.
47. *Boston Globe*, April 25, 1894.
48. *Boston Globe*, June 13, 1894.
49. *Boston Globe*, June 21, 1894.
50. Quoted in *Boston Globe*, June 26, 1894.
51. *Boston Globe*, July 14, 1894.
52. *Boston Globe*, September 7, 1894.
53. Ned Hanlon Hall of Fame file.
54. *Boston Globe*, May 7, 1895.
55. Quoted in the *Boston Globe*, May 21, 1895.
56. *Boston Globe*, July 5, 1895.
57. *Boston Globe*, August 2, 1895.
58. *Boston Globe*, August 8, 1895.
59. *Boston Globe*, August 16, 1895.
60. *Boston Globe*, September 18, 1895.
61. Billy Hamilton Hall of Fame file.
62. *Boston Globe*, June 8, 1896.
63. *Boston Globe*, August 6, 1896.

Chapter 4

1. *Boston Globe*, April 5, 1897.
2. *Boston Globe*, April 25, 1897.
3. *Boston Globe*, May 31, 1897.
4. *Boston Globe*, August 2, 1897.
5. *Boston Globe*, August 7, 1897.
6. *Boston Globe*, September 5, 1897.
7. For a much more complete description of the 1897 pennant race, see Bill Felber, *A Game of Brawl: The Orioles, the Beaneaters and the Battle for the 1897 Pennant* (Lincoln: University of Nebraska Press, 2007).
8. *Boston Globe*, April 14, 1898.
9. *Boston Globe*, June 13, 1898.
10. *Boston Globe*, September 4, 1898.
11. Hugh Duffy Hall of Fame file.
12. James, *New Bill James Historical Baseball Abstract*, p. 57, Nemec, *Great Encyclopedia*, 606–611.
13. Stanley Robison Hall of Fame file.
14. Nemec, *Great Encyclopedia, 629–651*.
15. *Boston Globe*, July 19, 1899.
16. *Boston Globe*, July 26, 1898.
17. *Boston Globe*, October 16, 1899.
18. Marty Bergen Hall of Fame file.
19. *Boston Globe*, April 10, 1900.
20. *Boston Globe*, May 13, 1900.
21. *Boston Globe*, October 9, 1900.
22. James, *New Bill James Historical Baseball Abstract*, 325–326.
23. *Boston Globe*, April 24, 1901.
24. *Boston Globe*, June 7, 1901.
25. *Boston Globe*, July 17, 1901.
26. *Boston Globe*, August 4, 1901.
27. *Boston Globe*, August 24, 1901.
28. *Boston Globe*, September 26, 1901.
29. James. *New Bill James Historical Baseball Abstract*, 906.
30. Frank Selee Hall of Fame file.
31. Frank Selee Hall of Fame file.

Chapter 5

1. James Hart Hall of Fame file.
2. Joe Tinker Hall of Fame file.
3. *Chicago Tribune*, April 21, 1902.
4. *Louisville Courier-Journal*, April 28, 1902.
5. *Chicago Tribune*, May 14, 1902.
6. Lawrence S. Ritter, *The Glory of Their Times* (New York: William Morrow, 1984), 39–40.
7. *Chicago Daily News*, May 24, 1902.
8. Ritter, *Glory of Their Times*, 46.
9. *Chicago Tribune*, June 3, 1902.
10. *Chicago Tribune*, July 27, 1902.
11. *Chicago Tribune*, July 31, 1902.
12. Johnny Evers Hall of Fame file.
13. Frank Chance Hall of Fame file.
14. *Chicago Tribune*, April 5, 1903.
15. *Chicago Tribune*, May 6, 1903.
16. *Chicago Tribune*, June 12, 1903.
17. Johnny Evers Hall of Fame file.
18. *Chicago Tribune*, September 19, 1903.
19. *Chicago Tribune*, March 7, 1904.
20. *Chicago Tribune*, July 17, 1904.
21. *Chicago Tribune*, September 4, 1904.
22. *Chicago Tribune*, October 18, 1904.
23. All major league statistics for 1901–1905 are from David Neft, Richard Cohen, and Michael Neft, *The Sports Encyclopedia: Baseball* (New York: St. Martin Griffin, 1999).
24. Frank Selee Hall of Fame file. *Baseball Magazine* article published in 1905.
25. *Chicago Tribune*, April 14, 1905.
26. *Chicago Tribune*, May 25, 1905.
27. *Chicago Tribune*, July 1, 1905.
28. *Chicago Tribune*, July 29, 1905.
29. Frank Selee Hall of Fame file.
30. James, *New Bill James Historical Abstract*, 81–82.
31. Bill James, *The Bill James Guide to Baseball Managers from 1870 to Today* (New York: Scribner, 1997), 33.

Chapter 6

1. Frank Selee Hall of Fame file.
2. *Pueblo Chieftain*, March 13, 1906.
3. *Pueblo Chieftain*, July 14, 1906.
4. *Pueblo Chieftain*, August 11, 1906.
5. *Pueblo Chieftain*, June 2, 1907.
6. Frank Selee Hall of Fame file.
7. Frank Selee Hall of Fame file.
8. James, *Bill James Guide to Baseball Managers*, 33–38.

Bibliography

Baseball Magazine
Baseball-Reference.com
Boston Globe
Boston Herald
Chicago Tribune
Cleveland Plain Dealer
Felber, Bill. *A Game of Brawl: The Orioles, the Beaneaters and the Battle for the 1897 Pennant.* Lincoln: University of Nebraska Press, 2007.
Gillette, Gary, Pete Palmer, and Michael Gershman. *The Baseball Encyclopedia: The Complete and Official Record of Major League Baseball.* New York: Macmillan, (1969) 1996.
Haverhill Evening Bulletin
Holtzman, Jerome, and Goerge Vass. *The Chicago Cubs Encyclopedia.* Philadelphia: Temple University Press, 1997.
James, Bill. *The Bill James Guide to Baseball Managers from 1870 to Today.* New York: Scribner's, 1997.
James, Bill. *The New Bill James Historical Abstract.* New York: Free Press, 2001.
Lawrence Daily American

Macht, Norman. *Connie Mack and the Early Days of Baseball.* Lincoln: University of Nebraska Press, 2007.
Melrose Record
Neft, David, Richard Cohen and Michael Neft. *The Sports Encyclopedia: Baseball.* New York: St. Martin Griffin, 1999.
Nemec, David. *The Great Encyclopedia of 19th Century Baseball.* New York" Donald I. Fine, 1997.
Omaha Daily Herald
Oshkosh Daily Northwestern
Player Files at the National Baseball Hall of Fame, Cooperstown, NY, which consist of newspaper and magazine articles, some of which are unattributed.
Pueblo Chieftain
Purdy, Dennis. *The Team by Team Encyclopedia of Major League Baseball.* New York: Workman, 2006.
Ritter, Lawrence. *The Glory of Their Times.* New York: William Morrow, 1966.
Roberts, Randy, and Carson Cunningham. *Before the Curse.* Champaign: University of Illinois Press, 2012.

Index

Numbers in **_bold italics_** indicate pages with photos

Abell, Fred 110–1
Allentown, Pa. 73
Alpha Team of Melrose 4
American Association 22–3, 36–7, 39, 47–55, 70, 79, 128
American League 121, 128–37, 140, 143, 145, 158, 168
Andrews, Willy 30
Anson, Cap 44, 50, 53, 65, 67, 70, 73–4, 86–7, 90, 98, 103, 114, 138–9

Bailey, Harvey 117–9
Baltimore (AA) Ballclub 39, 55
Baltimore (AL) Ballclub 128,
Baltimore (NL) Ballclub 55–120
Bannon, Jimmy 66, 72–92
Barnes, Ross 35
Barrow, Ed 1
Baseball Magazine 175
Bennett, Charlie 37, 40–72, 74, 78, 95
Bergen, Marty 84–120, **_115_**
Berry, Shad 129–36, 165–71
Biddeford Ballclub 9–12, 14
Billings, J.B. 35–6, 83, 116, 129, 136
Blake, Harry 111
Blue Laws 10, 27
Boston (AA) Ballclub 47, 52
Boston (AL) Ballclub 129–37, 156
Boston Globe 16, 44, 50–1, 54–5, 72, 74, 79, 82, 86, 88, 93, 99, 100, 104, 106, 116, 120, 122, 124, 126, 128–9, 131–4, 136
Boston Herald 40
Boston (NL) Ballclub 6, 10, 30–172
Boston (PL) Ballclub 37–55
Boston Reserves Ballclub 7–8, 10–1
Boston Resolutes Ballclub 15
Boston (UL) Ballclub 5–6
Breitenstein, Ted 102
Brockton Ballclub 12, 14–6, 18, 89
Brodie, Steve 39–56, 78, 127
Brookfield, Ma. 113, 116
Brooklyn (AA) Ballclub 30, 44
Brooklyn (NL) Ballclub 40–172
Brouthers, Dan 37, 39, 47, 78

Brown, Fred 130
Brown, Mordecai "Three-Finger" 147, 153, 156–7, 159–61, **_161_**, 162–74, 183, 185
Brown, Tom 38–9, 47
Brush, John 110, 120, 140, 168, 172
Brynan, Charlie 51
Buckenberger, Al, 136, 138
Burkett, Jesse 42, 111
Burnham, Walter 12
Burns, Tom 139

Callahan, Jimmy 143
Canavan, James 30, 32
Cantillion, Joe 176, 178
Carney, Bill 166
Carrington, Peter 16
Carroll, Cliff 63, 71–2, 95
Casey, Doc 152–72
Chamberlin, Icebox 70
Chambers, Rome 123–4
Chance, Frank 103, 140–74, **_150_**, 182, 185
Chesbro, Jack 101, 133, 143
Chicago (AL) Ballclub 143, 149–50
Chicago Daily News 144
Chicago Gravel Co. 172
Chicago (NL) Ballclub 29–35, 40–174
Chicago Tribune 139, 141, 144, 147, 149, 152–3, 156, 162, 164, 166, 170, 172
Chicago (WA) Ballclub 28
Childs, Cupid 111
Cincinnati (AA) Kelly's Killers Ballclub 51
Cincinnati Enquirer 96, 172
Cincinnati (NL) Ballclub 4, 40–172
Clarke, Fred 120, 124–5, 134, 146
Clarke, William "Boileryard" 111–30
Clarke, William (Omaha) 28–33
Clarkson, Dad 92
Clarkson, John 26, 37–62, **_43_**, 129
Clements, Jack 122
Cleveland, Elmer 30
Cleveland (NL) Ballclub 22, 40–120
Cleveland Plain Dealer 74
Collins, Jimmy 79–139, **_88_**, **_97_**, **_183_**
Colorado State Fair 178

193

Index

Comiskey, Charles 57, 69, 149, 152, 158
Congress Street Grounds 74
Connant, William 34, 36
Connaughton, Frank 72
Conroy, Wid 145
Cook, Jim 178
Corridon, Frank 159–65
Coyle, Bill 67
Crawford, Sam 143
cricket 4
Crolius, Fred 130
Crooks, Jack 30–1
Cummings, Arthur 7
Cuppy, Nig 111, 122
Currie, Lawrence 147

Dartmouth 122
Davenport Ballclub 27
Davis, George 138
Davis, Harry 48
Delahanty, Ed 143
DeMontreville, Gene 130–36
Denver Ballclub 31, 176–9
Des Moines Ballclub 22–36, 176–9
Detroit (AL) Ballclub 152
Detroit (NL) Ballclub 10, 34, 37, 78
Dexter, Charlie 141
Dinneen, Bill 121–37, 183
Dobbs, Johnny 131, 147–53
Dolan, Cozy 78
Donohue, Red 105
Doscher, Jake 155
doubleheaders 7, 53, 56, 5862, 105–7, 114, 116, 118, 135, 146–51, 155, 157, 163
Doyle, Jack 139
Dreyfuss, Barney 151
Drill, Lew 179–80
Duffy, Hugh 55–129, 137–8, 183
Duluth Ballclub 21–30
Durocher, Leo 182

Eason, Mal 143
Eastern New England League 12, 14, 44
Eau Claire Ballclub 21–26, 64
Elks 181
Emslie, Bob 96
Evers, Johnny 147, **148**–74, 183, 185
Ewing, Buck 20
exhibition games 6, 9–10, 16, 21, 25, 27, 34, 40, 48–9, 64, 72–3, 85, 87, 98, 101, 140–1, 152–3, 155–7, 160, 165–6, 169, 178

Fall River Ballclub 73, 86, 101
fires in ballparks 73, 75–6, 102, 104, 132
FitzGerald, John 99
flat bat 59–60, 63
Fogel, Horace 138
Forest City Streetcar Co. 104
Fraser, Chick 157
Freedman, Andrew 84, 87, 92, 120

Freeman, Buck 121–30
Frisbie, Charlie 114

gambling 22, 35, 83, 87
Ganzel, Charlie 37–101, 183
Gastfield, Ed 21, 27
Gastright, Hank 67, 73, 95
Getzein, Charlie 47–62
Girard, Pa. 23
Gleason, Kid 78
Gloucester Ballclub 12
Greensboro, NC 101
Griffith, Clark 81, 143

Hahn, Noodles 142
Halligan, Jocko 89
Hamilton, Billy 68, 84–137, **89**, 181, 183
Hanlon, Bib 152
Hanlon, Ned 2, 59, 78, 82, 96, 103, 111, 132, 142, 182
Hardie, Lew 38, 47
Hardy, Alex 147, 153
Harley, Dick 152–7
Harrington, Joe 83, 88
Hart, James 23–6, 28–30, 35, 37, 50, 54, 98, 122, 138, 140, 143–73
Harvard 6, 64, 111, 119, 122, 130
Haverhill Ballclub 12–19, 71
Haverhill Evening Bulletin 12
Heavenly Twins 70
Hemming, George 78
Henley, Clarence 177
Herrmann, Garry 151
Hickman, Charlie 98
Hines, Paul 39–48
Hodson, George 76, 79
Hofman, Artie 165–74
Holmes, Ducky 180
Holyoake Ballclub 7–8
Hoy, Dummy 21, 23, 26, 54, 122
Huff, George 140, 145, 159, 156–6, 171, 179
Huggins, Miller 182
Hughes, Jim 111
Hulbert, William 35–6
Hurst, Tim 33, 59

Indianapolis (NL) Ballclub 39, 102
International Association 36
Irwin, John 18
Isbell, Frank 180

James, Bill 36, 54–5, 62, 70, 128–9, 136, 174, 182, 187
Jennings, Hughie 63, 78, 82, 86, 93, 101, 108, 111
Johnson, Ban 122, 128–30, 134–5, 145, 151–2
Johnston, Dick 38–9
Jones, Davy 140, 143–68,
Jones, "Spit Ball" 176

Index

Kahoe, Mike 141, 143
Kansas City (AA) Ballclub 39, 63, 139, 168
Kansas City (WA) Ballclub 28–34, 88
Keefe, Tim 78, 82, 99, 101, 111
Keeler, Willie 99, 111, 143
Kelley, Joe 78, 99, 111
Kelly, Mike "King" 16, 27, 37–9, 46, 50–*53*, 54–64, 73, 129
Kennedy, Ted 29–33
Kiley, John 50
Killen, Frank 110, 113
Kittridge, Mal 129–137
Kling, Johnny 140–74
Klobendanz, Fred 73, 86–113, 183
Krock, Gus 21–2, 24

LaCrosse Ballclub 22
Lajoie, Napoleon 92, 101, 130, 183
Lampe, Henry 72
Latham, Arlie 45
Lawrence, Abbott 8
Lawrence Ballclub 7–18
Lawrence Daily American 9, 14
Leach, Tommy 107, 120
Lewis, Ted 88–130, 181–2
Lobert, Hans 171
Loftus, Tom 44, 139
Long, Herman 28–34, 37–*97*, 98–137, 164, 183, 185
Louisville (AA) Ballclub 23, 36
Louisville (NL) Ballclub 55–120
Lovett, Tom 22–30, 72, 75, 78
Lowe, Bobby 33–4, 39–137, *65*, *97*, 139–56, 183
Lundgren, Carl 141, 145–72
Lynch, Mike 141
Lynch, Tom, 96, 98
Lynn Ballclub 7–9

Mack, Connie 2, 4, 6, 48–9, 66, 182–3
Madden, Kid 38–9
Mains, Willard 85–6, 88
malaria 27
Maloney, Billy 169–71
Manning, Jack 36
Marshall, Archie 157
Massachusetts State League 5
Mathewson, Christy 130–4, 141, 151, 163, 171
McCarthy, Jack 157
McCarthy, Tommy 15, 22, 26, *26*, 30, 53, 55–85, 95
McChesney, Harry 166–7
McGarr, Chippy 17–8, 41, 47
McGilvary, Bill 178
McGinnity, Joe 113, 157, 163
McGraw, John 2, 59, 63, 78, 81, 88, 111, 113, 120, 123, 127–8, 145, 155, 163–4, 168, 182, 184
McJames, Doc 111
McLean, Larry 159
McMahon, Sadie 78

McPhee, Bid 61
McVay, Cal 35
Meekin, Jouet 117–8
Melchior, Harry 178
Melrose Record 4
Menefee, Jocko 141–58
Messitt, Jack 30
Miller, Dakin 141
Milwaukee (AA) Ballclub 55
Milwaukee (AL) Ballclub 143
Milwaukee (NWL) Ballclub 21–6, 28, 64
Milwaukee (WA) Ballclub 70
Minneapolis Ballclub 22–34
Mitchell, Mike 165
Moody, William 13, 16
Moran, Pat 130, 183
Moriarty, George 162
Morrill, John 37, 181
Morrissey, Frank 147
Mullane, Tony 124
Murnane, Tim 16–7, 40, 50–1, 53–137
Murphy, Charles 172–4
Murphy, Con 16, 25
Murphy, Danny 127
Murray, James 156

Nagle, Thomas 21, 24, 30
Nash, Billy 38, 47–84, 87, 95, 131, 183
National Association of Base Ball Players 4, 35, 37, 54, 65, 73
National Commission 168
National League 35–174
New York (NL) Ballclub 37, 40–174
New York Sun 38
Newburyport Ballclub 10–1, 14–5, 17–8
Nichols, Kid 28–34, 39–137, 139, 161–2, 167–8, 179, 183
no-hitters 60, 70, 119, 133, 157, 167, 171
Northwestern League 20–6, 28
Notre Dame 122, 159
Nyce, Charlie 80

Oakes Home for Consumptives 180
O'Connor, Jack 111
O'Hagan, Hal 141
Omaha Ballclub 26–36, 176–9
Omaha Daily Herald 27
O'Neil, Jack 159–71
Oshkosh Ballclub 20–6, 71
Oshkosh Daily Northwestern 20, 22, 24, 26
Overall, Orval 170–1, 174

Pedro, Chuck 147
Pfeffer, Fred 50
Pfeffer, Jeff 166–73
Philadelphia (AA) Ballclub 47
Philadelphia (NL) Ballclub 12, 17, 40–174
Phillippe, Deacon 145
Pickett, Dave 105
pitching distance 63

Index

Pittinger, Charlie 123
Pittsburgh Chronicle-Telegraph 128
Pittsburgh (NL) Ballclub 40–174
Players Association 126, 128
Players Brotherhood 37
Players League 37–47, 50–5, 70, 74, 84, 128, 137
pleurisy 149
Portland, Me. Ballclub 10, 12, 14, 18
Powell, Jack 111
Pretzel Battery 45
Princeton 73, 122
Proesser, George 30–1
Providence (NL) Ballclub 10, 16–19
Pueblo Ballclub 176–9
Pueblo Chieftain 176–80
Pulliam, Harry 151

Quarles, Bill 68
Quinn, Joe 38, 47–63

Radbourne, Hoss 38–9, 51
Raub, Tommy 153
Reach, Al 38
Reach Guide 63
Reisling, Doc 167
Reitz, Heinie 78
reserve clause 36–8
Rhoads, Bob 141, 146, 152
Richardson, Hardy 37, 39, 47
Richmond (AA) Ballclub 49
Richmond (EL) Ballclub 49, 86
Rickey, Branch 1
Ritchey, Claude 120
Robinson, Wilbert 78, 111, 120, 123, 127–8, 182
Robison brothers 104, 111–2
Rooks, George 50
Ruelbach, Ed 159, 166–74, 183
Rusie, Amos 41, 49, 58, 87, 92
Ryan, Jimmie 139
Ryan, John 72, 86, 102

St. Francis Hotel 167
St. Joseph Ballclub 31–4
St. Louis (AA) Ballclub 25, 27, 53, 55, 57
St. Louis (AL) Ballclub 143
St. Louis (NL) Ballclub 55–172
St. Louis Olympics 166
St. Louis (WA) Ballclub 28
St. Louis World's Fair 166–7
St. Paul Ballclub 22–33
St. Vrain, Jimmy 141, 144–5
Salem Ballclub 7, 9
Schaefer, Germany 141, 145–51
Schreckengost, Ossie 141
Schulte, Frank 165–74, 183
Selee, Annie 3, 154
Selee, Frank: Boston NL 35–137; Chicago NL 138–174; death and legacy 180–7; early life and semi-pro ball 1–19; minor league ball 20–34, 175–79; as umpire 12–4
Selee, Mary 139, 168, 175, 180
Selee, Nathan 3, 181
Selee Park 175–79
Sexton, Frank 66, 81–3
Sheckard, Jimmy 129
Sioux City Ballclub 28–33
Slagle, Jimmy 92, 131, 133, 140–74
smallpox 170
Smith, Alec 163
Smith, Harry 157
Smith, Pop 39
Sockalexis, Louis 94
Soden, Arthur 36, 56, 64, 67, 76, 78–9, 93, 96, 101, 114, 116–7, 129–30, 137, 140
South End Grounds 66, 73, 75, 78, 94, 116
Spanish-American War 104
Spaulding, Albert 2, 34–5, 37–8, 50, 110, 138, 140
Sporting Life 181
Springfield Ballclub 6–7, 9
Stafford, James 105
Stahl, Charles "Chick" 92–131, 183
Stahl, Jake 145, 153, 159
Staley, Harry 51–78, 80, 95
Stanton, Tom 160
Steinfeldt, Harry 124, 173
Stengel, Casey 182
Stenzel, Jake 94
Stivetts, Jack 53, 55–107
Stockdale, Otis 83
Stovey, Harry 47–58
Strauss, Joe 30
Streit, Oscar 112–3
Stricker, Cub 59
Sullivan, Billy 118–29
Sullivan, Jim 48–9
Sullivan, Joe 64, 98–102
Sullivan, John L. 61
syndicate teams 110–27

Taber, John 48
Taft, Charles 172
Taft, William Howard 172
Tannehill, Jesse 86, 116
tarpaulin 53
Taylor, Jack 107, 141–60, 168, 172, 183
Tebeau, Patsy 66, 111
Temple, William 78, 140
Temple Cup 78, 84, 90, 99, 102, 108
Tenney, Fred 56, 75, 75, 79–137, **97**, **121**, 183
Tinker, Joe **141**–74, 183, 185
Titcomb, Ledell 17
Tremont Ballclub 7–8
Tucker, Tommy 39–94
typhoid fever 68, 147

Union League 36, 54–5, 71, 128

University of Illinois 140, 145, 153, 159, 166
University of Virginia 56

Van Haltren, George 106
Viau, Leon 60
Von der Ahe, Chris 57, 60, 110
Von der Horst, Harry 111

Waddell, Rube 120, 125, 133, 140
Wagner, Honus 96, 101, 103, 107, 120, 134–5, 144
Wagners (owners) 67
Waltham Ballclub 5–8
Waltham Daily Tribune 5, 8
Waltham Watch Co. 5, 8
Ward, John Montgomery 37, 47, 70
Washington (AA) Ballclub 49, 55
Washington (AL) Ballculb 139
Washington (NL) Ballclub 55–124
Weimer, Jake 149–73
West, Frank 75

West Side Park 143, 164–5, 170
Western Association 26–34
Western League 175–9
White, Deacon 35
Wicker, Bob 152–73
Williams, Otto 156–69
Williams, Pop 139, 141, 147, 155
Williams College 88, 181
Willis, Vic 98–130, **130**, 131–137, 147, 183
Wilson, Zeke 78
Worcester Ballclub 7–9, 112
World Series 158
Wright, Harry 1–2, 35–7, 65, 79

Yale 56, 112
Yeager, George 93
Young, Cy 45, 51, 57–9, 62, 90, 94, 98, 103, 111, 126
Young, Nick 96, 140

Zimmer, Chief 120